P9-CCT-041

Italian Provincial Cookery

AUSTRIA
SWITZERLAND
YUGOSLAVIA
FRANCE
TRENTINO ALTO ADIGE
FRIULI VENETIA GIULIA
VALLE D'AOSTA
LOMBARDY
Milan
VENETIA
Venice
Turin
PIEDMONT
EMILIA ROMAGNA
LIGURIA
Genoa
Florence
TUSCANY
THE MARCHES
ADRIATIC SEA
LIGURIAN SEA
UMBRIA
LATIUM
Rome
ABRUZZI E MOLISE
APULIA
CAMPANIA
Naples
BASILICATA
TYRRHENIAN SEA
GULF OF TARANTO
CALABRIA
MEDITERRANEAN SEA
Palermo
SICILY

Italian Provincial Cookery

More than 300 Authentic Regional Recipes Adapted to the New World Kitchen

by
Bea Lazzaro
and
Lotte Mendelsohn

YANKEE® BOOKS
a division of
Yankee Publishing Incorporated
Dublin, New Hampshire

Illustrated by Elayne Sears

Designed by Ann Aspell

Special thanks go to Richard Elia of Quarterly Review of Wines *for his piece on wines in "The Italian Table."*

Yankee Books, a division of Yankee Publishing Incorporated
Dublin, New Hampshire 03444

First Edition

Printed in the United States of America

Library of Congress Catalog Card Number: 85-51876

ISBN: 0-089909-089-3

Dedications

. . . To my husband, Ralph . . . with appreciation for his support, kindness, and guidance.

Beatrice Lazzaro

. . . To the secret ingredient "Love," so generously given by both family and strangers, but most of all by my husband and closest friend, Bert.

Lotte Mendelsohn

Contents

Part I: The Italian Table

Part II: Cooking with Bea

Part III: The Italian Regions and Their Recipes

Chiacchierate

Author's Preface

When my husband Bert and I returned from Mexico City, after an absence of close to thirty years from our native United States, we rented a home in Weston, Massachusetts, a woodsy suburb of Boston. Our loving landlords were the Benotti family — Elena, Fred, and Joseph. It was Elena who, understanding and sharing my passion for the kitchen arts, said, "You must meet Bea." Bea was, and is, Beatrice Lazzaro, Elena's sister-in-law's sister.

This was soon accomplished, and so it happened that the idea for this book was born over a wooden pasta board, the stage for the venerable craft of making *tortellini.* The board was, of course, Bea's.

As a writer and food historian, I recognized at once the possibilities for getting down on paper Bea's exquisite ways with food. She is a joy to watch and a delight as a teacher and companion. Her astounding memory, energy, and practical knowledge acquired from almost seventy years in a continental kitchen are a gift — a rare and wonderful gift which I was anxious to document and am happy to share.

However, in discussing the scope for a possible book, both Bea and I were anxious to do more than simply share her fine culinary art. Thus, we focused on a regional recipe collection, designed to set down a rich assortment of authentic Italian regional recipes for all to enjoy.

In most cases it was necessary to go no farther than Bea's own files, or perhaps to those of her family and friends. However, our search for additional recipes occasionally led us even farther afield — into early Italian cookbooks and out into the New England Italian-American community. These excursions led us not only to more recipes, but to an unexpected mother lode of material offering fascinating insights into the lives of many Italian-American immigrants. It was these excursions that made possible the *chiacchierate* (chats) you will find scattered here and there throughout the book.

We have divided the book into three sections. The first discusses the Italian Table and its parts — from the antipasti through the desserts. The second, "Cooking with Bea," shares some of the Italian cookery tips Bea has found most useful over the years, as well as the basic pasta and sauce recipes she uses — recipes that also form the basis for many of the book's regional offerings. It also shares her rules for making pasta at home —

both by hand and by machine. The third is the regional recipe collection, each region with its own map and a brief summary of its own special contributions to the whole of Italian cuisine.

Bea joins me in wishing you happy reading and . . . *Buon appetito!*

Lotte Mendelsohn

Acknowledgments

Hundreds of caring friends of all nationalities, dedicated researchers, amateur historians, wine experts, ever-willing "tasters," and our patient editor, Neysa Hebbard, made this book a reality. But the great lady to whom we owe the most . . . that first kitchen introduction . . . is Elena Benotti. Thank you.

Beatrice and Lotte

Introduction

In New England, Boston is known as "The Hub," meaning all roads lead to the city, like the spokes of a wheel. However, it also means the *center:* the heart of the commercial, cultural, and culinary practices of the virgin settlements of our nation.

Greater Boston — which for eating purposes extends its historical roots south through Cape Cod to Providence (Rhode Island), north to Gloucester, and west past Springfield to the magnificent slopes of the Berkshires, and for that matter to much of New England — has a unique reverence for food. This may surprise the uninitiated, who, never having enjoyed its inns, restaurants, and — best of all — lovingly "home-cooked" meals, believe that our local kitchens produce only boiled dinners and simply prepared fruits of the sea.

The secret of the area's excellence at the dining table lies in its wealth of ethnic cuisines. These range from the Albanian to the French-Canadian, and from the Oriental to the Latin-American; but, as in all gold mines, there are certain veins which are richer than others. The tradition of Italian cookery in New England is a veritable culinary "Klondike."

The food-worshipping Italian immigrants who came to the Northeast in large numbers during the latter nineteenth and early twentieth centuries, and their now many American-born descendants, are the custodians of the regional treasure derived from the provincial, *country* cookery of the "Mother Cuisine," as it was so well christened by Waverly Root.

A study of the immigration patterns shows us that Southern Italy (in particular, the Abruzzi, Calabria, Campania, and Sicily) is most heavily represented in the New England area. Battered by drought, cholera, and earthquake and volcanic activity, these long-suffering lovers of their land undertook the frightening uprooting of family and tradition, and crossed the sea to America.

The largest percentage of these Italian immigrants remained in the New York area, where either a lack of money or the supportive presence of relatives was the principal factor. Some immigrants — those who either had trades identified with seacoast industries or were city claustrophobes — traveled farther north to New England — and, of course, many of their descendants eventually made their way to almost all corners of the country.

Both the Southern and the Northern Italians came in family groups which, in turn, soon expanded into ethnic enclaves, reassuring transplants of family and friends who brought with them the mores and traditions of the old country. *La Via Vecchia* ("the old way") represented security and sanity in the confusing readjustment years.

For the Southern Italians, the church and village of origin governed attitudes, behavior, and . . . one's address. Each block within the enclaves represented a living microcosm of *campanilismo.* As explained by William M. De Marco in his *Ethnics and Enclaves,* the village *campanile* (church bell) became the symbol of village to each family. The unique sound of the village bell not only announced all the important village events but, as time went by, defined the boundaries of the village. Those beyond the sound of the bell were generally considered foreigners to the "family" unit.

The new residents from the Northern provinces had an easier time. Often less impoverished than the *paesani* from the South, their circumstances allowed them to move farther from the city concentrations and to start myriad entrepreneurial enterprises all over New England and, as we have noted, eventually across much of the nation. From gardeners, they became nursery owners; from managers of "Mom and Pop" produce stores, they became the wholesale greengrocers of Boston's famed Faneuil Hall and Haymarket district . . . and beyond.

A common bond shared by the refugees from all of the Italian provinces was the dinner table. Hearty, simple fare, easily reproduced with the New World's wealth of prime materials and enhanced with imported olive oil and regional spices, became, among other things, an unguent for the uncertainties and frustrations of the new life.

As the years passed, New England, and much of the country, began to feel the vitality and creativity of the multifaceted immigrants of the "Boot." As New England and the rest of America gave shelter and succor to the Italians, the newcomers in turn deliciously nourished their adopted land. And, certainly, one of their most appreciated contributions has been in the area of the kitchen arts.

This book has been conceived as a salute to the regional, country-style Italian cooking which has so enriched our own country's culinary history and which continues to provide sustenance and pleasure to all who produce and partake of its wealth.

The Italian Table

Cuisines vary not only in the dishes served, but in the *order* of their serving as well. In England, tomatoes appeared at the breakfast table long before they enhanced the morning meal in America. In California, salads made their way ahead of the main course well before their arrival in that menu slot on the East Coast. And so it is around the world.

Italy is no exception. In Italy, there is no *main* course as we know it, but rather a series of courses. The antipasto, when served, always comes first, but it is sometimes followed by soup, sometimes not. The pasta, which follows, may on one occasion combine with the soup, and on another with the entrée. Breads (*pane*), strangely enough, though important — and good — are not as much a part of the Italian table as they are in much of the Old World. Salads (*insalata*) are most often found among the antipasti, although the purely "greens" salad as we know it most often comes to the Italian table after the entrée, much as here in America. And this is only the beginning.

To start our exploration of Italian provincial cookery, we (Bea Lazzaro, the cook, and myself, Lotte Mendelsohn, the scrivener) wanted to share with you a little about the order and various parts of the Italian table; thus, what follows. Remember, too, that the various recipes within the sixteen Italian regional collections are set out in much the same order — from the beginning antipasti; through the egg dishes, breads, and soups; on through the pastas and *polentas* and their sauces; to the fish, meats, and vegetables; and finishing up with the fruits, cheeses, and desserts. Included, too, is information on the fine Italian wines.

In truth, however, it is only the occasional Italian meal that makes use of the entire Italian table — and then usually only for very special family and village occasions. The more normal order would vary with the region, the occasion, the particular meal, and of course, the personal tastes of the cook and the diners.

The Antipasti

"What shall we have for an antipasto?" is a common question posed in restaurants of all "persuasions." The literal translation of the word — the dish that is served *ante* (before) the pasta course — is sometimes misused by us Italo-phile Americans, who often invoke it to signify only that marvelous mixture of spicy, olive oil–drenched vegetables, meats, and ocean treats that we expect to begin every fine Mediterranean meal.

In the mother country itself, antipasti can signify many different things; a broad designation that for our purposes includes the more familiar palate-awakening appetizers and special salads. (The more usual dinner salad as we know it is simplicity itself: a few slices of sun-ripened tomatoes or oranges, anointed sparingly with vinegar and oil; or a few leaves of the local lettuce fraternizing with a slice of snowy cheese and perhaps an olive or two.) Depending on the region in which you are seated when you tuck the white cloth napkin under your chin, your antipasto could be the current crop of either the host's garden or lands; the "catch of the day"; a collection of crisp, slivered, raw vegetables with an anchovy-based dip (Piedmont's *Bagna Cauda*); a deep-fried cheese-filled pasta (*Calcioni Rustici*); or simply the whim and mood of the cook.

Whatever your antipasto's *con*tent, its *in*tent is to alert your taste buds to the splendor that is to come. An old country saying, *"mostrare ospitalità è aver parte nella tavola degli angeli,"* ("to show hospitality is to be part of the table of the angels"), puts it well.

The ever-inventive antipasto is indeed a "heavenly" way to start a meal!

The Egg Dishes

Wooly lambs, plump porkers, and sad-faced calves may not be part of all rural Italian families' livestock inventory, but *everyone* has chickens!

Once out of the city, one often has the feeling that the chickens are the true landlords, with the resident family there merely at the sufferance of a strutting cock and his molting harem. No corner seems sacred to the scratching, clucking horde as they invade the bedroom, preen themselves on the kitchen table, and even lay their eggs in a half-opened drawer. But — aha — there's a justification: as long as the tithe is paid in poultry product, the cluckers have free run, for how else can one secure the evening meal in such a facile and frugal way?

Cheese, vegetables, and eggs represent the mainstay of the Italian farmer's diet. And, happily, no matter how many times one eats a *frittata,* each time, it seems, there is another twist, a new spice, or a different approach to this most delicious Italian egg creation. Peruse these pages and then invent your own. The cook can do no wrong here, for as our grandmothers used to say, "It can't be bad — it has good things in it!"

The Breads and Pizza

Bread is not the staff of life in Italy as it is in much of the rest of the world. Although important, it definitely ranks second to the vast variety of farinaceous dishes led by the ubiquitous "pasta." It is also very often served at the end of a meal as a bland vehicle for a dessert of cheese and fruit; or used as another ingredient in a wealth of recipes from an Avellino sponge cake to the famous *pappa col pomodoro* (bread soup) of Siena.

There are certain breads, however, that do merit attention all by themselves: the golden *grissini* of Turin; Ferrara's crunchy, four-cornered *ciupetta;* Basilicata and Calabria's circular *frisedda;* the Tyrol-inspired dark bread of Trentino-Alto Adige, coarse in texture and speckled with caraway seeds; and the huge bread "moons" of Apulia.

Sweet breads are to be found all over the country: *panettone, bicciolani, maritozzi, panpepato, pandoro* — all walk the line between "pastry" and "bread." These really sweet breads are served as a snack, are sometimes light substitutes for an entire meal, or are confected to satisfy that post-meal yearning for that little something sugary.

Naples' gift to the world's appetite, the pizza, is another subject entirely. Commonly misclassified as a junk food, pizza is truly a meal in itself, and a nutritious one. Over its yeast-dough base, there are no limits or rules to the kind or number of toppings. Fresh tomatoes, cheese, and olive oil drizzled with restraint form the delicious second layer, and from then on imagination and individual preference take over. Imitated and innovated all over Italy, it is now as much a staple in the "homeland" as it is in almost every modern shopping center around the world.

The Soups

In all ethnic cuisines originating from countries where there is a great variety of topography (which influences weather), where there are shared borders with sharply different cultures and languages, and where there is a necessity for frugality and a passion for creativity, soup will simmer in the pots!

Italy's Northern mountain soups tend to be legume-based and may have cubed potatoes, turnips, and carrots. All are laced with herbs and occasionally dumplings or small shavings of *gnocchi*. Everywhere, concentrated, golden broths are savory baths for homemade pasta in myriad textures and shapes, both simple and filled. ("Store-bought" pasta is also widely available.) The famous *minestrone* is served a hundred ways, depending on the region and the individual larder of the cook.

Not to be overlooked are the many versions of chowders and seafood-based liquid offerings that sometimes serve as first courses or even entire meals.

How better to energize a family at the ebb times of midday and early evening after a long day's labor? What more loving way to elasticize a budget while assuring good nutrition and good humor? The world loves soup, and its variety and quality are immeasurable. The soups of Italy are no exception.

The Pasta Sauces

"Appetito non vuol salsa" . . . "hunger is the best sauce!" While this may be true, in the Italian food experience it is the *salsa* that makes the dish and either glorifies or vilifies the cook.

The following list sets out the most common Italian regional sauces. The ones starred are some of Bea's favorites. You'll find recipes for her favorites and many of the others — and more — throughout the book, and of course listed in the index.

Common Regional Italian Sauces

Besciamella (flour and milk)*
Fonduta (cheese)*
Funghetto (mushroom)
Garofolato (Roman meat specialty)
Pesto (green, basil-based)*
Ragù Lazzaro (pork and beef)*
Salsa Agro-Dolce alla Parmigiana
Salsa alla Genoese
Salsa Bolognese
Salsa di Noci (nuts)
Salsa di Pomodori (plain tomato)*
Salsa di Pomodori Crudi (raw tomatoes)*
Salsa di Raffaele Lazzaro (classic tomato)*
Salsa Puttanesca
Salsa Siciliana
Sugo alla Toscana
Sugo di Carne e Funghi (meat and mushrooms)*

The Pasta

Pastaphilia is a serious malady afflicting, by very rough estimate, perhaps two-thirds of the world's population. It is marked by these common symptoms: a sudden, excessive salivation upon exposure to certain kitchen cooking odors (note: particularly those of garlic, butter, and olive oil, and possibly worsening with the addition of fresh tomatoes and spices such as basil and oregano), and an elevation of the complex "anticipatory" system, evidenced by severe mood changes. Many cooks find that such sufferers, at best, become grouchy, fretful, and impatient; at worst, who knows? An acute manifestation of the disease is the uncustomary offering of services to expedite the preparation process, sounding something like: "Hey, Mom, can I help . . . set the table, pour the water? . . . When *is* dinner, anyway???"

Pasta varies from one region of Italy to another. Not only are the shapes and fillings different, but the composition of the basic dough varies as well. Regional customs and the individual cook determine the culinary direction.

The generic term *pasta* includes all the shaped-dough preparations made from plain wheat, semolina, farina, and corn flours in their various textures. In most collections of Italian recipes the pasta section will include the commonest wheat flour pastas, along with the *gnocchi* and *polenta*. Bea and I have chosen to deal

The "Princes" of Pasta

A Chat with Joseph Pellegrino

"Dalle stalle alle stelle e dalle stelle alle stalle."

Old Sicilian saying: "From the stable to the stars and from the stars to the stable."

Not a trace of accent remains, but the musicality of his native Sicilian dialect occasionally whispers through his speech. The soft-voiced man who quoted the Italian folk maxim above is Joseph Pellegrino, the elder regent of Prince Spaghetti, the Lowell-based pasta empire. Seated opposite me, the sandy-haired man with the snapping black eyes was reminiscing about his own discovery of America, the land of opportunity.

"Back in those days I'd never even *heard* the word *entrepreneur,* let alone know what it meant, but nonetheless, at thirteen, I *was* one. Shopping bags, the brown paper ones, were probably my first big 'venture.' A bunch of bigger kids showed me how to buy them for two cents and sell them for three cents to the housewives making their way from the lower East Side (New York) pushcart markets, loaded with newspaper-wrapped packages."

"Joey" soon developed his own clientele, no doubt with the same soft-sell style that is still very much a part of the man today. Anyhow, it didn't take much to persuade Joseph Pellegrino to elaborate a bit.

"I'd say, 'Here, wouldn't it be easier for you to handle those in a nice shopping bag? Let me help you put all those things in. No, no, you don't have to pay me if you can't; . . . next time.' You see, sometimes they gave me a nickel and told me to keep the change, so it all evened out, and I made friends and customers. In a little while I was buying the bags wholesale for a penny each, and the janitor where I lived was letting me store them in his basement. After school, while the other kids were fooling around, I got to the shoppers first. By the time they finished with a game of catch and milk and cookies, I'd done all the paper bag business for the day. It was my first taste of profit. Because I worked harder, earlier, and later than anyone else, there were pennies to be made, and in those days pennies were important. Later, when I was older, I started contracting out shoeshine boxes. When some of the boys tried to cheat me, I took away their boxes with a firm but courteous demonstration of their 'difficulties' with arithmetic. As the 'Boss,' I even took my gang of shoeshiners on an annual outing to Coney Island. I treated them to hot dogs and paid for their rides; that was their reward for honesty. There wasn't a kid who didn't want to work for me. I was seventeen. I learned early: don't ever embarrass someone with his own failing. Find a way to have him discover it for himself. The people with whom you surround yourself are your strength, and their loyalty repays you a thousandfold."

Characteristically, Joseph Pellegrino speaks of the "others" in his life. With pride, he tells of only son Joseph's successful handling of and development plans for the 200-million-dollar company.

"He's a good boy. We always communicated. The only thing that I insisted on was one day a week for 'Papa.' He had six days for school and sports; Sunday was mine. We learned a lot from each other . . . . Oh yes" — and here he paused with a little grin — "he also had to learn the *pure* Italian from a weekly tutor. The Sicilian dialect he already knew." (Business magnate Joseph "the Younger" had a wry comment about that: most young ones of the thirties and forties would rather have played ball than labor over the conjugations of the mother tongues of their parents — hardly a surprise.)

"I was born in Mistretta, in the province of Messina," Joseph Senior continues, "but my mother died before I had any memory of her. My father died young, too. As a very small boy, I worked for my uncle in his macaroni factory in Sicily. It was my first 'taste' of the pasta business."

The first American pasta factory in which there were Pellegrino roots was the Roman Macaroni Factory in New York City. However, the dampness surrounding the pasta manufacturing process gave the elder Pellegrino a sudden and severe attack of arthritis. When a friend suggested the wonders of the "electric baths" in Brooklyn, Joseph went. There, another spa devotee, impressed by the energy and wit of his "partner in steam," introduced him to his doe-like young cousin Lena. No one has ever had a happier end to a period of pain: Joseph and Lena's marriage has lasted more than fifty years.

"My wife . . . she's an angel, and my mother-in-law and sisters-in-law. I had a ready-made family, a family of wonderful women —," he paused and then resumed with a twinkle, "to take care *of* and to have take care of *me*."

With the years, Joseph bought shares in the Long Island-based Roman Macaroni Company. His vision, capacity for work, and innate selling ability greatly increased the company's profits, and he eventually became a partner.

In 1938, at a festive gathering in New York's Westchester County, the Pellegrino family heard Walter Winchell announce the presence of Fiorello La Guardia (the famous New York mayor of Broadway musical, cartoon-reading, and fire-engine-chasing fame) at the site of a rampaging three-alarm fire on Long Island. Few details were given, other than that the blaze had started in a lumberyard. Joseph looked at Lena . . . "That's our factory!"

When the family scolded him for his pessimism, Joseph was firm. "It's *our* factory . . . I *know* it."

And he was right. Later, as they crossed the Triborough Bridge, the devastating fire was clearly visible. Arriving at the scene, Pellegrino's greatest concern (after learning that the night watchman was safe) was the Accounts Receivable records. Breaking away from restraining firemen, and with the help of La Guardia, he was able to salvage the precious spinal column of his business. No one had been hurt, the books were safe, and they could start again. He told the women to dry their eyes.

"Don't worry, we're all here, and we're all fine . . . but I don't want to rebuild in New York. I've *had* it with congestion, labor problems, and now the fire. There has to be somewhere else to make spaghetti!" . . . and he headed north.

What is today "Spaghettiville's Pride" started on Prince Street in Boston in 1912. Beginning its life as the Prince Macaroni Company, the company was started by three partners. Gaetano La Marca and Miccaele Cantella each invested $300, with the third partner, Giuseppe Seminara, using his horse and wagon as "sweat equity." In those days, pasta was sold wet by the pound: five to ten pounds for a family, and in twenty- to fifty-pound barrel lots for wholesale distributors. This barrel trade made the horse an important member of the company!

As the years passed, the company grew without direction or organization, a ragged mass of potential with a faltering everyday presence. This was the company that Pellegrino bought.

With his portfolio of customers from the burned New York facility and his gifted commercial vision, Joseph Pellegrino instituted changes (packaging in lots of 12 instead of 24 to broaden the customer base), revved production up from three days to five days a week, and turned a small *home-style* operation into a profitable business.

In 1939, bursting at the seams, the company moved into the former Lowell textile mill that is its expanded home today. The following year, Pellegrino purchased controlling interest of Prince . . . the rest is history.

The maxim that starts this tale of guts, imagination, and no small amount of grueling labor, of course, alludes to the possibility of capturing your star, wherever you stand to view it; and the last Pellegrino anecdote has to do with the psychic *push* that precipitated Joseph Pellegrino's "long reach."

"I hadn't been in Boston too long when I went into a busy grocer's and found myself standing next to the sales representative of a then-giant pasta producer. The store owner came out from behind the counter and extended a check for seven hundred dollars to the man. My eyes bulged and my mind reeled. 'Sir,' I interrupted, introducing myself, 'my name is Joseph Pellegrino, and I'm honored to make your acquaintance. I sell macaroni also.' The salesman's belly shook with laughter. 'Well, young fella,' he said, 'we're so big we can afford to let you little guys have the *crumbs*.' "

It was at that moment, it seems, that the slender, beginning-again "Joey" firmly set his stellar staircase. The company to which the large check was written is today all but invisible in the business firmament. So, to quote again the "Prince of Pasta":

"Don't look with your eyes; see with your heart — and *go get 'em!*"

with rice, *gnocchi, polenta,* and fritters separately, allowing pasta, as most of us know and love it, an unshared stage and a single spotlight.

Our American interest in nutrition has taught us about the food "families" and the necessity of a healthy balance of fresh fruit, vegetables, and a starchy carbohydrate along with meat, fish, or fowl. The rich assortment of basic pasta recipes and the large selection of regional sauces (and their variations) following throughout this book allow today's cook a broad base for both salutary meal planning and creative cookery.

Bear in mind that what is known as the "Motherland of Pasta" traditionally serves this hearty and filling dish *after* the antipasto. It may take the place of soup, or may share the table with a protein-rich entrée. There is no *main* course as we know it here, rather a *second* course, or courses — and the variations are endless. As the French may pique your appetite with a few mouthfuls of fish fillet, or a nicely sauced crêpe or timbale before the extravaganza that is their principal course, so the Italians dull the sharp edge of hunger with a moderate serving of *pasta asciutta* (*dry* pasta with sauce) or a simpler pasta *in brodo* (pasta in broth).

Most of us are willing prey to sporadic bouts of *pastaphilia,* and the authors of *Italian Provincial Cookery* fervently hope that the pages of this book will serve as a happy and handy cure.

It is said that the true Italian can name over two hundred different kinds of pasta. Because Bea has been too busy *making* it, and my research to date has revealed only fifty or so, we offer you here an abbreviated, but still impressive, list.

Italian Pastas: A Partial Listing

Acini di Pepe
Agnolotti
Anellini
Cannelloni
Capellini
Cappelletti
Conchiglie
Conchigliette
Curly Lasagne
Fedelini
Fettuccine
Fusilli
Gomiti
Gramigna Rigata
Grosso Rigato
Lasagne
Lasagnette
Lasagne Verdi

Lingue di Passero
Linguine
Lumache
Mafalde
Mafaldine
Maltagliate
Manicotti
Mezzani
Nocchette
Occhi di Lupo
Pappardelle
Pastina
Penne
Pennine
Perciatelli
Quadrucci/Quadrini
Ravioli
Ruote
Semi di Mela
Spaghetti
Spaghettini
Spiedini
Stivaletti
Strichetti
Tagliarini
Tagliatelle
Tortellini
Tortiglioni
Trenette
Ziti
and Zitoni

Note: The pasta names are usually derived from their shapes or from folk tales about their evolution. When traveling to cook in Italy, it is wise to choose "by sight," as names vary from region to region.

Rice, Polenta, Gnocchi, and Fritters

The Po Valley is the nurturing bosom for Italy's excellent Piedmontese rice. While the first step in the cooking process — browning the short, plump grains in butter or oil — is similar to that of Spain and the Middle East, step two — the addition of water or broth — is quite different. Elsewhere, the liquid is added all at once, and the rice covered and left undisturbed until done; the Italian cook adds water little by little and then carefully "guards" the pot, stirring every few minutes with a wooden spoon. Why the totally different approaches to the art? Because each culture's ideals of culinary perfection are unique. *Risotto* should have a rippling liquid (*all'onda*) quality, whereas other countries value a dry consistency. The artistry of the Italian dish is that while it must be moist, each grain must also be separate — "mobile," not sticky — no easy feat for the kitchen neophyte.

Polenta, made with the coarse cornmeal flour *granturco,* is the Northern Italian's answer to pasta. This staple food, which could be a first cousin to our "grits," hominy, or early American porridge, ranges in color from a creamy to a golden hue (usually the coarser the grind the deeper the color). It may be eaten hot, or allowed to cool and sliced in squares. Eaten alone, *polenta* is the same kind of satisfying, but bland, filler as bread; eaten with a savory sauce, it competes with the best flavor treats of the Southern Italian cooks.

While rice and *polenta* are most often found on Northern tables, *gnocchi* are a national treat served throughout Italy in place of pasta. Their forms and substance vary according to region: they may look like giant eyelashes, fat coins, or be almost bullet-shaped; they may be made from potato flour, cooked potato, farina, or bread. Whatever their base, these little dumplings are everybody's darlings because, chameleon-like, they marry well to sauces from sweet and sour to classic tomato; or, in another vein, with the addition of a bit of sugar and cinnamon, they can be prepared as a simple dessert. Further proof of their versatility is that they take as easily to an oven-baked casserole as they do to a steamy *minestra,* or to solitary splendor on your *primo piatto* (first-course plate).

Fritters, for their part, appear in the cuisine of most of the world. They are a delicious way to use up leftovers, to disguise a vegetable that may be less-than-loved, or simply to add texture and interest to an otherwise ordinary meal.

The Fish and Seafood

Italians have long been fish enthusiasts — and, according to the lore, sometimes rather naive ones. As Waverly Root tells us in his *The Food of Italy,* when the waters of Italy were stocked by the Etruscans, they were stocked with sea fish. "The ancients," Root writes, "apparently did not know that saltwater fish cannot live in fresh water, but neither did the fish, which adapted themselves to the new environment."

And when it comes to fish, the Italians are also purists. Not for them the modifying, or actually disguising, sauces of the French. Their palates demand that fish from the sea taste of the sea, as should all the mollusks and crustaceans that grace their tables. Herein lies the origin of the true Italian's indulgent shudder when someone from another part of the world asks to have grated cheese with his or her *pasta alla marinara.*

There is also a plentitude of fresh water found on the Italian peninsula. Lakes, crystalline streams, and rivers large and small all give of their vast and varied inventory to supply additional fish

Chiacchierata con un Pescatore

Chat with a Fisherman

Rosario Salvatore Testaverde is a retired fishing-boat captain. Three of his four sons have followed in their father's footsteps. The fourth is a marine biologist. This "family of the sea" makes its home in Gloucester, Massachusetts, one of our country's most famous fishing ports. Testaverde is a handsome, robust man with a shock of seafoam-colored hair. Even with his enchantingly fractured English and little formal education, he is a frequent guest columnist for a Massachusetts North Shore newspaper and a sought-after lecturer at local schools and clubs. His magic? — a prodigious memory, the sailor's way with a yarn, and a joyous celebration of life. "Salvi" (as he is called by his friends) is also a *great* cook!

"It'sa gotta be fresh!" and fresh it was on the day that the Captain cooked for us. The only ocean treasure served that had not breakfasted on the ocean bottom was the *calamari in scabeccio*. "They hafta rest in the juices," Salvi told us, referring to the slender marinated slices of squid that were to be our appetizer or *antipasto*. The chewy treat, he elaborated, had been seasoning for a week in the refrigerator.

The whole of Salvi's menu was a hymn to the North Atlantic's bounty. Baked stuffed lobster (see Salvi's recipe on page 323), breaded sand dabs, fillet of grey sole, shrimp, skate wings, and *calamaretti* (finger-sized squid). A salad of mixed greens tossed with baby shrimp, and fresh mushrooms sautéed in garlic and oil complemented the fish.

Sicilian-born, our captain-cum-chef shares with his fellow countrymen an abiding love for the gifts of the sea — a love he, in turn, shared with us over his fine meal that day. You may not be able to duplicate Salvi's salty *tales* with your Italian "fruits of the sea" dinner, but with some of his, and other, recipes from this book, you can duplicate the menu — and the good eating!

dishes for the Italian table. The preparation of these freshwater finny, spiny, or wriggly creatures is also always simple — pan-fried, spit-roasted, or oven-baked. Herbs are used to season, but judiciously.

A passion that Italians share with most of the Latin peoples of the world is their enthusiasm for *baccalà*, or dried salt cod. The Spanish and Portuguese, as well as many in the southern half of our own Western hemisphere, join the native Italians in considering the complicated several-step method for its preparation well worth the effort. You'll find rules for its use as you peruse the pages of *Italian Provincial Cookery.*

Although many of the fish and shellfish of the Adriatic, Mediterranean, Tyrrhenian, and Ligurian seas are not available here in the West, the catch of our American waters adapts itself handily to the recipes of the Old Country. Included in our book are many Old-Country recipes for both fresh- and saltwater inhabitants. And, for your convenience while traveling or when buying fresh fish in ethnic markets, there follows a brief glossary of fish names in Italian with their English equivalents.

Good Things That Swim and Have Gills

ITALIAN	ENGLISH
Anguilla, Capitone	Eel
Canocchie	Squill
Cefalo	Grey mullet
Lasca	European roach
Lucio	Pike
Nasello	Cod
Pagello	Red snapper
Palombo	Dogfish
Pesce da Taglio	Halibut
Pesce Persico	Perch
Rombo	Turbot
Rospo	Angler fish
Sardina	Sardine
Sardone, Acciughe	Anchovy
Scombro, Sgomberi, Maccarello	Mackerel
Scorpena	Hog fish
Sogliola	Sole
Storione	Sturgeon

Tonno	Tuna
Triglie	Red mullet

And More Creatures of the Sea

ITALIAN	ENGLISH
Aragosta	Spiny lobster
Calamaro	Squid
Cappa	Scallop
Cozza, Datteri	Mussels
Delfino	Dolphin
Gambero	Small shrimp
Granchio	Crab
Polipo	Octopus
Ostrica	Oyster
Scampi	Shrimp
Seppia	Cuttlefish
Vongola	Mussel-like shellfish

The Meats

Unlike most classic Western cuisines, in Italian cooking the meat course is not the *main* course. Meat falls into the broader category of *second* courses, usually sharing the spotlight with a pasta or a substantial vegetable dish (or a combination of the two, as in *spaghetti coi punti d'asparagi).*

Synonymous with most thoughts of the ideal Italian meat dish is the vision of a tender, pale veal entrée, delicately sauced. Integral to this, of course, are the freshly cut herbs, slices of lemon, and the many fine wines of the country, all put to fragrant use in the embellishment of this popular milk-fed viand. For the purist, there is the magnificence that is the charbroiled *costata di vitello,* crusty on the outside and pink at the heart, and which Naples, for one, counterpoints with a fresh tomato sauce (*alla pizzaiola).*

Agnello is the Italian word for lamb as we know it here. *Abbacchio* is the suckling lamb that has never eaten grass. It is one of Latium's culinary triumphs, spit-roasted whole and basted with rosemary, garlic, wine vinegar, anchovies, and fine olive oil. There are times when the hills of Rome carry the fragrance of this dish on the wind, and one would swear that all the cooks of the ancient city chose the same menu for the day!

Northern Italy is the center for the beef breeders and beef eaters. The Alpine grazing cattle are bred more for dairy use than for their meat. However, Tuscany's *Val di Chiana* steaks are deservedly famous; some say on a par with the Japanese Kobe beef. The slow-cooked stews of the colder regions make tasty use of the cuts that may be tougher than desirable. Paired with a hearty wine in the pot and wine in the diner . . . delicious!

Pork is popular all over the "Boot," and enjoyed in dozens of ways whenever it is available. Fatback lard is almost as much a staple as olive oil; therefore, pigs are kept even in the poorer Southern reaches. Suckling pigs are holiday fare, and the extremely popular variety-meats (offal) use pork in spicy combination for sausages, pâtés, stuffings, and meat loaves.

In a country where waste is considered sinful, there is no part of the precious Italian livestock that is not used and savored.

Poultry and Game

As already mentioned in the Egg Dishes section, chickens are "first-class citizens" of the Italian country household, but ducks, geese, and turkeys are also raised to grace the Italian table. Here in the United States, the varied use of turkey — in thick steaklike slices, pounded thin to substitute for the more expensive veal scallops, and in combination with other meats for sausage — is a relatively new marketing idea. In Italy, because of both a poor economy and adherence to the age-old admonition, "Waste not, want not," their "big birds" have been used creatively for centuries.

Game, another gift from nature, is prized in Italy not only for its economics, but also because there are so many wonderful things the Italian cook manages to do with this hearty-flavored prime ingredient of the forest. An acquired taste for many American palates, seasonal game birds, rabbit and hare, venison, and other smaller game are a vital part of the European rural diet.

The Vegetables

Nature's own vibrant hues of red, white, and green are not only the colors of the Italian flag; they are the country's kitchen palette as well. Nowhere in the world are the tomatoes more brilliantly crimson, the onions and garlic heads more snowy, or the variety of fresh, leafy vegetables more extensive and *green*! Even the most hard-core "meat and potatoes" eater will salivate over a subtly seasoned serving of Lombardian *peperonata* or the irresistible *carciofi fritti* of Tuscany.

Like many objects of beauty, the fresh produce of the "Boot" is spoiled to death — cultivated with care, handled gently, and nurtured to maturity with expertise and pride. The manner and treatment of bringing harvest to table is equally creative and loving. For example, fresh butter, heavy cream, and truffles (both white and black) are used to complement the vegetable dishes of the Northeast. There, too, pasta is paired with, among other things, pumpkin (as in the filling of the *cappellacci* of Ferrara) and spinach (which gives color and flavor to the exquisite Emilian *lasagne verdi*).

Less brilliant in color, but nonetheless a world dietary staple, are the members of the legume family. Popular in our own country, they are equally enjoyed all over Italy, particularly in soups. Prepared with rice or the whimsically shaped small pastas, the beans, peas, and lentils lend taste and substance to hearty country fare.

Because vegetables play such an important role in the Italian diet, note should be taken of our common misconception about "the BIG taste" of Italian cuisine. When invoked, this phrase usually conjures up taste memories of piquant spices, fried onions, and enormous quantities of too-pungent garlic. While the Southern provinces may lean more heavily on these flavorings than our Anglo palates appreciate, the rest of Italy seasons more delicately, using a vast but subtle bouquet of freshly grown herbs; pistachio, pine nuts, and walnuts for texture; and the local wines for zest. Nutmeg, cinnamon, and ginger may also make unexpected appearances — the results, a kind of Latin *nouvelle cuisine* that has been in use in Italy for more than a thousand years!

The Fruits and Cheeses

Food memories are most often provoked by our sense of smell, but of all the happy moments the traveler to Italy stores, likely the one most often shared is the feeling of refreshing delight when the belt is slyly eased, the table cleared, and the waiter appears with the sparkling bowl of water, ice, and submerged branches of green, magenta, and purple grapes.

The next arrivals are the pears, also multihued according to the season; peaches, apples, cherries, apricots, and the Southern exotics — the figs, tangerines, and prickly pears. What a juicy cornucopia to empty its ripe wealth on a plate readied for your choice!

". . . and now, Signore, which of our wonderful cheeses will you try? Or perhaps you'd like a sliver of this Bel Paese or Gorgonzola. Strong? Oh my, no. . . . Flavorful . . . noble . . . assertive, but not strong." The waiter was right, deliciously, unforgettably, *right*!

Oh Italy, you are a charmer and a disarmer. To compensate, we shall have to climb at least two *campanili* (bell towers) in the morning!

The Desserts and Pastries

Generally speaking, every Italian travel, food, and cookbook written states that Italians are not great dessert eaters. In fact, somewhere in *these* pages are words to that same effect, propagating a myth that my collaborator drowns in whipped cream and chocolate sauce whenever she gets a chance.

This is the section of the Italian table that Bea Lazzaro really "gets into." In all my years of passionate devotion to pastry, "chocoholism," and just, "if it's sweet, I want it!," I have never been more impressed, more tempted, or *fatter* than during the time Bea and I worked on the various regional Italian desserts.

In these pages, you'll find not only the recipes for Italy's famed *gelati,* but the "how to" for Bea's own *Cassata Siciliana,* which surpasses anything eaten either *here* or *there,* along with recipes for *gianduia,* which should be forbidden by law, and for the simpler stewed fruits and economical, hearty puddings more commonly served when, indeed, desserts *are* served.

The Wines

For centuries Italian wine was largely taken for granted by Italians. To them, it was a drink as common as an Italian fountain in any one of their picturesque squares in virtually any village.

It was not, however, until the twentieth century, and the 1960s specifically, that Italian wines were recognized and introduced to the world. The discovery proved exciting: Italy had ideal weather conditions, perfect hills with immense southern exposures, and extraordinary soil. Now Italy produces over twenty percent of the world's wines.

More important, Italian wines have become not only "fine" wines, but incredibly, extraordinary "buys" as well. In the jargon of the day, Italy's wines represent the best quality-to-price ratio of any wine in the world. And to add to it, Italy's wines marry especially well with the various cuisines of the world.

Banish the notion that fine Italian wines are red only. Over the last twenty years, Italian winemakers — now some of the best in the world — have shown what great white wines can be like when produced from the areas of Piedmont, Umbria, and Campania. The Italians, at last, have recognized what an export item they have, and have protected it by creating DOC (Denomination of Control) and DOCG (Denomination of Control Guaranteed) — assurances that the wine is what the label says it is.

Wine buyers must be patient when dealing with Italian red wines, whose grapes take considerable time to mature. Vinification processes over the years have improved and as a consequence wines can now be matured earlier; but overall, the majority of reds on the shelves today were made by the older method and subsequently need time to mature.

Cooking with Bea

The combination of taste, color, and texture makes Italian cuisine a universal favorite. This is certainly true where the Italian population continues to guard zealously the sanctity of their native cuisine and the fragrances of *home*. The kitchens of the second and third generations of Italo-Americans are still regularly dusted with the fine flour used for making golden-crusted bread and pastas. Huge, shiny aluminum pots (or in some treasured cases, *Nonna*'s chipped blue and white enamel soup kettle) cradle the steaming *brodo* used for a variety of sauce bases and as a liquid accompaniment to fanciful filled pasta shapes such as *tortellini* and *agnolotti*.

So it is with Beatrice Lazzaro. Although Bea is in many ways as modern as today's latest innovation, when it comes to cooking, hers is still "the old way." Therefore, it is no surprise, when watching a television cooking show with her, to hear Bea burst out:

"That's sloppy cooking. That's not *right!*"

Because I am a pot slammer and always somehow manage to get half of the vegetables I'm chopping on the floor, I turn in wonder:

"Does it matter, Bea, as long as the eating is good?"

"Of course it matters. . . . It's not the way to *do* things!"

My friend Bea is an exquisitely tuned, highly efficient, and loving "cooking machine." Her julienned carrots could have been cut by computer. Each ravioli "pillow" has the exact amount of filling couched in its beautifully symmetrical pasta casing. Her minestrone is always the correct consistency and her Bolognese bread is, quite simply, an art form. How does she measure? — by eye and that inimitable cook's *instinct*. Of course, all of this care could mean anxious clock-watching if it were practiced by someone less skilled, but Bea's chubby hands fly, with everything looking so effortless, and the results are ambrosial!

Those of you who have undertaken the labor of love that is homemade pasta know it's not the *neatest* occupation in the world. My kitchen gets even messier than when I make bread! However, by some magic, this doesn't seem to apply for Bea: somehow the Lazzaro kitchen remains pristine — or nearly so.

Bea does of course dirty her share of pots and pans. However, cooking with Bea, learning her personal cooking techniques, and sharing her treasury of familial folk cookery knowledge makes even the "detergent and sink duty" a festive occasion. Her wisdom, humor, and simple practicality turn even the pot scrubbing into a pleasure; a pleasure enhanced, to no small degree, by the knowledge that all the good things that created the mess are soon to be savored. In the meantime, have a glass of wine, and . . .

"Get a fresh dishtowel. . . . That one's all wet."

There are many fun parts to "Cooking with Bea," but perhaps the most invigorating is not knowing exactly when Bea will suddenly share one of her pithy, and often sprightly, insights into the world of Italian cooking. During the time we worked together on this book, she peppered our conversations with many of her "Bea-isms," as I like to call them, and sometimes in the most unlikely places and at the most unlikely times. I tried to make note of the best of them to share them with you here: Bea on Italian cooking, Bea on tomatoes, Bea on leftovers, and so on. Then, to end this section, Bea spelled out her way of making pasta, along with the recipes both for the basic pastas she uses and for her own very special *pesto.*

We hope you will find these insights and "old ways" of doing useful . . . and inspiring.

Bea on Regional Italian Recipes

Going through our collection of recipes for the regional section of the book, I was perplexed:

"Bea, some of these recipes seem to be repeated."

"They're not really; study them carefully."

"Olive oil is olive oil is olive oil, isn't it?"

"I'm ashamed of you." Bea's admonishing looks are like melting butter. "Look carefully at all the ingredients. Each little variation makes a big difference to the cooks from the different provinces," she insists.

And so I learn that the slight variations in amounts as well as basic ingredients are of utmost importance to the purists of regional cooking, and I am careful to copy Bea's specified proportions, just as she's written them in her clear, firm hand.

As I continue to fan pages, another "constant" strikes me, and again I am puzzled:

"Every third recipe has the same vegetable 'triumvirate': carrots, onions, and celery!"

Beatrice straightens to her full five feet, directs her wooden spoon like a professorial pointer, and intones, "That's a *soffritto*, or *battuto*, the backbone of the entire cuisine of Italy! And, unlike many other elements in the cooking, it's found in every regional kitchen in the country."

And so, I realize, in Italy the *soffritto* is what the *mirepoix* is in France. The message: never start an Italian dinner without the crunchy three in your vegetable inventory.

Bea makes me understand that, as the gifted oenologist can name the year and the vineyard from which his glass of wine comes, so too can the seasoned Italian pasta lover name the cook's place of origin — this from both the consistency of the noodle and the special, good things in the sauce. For most of us the small differences in texture and flavor, and the great variances of shape, are only interesting; for the Italian food expert they present a definitive clue. They also are the stuff memories are made of . . . the meeting of "brain and belly."

"Just like Mamma's. . . . That's Italian!"

Bea on Tomatoes

As evidence of the importance to Bea of tomatoes in her cooking, when she says *small* can she means a 1-pound can, and so on. A can has to be 32 full ounces before she'll call it *large*. But when Bea and I discussed tomatoes, it was more than can size that perplexed me.

"Bea, I'm in a total state of confusion about tomatoes. Remember the old song, 'You say tomatoes and I say tomahtoes?' Well, that's kind of the way I feel, particularly the part about 'Let's call the whole thing off!' What's with the fresh tomatoes, the canned tomatoes, and now there's this new carton of 'kitchen ready' tomatoes. Are they all the same or is there *really* a great difference in taste . . . and when can we substitute one for the other?"

Bea has the most beautiful smile in the world, and she's not the least bit miserly with its use.

"Of course there's a difference in taste, but it's not all that important in family cooking. Let me explain. I find that the best way to cook is the way the cook finds easiest and that still lets her enjoy putting that meal on the table for her family. Time is an enormous factor and so is the budget a cook has to work with. If one has the will and the free hours to 'put up' fresh tomatoes when they're at their peak and cheap, great — do it!"

"Bea, I'm still not quite satisfied. I spent days at your elbow last summer while you were canning those tomatoes from your garden, including the big, big ones. You have three kinds of tomatoes from which to choose, and you do use them all for different dishes. . . . Why?"

"It has to do," Bea replies, "with how I feel about a recipe, and also what's on my schedule for that day. I suppose in most cases it has to do with what the cook has available. If you run out of one thing, you substitute another. I never feel that the end result is not going to be good if I make a change; sometimes it's *better.* The important thing is not to be too rigid about cooking. If your sauce is a little less concentrated than you'd like, add a little tomato paste, or stir in a bit of flour. If the tomatoes you used are a bit acid, use a pinch of sugar and a pinch of baking soda. Another way is to mix fresh and preserved. Don't forget, no two tomatoes are going to have the same taste no matter *what* is done to them."

I pause in my frantic scribbling to agree with Bea that "tasting food as you go along" is really what it's all about.

"Maybe you also want to add that an easy way to peel tomatoes is by dropping them in boiling water for thirty seconds or so — that might help — and don't forget to include that overcooking tomatoes makes them bitter. The way to tell whether a tomato sauce is done is by the color of the oil or fats that surface. When the fat is a deep, rich red, your sauce is ready."

So it's not only *tasting* as you go along, it's also a general vigilance. You might say that cooking is like baby-sitting: never take your eyes off your charge . . . your eyes *or* your nose!

Bea on Seasonings

"Why do your seasonings always have such a special taste?" I asked Bea. "They are *defined* but not pervasive or overpowering. Some cooks seem to feel that if one is able to pinpoint a spice, the cook has used too much."

"That's nonsense," Bea retorts. "What's the point of making 'tarragon chicken' if it doesn't taste like tarragon? It's one of the reasons why I use my own homemade garlic salt (see recipe following). The flavor is 'true.' There aren't any preservatives or additives; it's all fresh and natural, and because of that you need much *less* to season. If a recipe outside this book were to call for half a teaspoon of garlic salt, using my own fresh, I would use about one-eighth of a teaspoon measure, or about a quarter of the amount called for. Oh, and another thing about garlic. I always use a garlic press and *discard* what's left in the little bowl. You get a much purer flavor and no bitterness without the outside layers of the peeled clove.

Bea Lazzaro's Homemade Garlic Salt

Bea uses this fine seasoning as a light "overcoat" for many of her ethnic specialties. It also makes a wonderful kitchen gift. Bea keeps one jar always ready in a screw-top container on one of her refrigerator door shelves: it gets dried out and rancid if not refrigerated. You'll find we have recommended its use throughout the book when garlic seasoning is called for. You can use others but this does something special.

- 1 large whole head garlic, peeled
- 2 containers Morton's LITE salt or ½ pound regular salt
- Freshly ground black pepper to taste

Grind all seasonings together thoroughly in a food processor or with a mortar and pestle. Fill sterilized jars with the mixture and store in a refrigerator. It will keep for several months.

Makes 1 pint

"And there are other little cook's tricks," Bea continues, "not really 'tricks' but things that cooks find work for them. For example, when I'm cooking with fresh mushrooms, I like to chop in a few of the dried Italian mushrooms; they lend that extra 'earthy' flavor. Or, if I find I'm short of fresh basil or rosemary and only have a few sprigs, then I put some of the dried spice on top of the fresh and chop them together to 'release' the flavor."

"Don't stop now, Bea, we're on a roll. Let's have some more of these seasoning tips."

"Well, some folks like bay leaves, others don't. I cook with them and then remove the leaf itself before serving. I find it's not the flavor that bothers some people, but the actual presence of the tough leaves."

"What about parsley: which is better, the curly or the flat variety, and why?" I was curious even though I thought I knew Bea's choice: I knew I had never seen the common curly variety in *her* kitchen.

"The flat Italian parsley is best for cooking. It has more flavor, but the curly is pretty. If you can't find the flat parsley for a special dish, then use about half again as much of the curly for almost the same flavor. I said 'almost': the two varieties are a little bit like pot marjoram and oregano. Pot marjoram is in the same family of herbs as oregano, and the flavor is similar but much less pronounced."

Bolognese Spice Mix

Use judiciously when a dish seems to "need" something.

- 4 teaspoons cinnamon
- 1½ teaspoons grated nutmeg
- ½ teaspoon ground cloves
- 1¼ teaspoons ground cardamom
- 1½ teaspoons pepper
- 1 teaspoon ground coriander seeds

Pulverize all together in a food processor or with a mortar and pestle. Sift, and put in a tightly closed jar. Refrigerate.

Makes ⅔ cup

The popular spice mixture listed above is "put up" by the housewives of Bologna and is similar in some regards to *Spezie Lombardina* — a spice mix used widely in Lombardy (the recipe for which can be found on page 98 in the Lombardy section).

Bea on the Italian Cook's Pantry

When asked which ingredients are basic to a proper Italian cookery pantry, Bea compiled the following "beginner's" list.

The Italian Cook's Basic Pantry

- Good, imported olive oil (Bue or Pastene)
- Balsamic vinegar (a fine, concentrated wine vinegar from Modena)
- Wine vinegar (good quality of cook's preference)
- Tomato paste (6-ounce cans)
- Tomato purée (1-pound cans)
- Plum tomatoes, peeled San Marzano (28- and 35-ounce cans)
- Arborio rice (a 5-pound bag)
- Cornmeal, ground (a 5-pound bag)
- Semolina flour (a 5-pound bag)
- Canned anchovies, both rolled and flat (Pastene)
- Good quality white meat tuna
- Grated Parmesan cheese (mild)
- Grated Romano or pecorino cheese (stronger)

and

The Following Spices

- Bay leaves
- Cayenne
- Ginger
- Marjoram
- Mint
- Nutmeg
- Oregano
- Rosemary
- Sage
- Thyme

These spices should be in your cupboard in their dried form. When fresh herbs are available, by all means use them. A rule of thumb for herb use is one-third of the amount of dried herbs equals the full fresh herb measure. For example, 1 *teaspoon* dried equals 1 *tablespoon* fresh. When using dried herbs, rub them between your hands to allow your body heat and oils to release the flavor. Another tip, mentioned elsewhere in these pages, is to chop fresh and dried together.

Bea finishes her advisory on herbs by urging all cooks to grow their own. In her words, "It's a delightful and rewarding hobby."

Bea on Leftovers

"Bea, what in the world are you doing with all of those?" I wanted to know, "those" referring to a nightmare number of plastic refrigerator dishes: tall ones, short ones, square ones, round ones, *plus* several irregular-shaped foil packages of mystery foods.

"I'm going to use them — or what's in them — for lunch today. Let's see, green beans in here. I remember that there was a bit of cucumber salad somewhere. Here it is. Into the salad bowl with both of them. Now I'll just thinly slice an onion on top, add a bit more Balsamic vinegar, olive oil, and a pinch of my garlic salt, give it a stir. . . . There, salad's ready!"

"Now, what's in this one?" she continued. "A cup of cooked *ziti*. And *that* little blue container has a few serving spoonfuls of *penne*. Those mixed with what's left of the *lasagne* should give me about four cups of pasta. I'll just beat up two eggs. Where's the grated Parmesan? Here it is, and in it goes, about half of a cup. I'll just roughly mix this all together, put it into a buttered casserole, and let it bake at about 375°F., just until the top is brown and crispy. We could also make a *frittella* like my grandmother used to make, egg noodle fritters, or if it was rice that was left over, *frittella di riso*. Same idea as the casserole: you'd add several eggs depending on the amount of leftover pasta or rice. If it was mixed with soup, you'd sprinkle in a little flour and a pinch of baking powder, and then add grated cheese. The batter should be about the consistency of pancake batter and dropped by spoonfuls into hot oil or lard . . . then *presto . . . frittelle!*"

After about ten minutes of Bea's "show and tell," I'm getting into the spirit of things. Peeling open a foil-wrapped packet, I find a lamb bone with a few lonely shreds of meat still intact (most of us would have thrown this away), and being basically a grown-up "bad kid," I challenge:

"And what are you planning to do with this?"

"Oh, you found my lamb bone . . . . Good, that's the base for my white bean soup for tomorrow!" And away she twinkles to put the beans on to soak.

The message here is clear: in the hands of a master, no morsel of food is without use, nor will it go unappreciated if treated with loving creativity and concern.

That was the *best* lunch! — and a good lesson for us all.

Bea's Basic Pasta Recipes

During the extensive research that went into this book, I spoke with dozens of fine Italian *natural* cooks; women and men who have spent a lifetime making pasta at home, in the time-honored "by feel" fashion. There are two areas in which there are as many variations as there are cooks: first, the precise step-by-step process for homemade pasta, including the exact proportion of the ingredients; second, what constitutes the *proper* tomato sauce.

What follows is a primer on the basic pasta recipes from Bea's kitchen. In addition, there is a series of variations for your pleasure, experimentation, and cookery trivia inventory. Unless otherwise noted, these recipes will make enough dough to prepare pasta for 10. It is a good deal of loving work, but work that will yield you ample for a large group, or if you are a small family, enough to freeze for another time. Beginning on page 38, you will find complete instructions for making Bea's basic pasta recipes either by hand or by machine. Bea does both.

Basic #1: Eggless Pasta

4 cups flour
1 cup water
1 tablespoon olive oil

Prepare per instructions for handmade or machine-made pasta, beginning on page 38.

Note: This cooks faster than classic, dry pasta.

Basic # 2: Classic Egg Pasta

Because this is the most common kind of pasta made, we are giving you an ingredient breakdown for 4, 6, 8, and 10 persons.

For 4:	2 extra-large eggs	1½ cups flour
For 6:	3 extra-large eggs	2¼ cups flour
For 8:	4 extra-large eggs	3 cups flour
For 10:	5 extra-large eggs	3½ cups flour

Prepare dough as per Homemade Pasta Bea's Way or by machine (see page 38 and pages following).

Basic # 3: Green Spinach Pasta

- 2 extra-large eggs
- 3½ cups flour
- 1 package (10 ounces) frozen spinach, cooked and squeezed dry

Purée spinach in blender or food processor. Make flour well as described on page 39, and add spinach purée and eggs alternately. Continue process as described.

Basic # 4: Pasta for Filling (e.g., ravioli, tortellini)

- 3 extra-large eggs
- 1 to 2 teaspoons warm water
- 3½ to 4 cups flour
- 1 teaspoon salt

Prepare dough as on page 38, and divide into thirds for easy handling.

Note: See index for specific *ravioli* and *tortellini* recipes and for handling techniques.

Basic # 5: Semolina Pasta

- 4 cups all-purpose flour
- 1 teaspoon salt
- 2 cups semolina flour
- 2 to 3 tablespoons warm water

Prepare dough as for Basic #1, #2, or #3 Pasta.

Basic #6: Tomato Pasta

2 tablespoons chopped basil
3 tablespoons chopped parsley
5 extra-large eggs
3¾ to 4 cups flour
1 can (6 ounces) tomato paste

Chop the basil and parsley together (very fine) in the food processor, or by hand if need be.

Proceed as with the other pastas, alternating the mixing of the eggs with like amounts of the herbs and tomato paste.

These are the six basic pastas made in the good Italian kitchen, but as with all creative work, occasionally the cook gets bored and then there's no end to the mischief that she or he can get into with pasta dough. The following pasta recipes translated from an old Northern Italian cookbook are only two examples. The "yield" was not indicated, but with the given quantities, this would make *a lot* of very expensive pasta!

Pasta al Salmone Affumicato

Smoked Salmon Pasta

4 cups semolina flour
2 cups all-purpose flour
9 or 10 eggs
1¼ pounds smoked salmon, chopped

Proceed as with other pastas, alternating addition of eggs and salmon.

Pasta al Basilico

Pasta with Basil

4 cups flour
4 eggs
¾ cup chopped basil

Mix as with others, alternating addition of eggs with addition of basil.

Pasta di Cacao

Pasta with Cocoa

This is a pasta which, although flavored with cocoa, is not sweet. Angelina Zanleoni makes a dish called five-colored pasta. This is one of the colored pastas she uses.

2½ cups flour
1 tablespoon oil
4 eggs
2 heaping teaspoons unsweetened cocoa
Warm water as necessary

Mix as above, adding eggs alternately with the cocoa, and adding warm water as needed to make a workable dough.

Pasta Fatta in Casa Stile Lazzaro

Homemade Pasta Bea's Way

Equipment Needed:

A plain (unfinished) heavy board. The board should measure at least 24 by 40 inches. Formica will serve as well, as will marble.

A *mattarella.* This is a 36-inch long and 1¼-inch in diameter rolling pin. A hard, wooden shovel handle will also do nicely. Either can be purchased in a good hardware store.

A broad-bladed *sharp* knife.

Process:

1. Rub rolling pin lightly with olive oil, then wipe and dust with a light flour coating. Wipe down with a paper towel.
2. Dust the work board lightly with flour.

3. In the center of the work board make a "well" or "ring" of flour and into this break the eggs (sometimes all at once, sometimes alternating with other ingredients as per the recipe). Beat eggs lightly as they are added.

In mixing pasta dough, work carefully from the inside of the "well" to draw the flour into the beaten-egg mixture.

4. Work from the inside of the well with a fork to bring, and mix, the flour into the eggs.
5. Mix well, and form into a ball.
6. Place the dough ball into a plastic bag and allow it to "rest" for 5 minutes (first resting period).
7. Clean off your kneading board; lightly reflour it if necessary.
8. Remove dough from the plastic bag to the board and *work* it with the hands, pulling, folding, and punching until the dough is smooth and blisters form on the top of the mass.

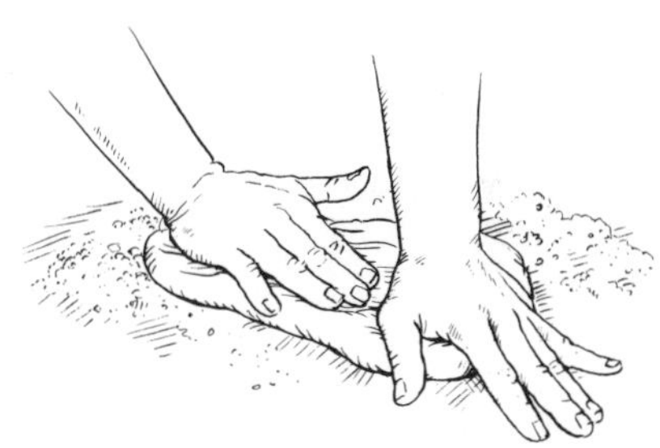

To knead properly, work the dough firmly, but not roughly, with first one hand and then the other.

9. Return the dough to the plastic bag for another 5 minutes (second rest). Note: If dough still seems too dry or crumbly, add a few spoonfuls water (just enough to soften the mass); if it seems too sticky, add a bit more flour.

10. Rework dough until smooth, then return it to the plastic bag for its third rest, this time for 30 minutes. These relaxation techniques make the dough more pliable and easier to handle. (Bea comments wryly, "Doesn't everything behave better after it's had a bit of rest?") In fact, all doughs benefit from the "rest" process — bread, pasta, and also pie crust dough. It allows the dough to stretch while it is being worked with; otherwise it has a tendency to "spring back."

11. Put the ball of dough on the floured board. Press down to flatten.

12. With the rolling pin, begin to form it into a circle, rolling away from your body, turning the dough a quarter turn each time — *counterclockwise.*

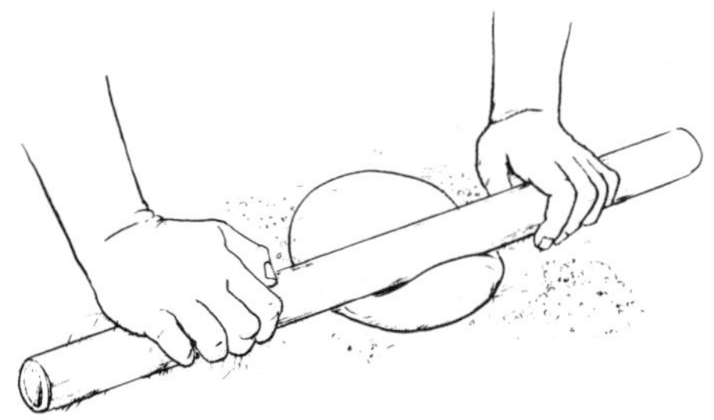

Use a mattarella *(or other rolling pin) to roll out the pasta dough. After each roll, the dough is turned a quarter turn counterclockwise and then lightly rolled again until it is about 1/16-inch thick.*

13. Continue to roll and turn, using a smooth, light motion, keeping the circle of dough as symmetrical as possible, until the dough is about $\frac{1}{16}$-inch thick. (Bea uses an ancient way of rolling dough which involves draping the far side of the pasta round over the *mattarella* towards her body. She then rolls the *mattarella* counterclockwise to furl and unfurl the pasta until it is Kraft-paper thin.)

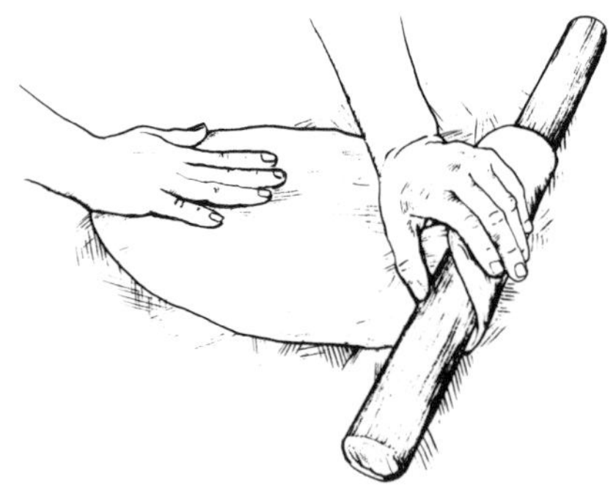

When the dough is close to its desired thickness, the mattarella *can be used to stretch it out even further and to smooth out any uneven spots.*

14. Gently pick up the circle in both hands. Hold it up to the light to check for places where the dough is too thick.
15. Return dough to the board and even out any thick spots. The dough should be as thin as possible and thoroughly "even."
16. After dough is rolled out to desired thickness, put it on a cotton cloth to dry — just to the point where it can be handled without breaking. (You may want to divide the dough into several parts if you are making large batches; it will be easier to handle.)

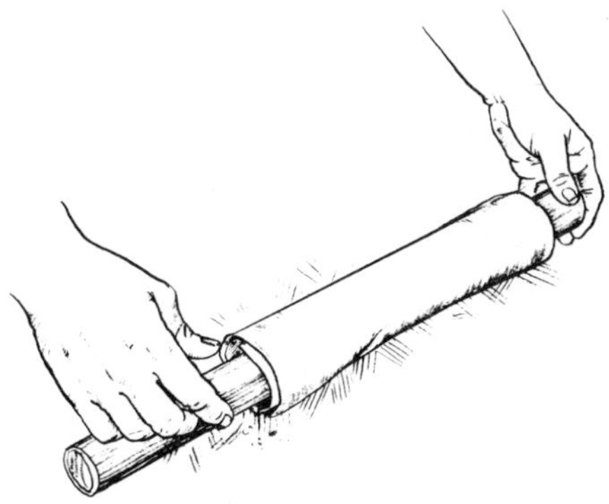

One method to ready the stretched pasta dough for cutting is to reroll it lightly around the mattarella.

17. Roll the circle of dough loosely back on the *mattarella*. Slide the pin out, press gently down on the rolled dough with your hand, and cut the pasta the desired width for your recipe. (See list and illustration following.)
18. To unfold the pasta, toss it gently with your fingers.

Cutting Widths:

Cannelloni: first cut 4-inch strips, then unroll and cut crosswise to make squares.

Fettuccine: cut 1/16-inch-wide strips (dough for fettuccine is rolled out a little thicker than the standard 1/16 inch).

Lasagne: 1 inch to 4 or 5 inches for the extra-wide variety.

Manicotti: first cut 3½-inch strips, then make squares.

Pappardelle: cut ¾- to 1-inch strips.

Quadrini/Quadrucci: first cut ¼-inch strips, keeping them together. Then cut across strips; loosen and repeat to cut into tiny squares.

Ravioli: cut into strips 2 inches wide, then unroll and cut every 4 inches to make 2-inch squares.

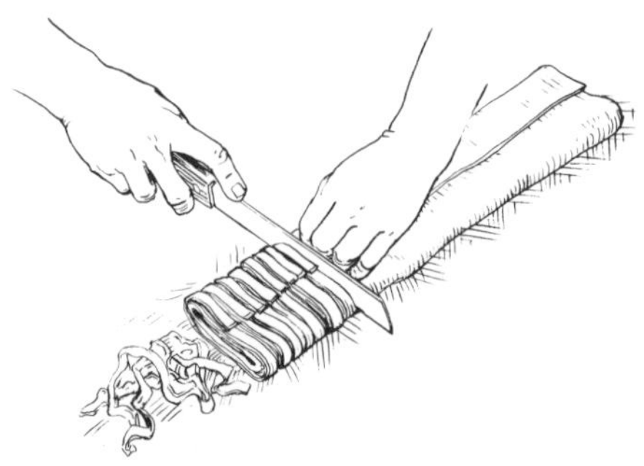

Holding the dough lightly and keeping the knife straight, pasta strips are cut to the desired width. Be careful: the knife is sharp.

Tagliarini: narrowest cut (used in chicken soup).

Tagliatelle: cut ⅛- to ¾-inch strips.

Trenette: narrow cut (used with *pesto*).

Machine-Made Pasta

1. Make dough as described; roll a bit with the *mattarella*.
2. Cut into strips 3 inches wide and 5 to 6 inches long.
3. Feed strips several times into the rollers of the machine, changing notches for thickness wanted (see guide below). Dry on a cotton cloth.

One of several available pasta-making machines.

Notch Guide

ROLLING	CUTTING
Fettuccine: use third to last notch.	*Fettuccine:* use wide cutter.
Tagliarini: use last notch.	*Tagliarini:* use narrowest cutter.
Tagliatelle: use second to last notch.	*Tagliatelle:* use medium cutter.

Bea's Do's and Don'ts for Making and Using Pasta

1. Add a bit of water if dough is dry.
2. When mixing flour and eggs, don't try to save time by doing it all at once. Incorporate slowly and smoothly. Be gentle.
3. Cover pasta and allow it to relax for 30 minutes before rolling. Relax dough for several minutes *covered* before handling.
4. During any part of the process, reflour board and the pasta mass itself if either gets sticky.
5. Don't leave pasta dough for filling uncovered. It will dry out and the edge seals won't stick.
6. Don't cut pasta (either by hand or by machine) if the pasta is not dry to the touch. This causes the ribbons to stick to each other.
7. Don't plan to make pasta on a hot, muggy summer day. Choose a cool day, preferably when house heat is on and the atmosphere is dry.
8. When cooking her finished homemade pasta — as with prepared — Bea likes to add a tablespoon of oil to the cooking pot; it keeps the pasta from sticking.

Pasta Sauces

No matter how good the pasta, there are few Italian pastas that stand alone. Like sunshine, it is the sauce that makes the day. In *Italian Provincial Cookery* you will find many sauces from the various Italian regions. There was also a short list of them on page 9, noting, too, some of Bea's favorites. You will meet many more as you cook your way through this book — and, of course, in the index. In planning how much sauce she will need, Bea plans on 1 pound of pasta for every 6 people, and 2 to 3 cups of sauce for each pound of pasta.

Beyond that, Bea shares with you here her own *pesto* recipe.

Pesto alla Beatrice

Bea's Pesto

Makes ¾ to 1 cup

If you judge the pedigree of this famous sauce by the supermarket prices for several ounces, you'll be impressed indeed. Substituting walnuts for the very expensive pine nuts (pignoli) *alters the exquisite results very little. Try it and see. Bea and I both keep several plastic containers of this in the freezer at all times and spoon out whatever quantity we will use immediately. It's not only an unequaled topping for pasta, but the Northern Italians stir a spoonful into soups and egg dishes as well. You'll find other* pesto *recipes as you travel the pages of our book.*

1 package (3 ounces) cream cheese
1 cup *fresh* basil leaves
2 cloves garlic
½ cup olive oil
Good handful of parsley
⅓ cup walnuts or pine nuts
Salt and pepper to taste
¼ cup combined grated Romano and Parmesan cheeses

Place all of the ingredients in the glass container of your blender. Grind to a grainy consistency. It should *not* be paste-smooth.

The Italian Regions and Their Recipes

Piedmont/Valle d'Aosta

The Special Wines, Beer & Cheeses of
Piedmont/Valle d'Aosta

Wines and Beer of the Regions

The Home of Vermouth: *Vermouth di Torino*

Dry reds: *Barbaresco, Barbera, Barolo, Dolcetto, Donnaz, Enfer d'Arvier, Gattinara, Ghemme, Grignolino, Prunotto*

Demi-sec red: *Freisa*

Dry whites: *Cortese, Cossan, Gavi, Marchese Spinola, Morget, Pinot Bianco, Riesling*

Sweet whites (sparkling): *Gancia,* and the famous and delicate *Asti Spumante*

Beer: *Zimmermann* (Gressonay)

Wines Available in the United States

Dry reds: *Barolo, Gattinara Dessilani, Prunotto*

Dry whites: *Gavi, Marchese Spinola*

Sweet whites (sparkling): *Asti Spumante, Gancia*

Cheeses of the Regions

Bross, Castelmagno, Erborinati, Formagette, Frachet, and the outstanding *Fontina (d'Aosta)*

Vielle marmitta, buona sopa.

The older the pot, the better the soup.

For those travelers who have been blessed enough to enter Italy through its northernmost door, the Matterhorn at their back and the lakes at their feet, it's difficult to understand how the citizens of this Italian border area could bring themselves to abandon their homeland for the uncertain fortunes of the New World, and New England in particular.

But the decision once taken, perhaps they found the adjustment not so difficult. Personal industriousness and dynamism are traits of both regions; then too, remember that the climate of our Eastern shores, where most of the emigrants from Piedmont/Valle d'Aosta made their homes, was less shocking to folk accustomed to the caprice and intensity of Alpine weather. In addition, one can find considerable Celtic influence to use in comparing Boston, "The Hub" — one of New England's central cities — with Turin, the capital of Piedmont. Of course, the historic time frames are completely different: Boston's Celtic influences are mostly of this century, whereas on the shores of the River Po it was the elephant-borne army of Hannibal that was harassed and resisted by the early (pre-Roman) Celt tribesmen. The cooperative farming that is today practiced in the Tanaro and Po valleys may well stem from the early banding together for safety and better land yield — the "clan" concept, then as now.

The cuisine of Piedmont/Valle d'Aosta is at its honest best in the healthy mountain dishes indigenous to the area north of Turin. The city itself, as the magical meeting point between the French and Italian cultures, offers some of the most elaborate cuisine in all of Italy.

Waverly Root, in his *The Food of Italy*, says of the regional table, "It depends on food resources peculiar to the region, or concoctions born of local genius and found nowhere else; and then there are echoes of dishes from across the border . . . not so much borrowings as sharings with adjacent areas. . . ."

Culinary specialties of the Piedmont/Valle d'Aosta area often center around the white truffles (*trifola d'Alba*) that are the "jewels" of these regions. They are used in many ways, including in omelets, in antipasti, sliced over tossed salads, and in several of the area's very special dishes, recipes for which follow. The round-grained rice from the Vercelli and Novara farming districts is another specialty also represented in the following recipes. The Turin area, in turn, boasts among other things the especially well-known and delicious *grissini* (bread sticks). Among the area's most renowned dishes are *Bagna Cauda,* a hot anchovy dip; *Bollito Misto,* Italy's version of the New England boiled dinner; *Fonduta,* a velvety fondue; and *Agnolotti,* over-sized ravioli: recipes for all four are among the others that follow here.

Both Piedmont and Valle d'Aosta use fresh butter in their cooking — butter made from the milk of the cattle that graze on the Alpine grass and wildflowers, while the sweet cream from the same cattle also creates cheeses which are a connoisseur's delight. Game is also plentiful in the rocky reaches of both provinces; deer, hare, and marmot coexist in abundance with domestic animals.

Food fairs or *feste* are a happy local custom, and there are charming country inns which exist to honor and perpetuate these rites. It's interesting to note that the names of the hostelries translated could put one in the English countryside: "The Golden Cannon," "The White Horse," "Dead Tree Inn," and the "Red Oxen," for example. Colorful folk dances (the *Monferrina* and the *Corrente*) are still enjoyed in their courtyards and barns.

In the Asti environs (home of the bubbly grape delight, *Asti Spumante*), there are *feste di polentone,* during which gargantuan quantities of *polenta* are prepared, consumed, and "chased" with the famous wine. Maize, the base ingredient of the specialty, has a second carnival day annually, which coincides with grape-pressing time — dual reason for celebration. Corn-husking competitions, bonfires, ancient ball games, and the usual marathon dining also mark these days of innocent merrymaking.

What greater moment of bliss than when sampling one of the Piedmont/Valle d'Aosta truffle-adorned *Camoscio in Salmi* (chamois in sauce), with a bottle of Bramaterra or Caramino. And, it is worthy of note that the wine-cellar treasures of the region are surpassed only by the wealth of its liqueurs and vermouth.

Tarry awhile; we've things yet untasted!

Antipasto Nicolino

Makes 12 pints

Do you know what antipasto really is? This is a version shared with us by Pace Nicolino, one of our friends in Barre, Vermont. Bea likens it to the dish known as caponata *in Southern Italy.*

- 2 to 3 stalks celery
- 1 small carrot
- 1 small green pepper
- 1 can (6 ounces) tomato paste
- 1 pint cider vinegar
- 2 tablespoons sugar
- 4 cans (2 ounces each) anchovies
- Scant pint olive oil
- 1 cup water
- 3 tablespoons flour
- Pinch of ground cloves
- 1 cup green olives
- 1 cup black olives
- 2 pounds pearl onions
- 1 jar (14 ounces) artichokes (in water, not pickled)
- 1 small jar gherkin pickles
- 1 pint button mushrooms (fresh preferred)
- 3 large cans (12 ounces each) chunk tuna
- Salt to taste

The night before, cut the celery, carrot, and green pepper into random chunks and soak them in salted cold water overnight. Then drain and blanch the soaked vegetables. When ready, boil the first 11 ingredients (through the cloves) together for 10 minutes. Then add the green and black olives, onions, artichokes, pickles, and mushrooms. Allow to continue simmering for about 15 minutes. Then add tuna and simmer an additional 10 minutes. Salt to taste and put in sterilized pint jars, lightly covering top with oil before capping. Keeps in a cool place indefinitely.

Note: It is not necessary to process this mix. Just keep cool — and then enjoy!

Bagna Cauda

Hot Raw Vegetable Dip

For 4 to 6

The Italian answer to happy calorie watching, an ancient dish which suddenly has found itself both healthful and "chic."

- 1 cup olive oil
- ½ cup butter
- 6 cloves garlic, sliced
- 1 can (2 ounces) flat anchovies, rinsed
- A few grindings black pepper
- 2-inch strips of raw carrots, celery, fennel, green and red sweet peppers, radish roses, broccoli and cauliflower florets, scallions, zucchini strips, pea pods, etc.

Melt oil with butter. Add garlic; when it begins to turn golden, add anchovies and mash. Season with pepper. Put into small chafing dish over low heat and surround with the vegetables.

Note: In a very old recipe book from Cigliano, walnut oil was used in place of the mixture of olive oil and butter. Because it is difficult to find and also quite expensive, Bea suggests a "mock" walnut oil that she makes by putting ⅓ cup of walnut halves in ½ cup of corn or safflower oil. Whir in the blender until nuts are puréed. Place in a covered jar for a few days. When ready to use, strain through a cloth and use for the *Bagna Cauda* if you desire.

Frittelle di Fontina d'Aosta

Cheese Fritters

For 4

- ½ pound Fontina cheese, finely diced
- ½ cup bread crumbs
- Herb bouquet of 1 heaping tablespoon each fresh chopped rosemary, basil, and parsley
- ½ pound leftover meat, diced
- 2 eggs
- 2 to 3 tablespoons milk
- Salt and pepper to taste
- Deep fat, for frying

Put diced Fontina into a bowl with the bread crumbs and the herbs. Mix in diced meat, eggs, milk, salt, and pepper. Heat the oil in a deep fryer or deep heavy saucepan. Drop the fritter mixture by spoonfuls into the oil. Allow to brown on all sides. Drain on paper towels and serve at once as an hors d'oeuvre or as a side course.

Valle d'Aosta Fonduta

Fondue

Makes 2 to 3 cups

Has anyone ever written a sonnet about fondue? This creamy delight deserves no less. The color comes from the large, golden wheels of the local Fontina cheese, and unlike some of its cousins, this fondue is made without alcoholic help! Perhaps one is expected to become intoxicated with the truffle topping.

- 1 cup milk
- ¾ pound Fontina cheese, thinly sliced
- 3 tablespoons butter
- 4 egg yolks
- 1 small white truffle, thinly sliced
- Dash of white pepper
- Chunks of French or Italian bread

In a stainless steel pot, combine the milk and the cheese; cover and leave at room temperature for several hours. Then, in a fondue pan or double boiler, melt the butter over low heat, and add the cheese and milk mixture, whisking constantly until the cheese is stringy. Intensify the heat slightly and whisk faster. Next, add egg yolks, one at a time, continuing to whisk. If the 4 yolks do not make a foamy fondue, add another yolk. The consistency should be thick and very creamy — just right for clinging to the dipped bread chunks. Garnish with white pepper and the truffle slices.

Note: If truffles are not in your budget or not available, substitute a diced medium white mushroom. The palate will know the difference, but perhaps for one happy moment the eye will not!

Riso alla Piemontese

Rice, Piedmont-Style For 6

This dish is identical in preparation to the Risotto alla Milanese *(see page 101) except that 2/3 cup of dry white wine is included in the last liquid addition. The finished rice is adorned with the famed truffles of the Piedmont region, sliced or chopped on top, and is served with a simple meat sauce.*

Agnolotti Lago Maggiore

Ravioli, Piedmont-Style For 6

This is an ancient recipe of the region which Bea has revised. It is normally made on Mondays because it is an ideal way to use up leftover bits of meat. The flavor varies with the meats used.

Pasta:

1 recipe Pasta for Filling (see page 36)

Make pasta. Set aside while you prepare the filling (below).

Meatball Filling:

- 3 tablespoons olive oil
- ½ stick (4 tablespoons) butter
- 1½ pounds ground leftover meat
- 4 Italian sausage links
- 1 small onion
- 1 clove garlic, crushed
- 2 sprigs fresh rosemary
- 2 tablespoons flour
- 1 cup stock
- 3 whole tomatoes
- 1 head escarole
- ¾ cup grated Parmesan cheese
- 3 eggs, well beaten
- Dash of nutmeg
- Salt and pepper to taste

In a large skillet, melt the oil and butter; brown the ground meat and the sausages from which the casings have been removed. Then remove the meat and place aside. In the same skillet, sauté onion, garlic, and rosemary. Sprinkle with flour, stirring constantly, and add the stock. Peel, seed, and crush the tomatoes and add to the onion mixture. Replace the meat and simmer over low heat for about 1 hour, stirring occasionally. Cook the escarole; drain and chop fine. When the meat mixture is done, add the escarole, cheese, and well-beaten eggs. Mix well, season with nutmeg, salt, and pepper; then, with your fingers, shape into marble-sized meatballs.

Assembly:

Roll out pasta and cut into 3-inch-wide strips. On half of a strip of pasta, place the meatballs every 2½ inches (see sketch). Fold over the remaining half and seal between the meatball fillings and around the edges by pressing down with your fingers. Cut, using a pasta wheel. The end product should be even(ish) 1½-inch filled squares. Place *agnolotti* on a floured cloth, and allow them to dry. Boil in salted water until *al dente,* and serve in broth or topped with a favorite sauce.

Note: Cooked spinach may be substituted for the escarole. *Agnolotti* should be made smaller for broth.

The agnolotti *strips are first filled, then folded, and then cut into their individual packets.*

Cannelloni di Limone

Filled Pasta Tubes

For 6

A specialty of the city of Limone, the fragrance of this dish warming in the oven is the "stuff" of which food dreams are made.

Filling:

1 pound stewing veal
4 tablespoons butter
Water or broth as needed
1 pound fresh or 1 package (10 ounces) frozen spinach
¼ pound boiled ham
2 eggs
Salt and pepper to taste
½ cup grated Parmesan cheese
¼ teaspoon nutmeg

In a Dutch oven, braise the veal in butter over low heat, adding water or broth if necessary to keep the meat moist. Cook, squeeze dry, and chop spinach and mix thoroughly with remaining filling ingredients. When veal is done, grind it with its juices and combine with the spinach mixture.

Pasta:

1 recipe Classic 3-Egg Pasta (see page 36)

Make pasta, roll it out thin, and cut into 5-inch squares. Boil pasta squares in salted water for 1 to 2 minutes, a few at a time so they do not break. With a slotted spoon, remove pasta to a cloth to dry.

Assembly:

Salsa di Raffaele Lazzaro (see page 316)
Grated Parmesan cheese, for topping
1 recipe *Besciamella* (see page 133)

Place a tablespoon of filling in the center of each pasta square. Lap opposite sides of each square over the filling and place the "tube," seam side down, in a buttered baking dish, lining up the *cannelloni* close together "like soldiers." Cover with the simple tomato sauce, sprinkle with additional grated cheese, and top with *Besciamella.* Bake for about 20 minutes in a 375°F. oven. Serve at once with additional grated cheese.

Zuppa di Castagne

Chestnut "Stew"

For 6

There is no exact translation for this recipe. It is one of those country supper dishes that has simply evolved over hundreds of years. This recipe is an adaptation of two households' ways of preparing the "stew."

- 1 pound chestnuts
- 3 cups milk
- 1 tablespoon butter
- ¼ teaspoon cinnamon, plus extra for sprinkling
- Salt to taste
- ¾ cup uncooked white rice
- ½ cup white raisins, plumped (optional)
- Sprinkling of cinnamon

Soak the chestnuts in boiling water. Then clean them, removing the skins and membranes. Soak the cleaned nuts overnight. When ready to prepare the "stew," put the nuts in clean water and boil until tender. Add cold milk, butter, ¼ teaspoon cinnamon, and salt, and boil for 5 additional minutes. Rinse rice in sieve, add to the chestnut liquid, and boil slowly until rice is tender. Add plumped raisins if desired. Let stand, covered, for 5 minutes. Serve in a deep bowl, sprinkled with cinnamon.

Note: After the chestnuts have been boiled, they may be coarsely chopped or left whole.

Polenta Piemontese

Classic Cornmeal "Mush" For 6

The English word "mush" seems most unflattering for the starchy staple that is the heart and soul of the cooking of Italy's North. It is to these cooks what "pasta" is to the South. In fact, it's so important that Piedmont has a yearly festival called Il Polentone *("Big* Polenta *Day"). The recipe given here is a basic* polenta; *elsewhere on these pages you will find versions from other provinces.*

2 cups cornmeal
6 cups water
1½ teaspoons salt

In a bowl, mix the cornmeal with 3 cups of cold water, blending well. Next, into 3 cups of *boiling* water, add salt and the moistened cornmeal, and stir with a wooden spoon. Keep stirring for 20 to 25 minutes until the mass begins to leave the sides of the pan.

Pour the *polenta* onto a wooden board, and shape it into an approximate square with a broad spatula or the side of a cheese grater. Let it sit for a few minutes, then slice. (The "authentic" way to slice is with a heavy thread. Hold the ends of the thread firmly in both hands and slide under squared-off *polenta.* Bring up through the mass, holding the thread taut. Repeat until you have the number of squares of the thickness you desire.)

Serve with a hot, favorite sauce or as a side dish for Italian sausages, Chicken Cacciatore, or any meat stew. *Polenta* can also be eaten cold, or fried in butter and topped with syrup or jam for a fine cold-weather breakfast.

Rane Verdi

Green Frog Legs

For 6

The reference to the color green has nothing to do with the frog itself, but rather with the crunchy outside coating that is indeed the color of early spring grass. The recipe is a specialty of Cigliano.

- 1½ pounds frog legs
- ½ cup finely ground cornmeal
- 3 tablespoons chopped parsley
- 3 branches sage, bruised
- 4 basil leaves
- 1 clove garlic, crushed
- ¼ cup grated Parmesan cheese
- White wine (about ¾ cup)
- 3 to 4 tablespoons olive oil

Wash, clean, and dry the frog legs. Make a mash (using a mortar and pestle or a processor) of the cornmeal, parsley, sage, basil, garlic, and Parmesan. Dip each frog leg into white wine and then roll it in the mash, "leaning" into it so that the breading sticks. Heat the olive oil in a large skillet and fry the frog legs gently until tender. Watch them carefully so as not to overcook — 5 to 7 minutes should be sufficient.

Trota alla Piemontese

Piedmont-Style Trout

For 4

Piedmont, the region of blue lakes reflecting snow-capped mountains, has a wealth of freshwater fish. Trout is a local favorite.

- ¼ cup sultana raisins
- 1 stalk celery
- 1 onion
- 1 clove garlic
- ¼ cup olive oil
- 2 medium or 4 small trout
- 1 tablespoon Balsamic vinegar
- 2 teaspoons grated lemon rind
- 1 sprig rosemary, bruised
- 6 sage leaves, bruised
- ½ cup broth
- Salt and pepper to taste
- 3 tablespoons butter
- 3 tablespoons flour

Soak raisins in warm water. Wash and chop celery, onion, and garlic. Pour olive oil into a large skillet and braise the chopped vegetables. Add the whole fish to the skillet: sprinkle the vinegar over all, along with the lemon rind, drained raisins, bruised rosemary and sage, and the broth. Add salt and pepper if desired. Cook about 5 minutes on one side, then turn fish and cook another 4 minutes. Remove the fish; skin (and bone if wanted). Transfer to a heated platter and cover until ready to serve.

Make a paste of the butter and flour. Add it to the pan juices, whisking to prevent lumps, and cook until the consistency of gravy. Pour over trout and serve at once.

Bollito Misto Piemontese

Piedmont Boiled Dinner

For 10 to 12

This is, of course, one of the specialty dishes for which the Piedmont area is well known. Some compare it with the New England boiled dinner.

- 2 to 3 pounds beef chuck or rump
- 2 pounds boneless veal roast
- 3 stalks celery
- 2 onions
- 2 carrots
- 1 whole roasting chicken
- 2 pounds Italian sausages
- 2 whole cloves
- 1 bay leaf
- 4 sprigs parsley
- 2 teaspoons Bea's Garlic Salt (see page 31)

In a large kettle, place the beef, veal, vegetables, and water to cover. Boil slowly for 1½ hours. Add chicken; boil 1 hour more. Add sausages, cloves, bay leaf, parsley, and garlic salt; cook an additional 30 minutes. Remove meats to a large platter. Skin the sausages; slice the meat evenly and arrange attractively. Cut chicken into serving pieces and add to platter. Serve hot, accompanied by *Mostarda di Frutta* (see page 105) or any sweet and sour sauce.

Note: In Lombardy or Latium, a *salsa verde* (see page 229) would also be served.

Carpaccio (Insalata di Carne Cruda)

Marinated Beef For 6

Whether the Renaissance painter of the same name had a predilection for this dish or not, its provenance is not nearly as important as its present-day discovery. When served in its native Piedmont, the dish is usually accompanied by thin slices of the wild mushrooms of the region and equally slender slices of a strong local cheese. On the traditional Italian menu, salads containing cold meats would usually be served as an antipasto or perhaps as a second course, rarely as a salad as we know it.

- 1½-pound piece sirloin or top round, cut thick
- Salt to taste
- Juice of 3 lemons
- 2 cloves garlic, sliced
- ½ cup olive oil
- Black pepper to taste
- Sliced fresh mushrooms and finely chopped sour pickles, for garnishes

Put beef in freezer long enough to become firm but not frozen. Slice paper-thin, and sprinkle each slice with salt to taste. Then put the sliced meat in the refrigerator while you prepare the marinade.

On a deep platter, put the lemon juice, sliced garlic, and olive oil. Season with pepper and whisk to blend well. Then allow marinade to sit at room temperature for about an hour. Coat each of the meat slices with the marinade, turning each once or twice. Let sit several hours refrigerated. Circle a serving platter with a ring of raw sliced mushrooms, place the marinated meat in the center, and top with sprinkled chopped pickle.

Stufato di Cervo Pacetti

Venison Stew with *Polenta* For 4 to 6

Angela Pacetti's favorite memories of her childhood have to do with happy afternoons spent searching for mushrooms in the wooded areas around her native village, Feriolo, in the Novara district of Piedmont. Because game was plentiful, this recipe is one which she has treasured all her eighty-eight years.

2 pounds venison, cut in 1-inch chunks
1 medium onion, sliced
¼ cup cooking oil
1 chunk salt pork
Handful of parsley
2 cloves garlic
2 stalks celery
¾ cup white wine (muscatel)
¼ teaspoon allspice
1 bay leaf
Salt and pepper to taste
1½ cups chopped mushrooms
1 cup beef broth
1 teaspoon tomato paste

Sauté the venison and onion in the oil until the released juices have almost evaporated. Remove venison and discard onion. Combine the salt pork, parsley, garlic, and celery; put through grinder and then sauté. Return the venison to the skillet and allow it to brown slowly. Add the white wine, allspice, bay leaf, salt and pepper, and allow sauce to reduce. Then add the mushrooms, beef broth, and tomato paste and continue cooking until meat is tender to the fork, adding more broth if necessary. Serve with squares of *polenta.*

Pollo alla Marengo

Chicken Marengo

For 4

This exotic combination of ingredients is said to be the result of Napoleon's chef's desire to please after his master's victory at the battle of Marengo. Some recipes suggest crabmeat instead of shrimp.

- 1 broiling chicken (2½ to 3 pounds)
- Flour, for coating chicken
- 4 tablespoons olive oil
- 1½ pounds tomatoes, seeded and chopped
- 1½ pounds fresh mushrooms, sliced
- 1 teaspoon meat extract
- 2 cloves garlic, crushed
- 2 to 3 basil leaves
- ¾ cup dry white wine
- 4 to 6 large shrimp
- 4 slices bread
- 4 eggs
- Salt and pepper to taste
- Juice of 1 lemon
- ¼ cup cognac (optional)
- ¼ cup chopped parsley

Wash, dry, and cut up the chicken into 4 serving pieces. Coat with flour and fry in hot oil in a large skillet. Cook legs and thighs first (they take longer), and continue turning the pieces until they are golden brown. Drain some oil from the pan, putting it aside for later; add the tomatoes, sliced mushrooms, meat extract (to provide rich color), crushed garlic, basil leaves, and ¼ cup white wine. Cover and cook for 20 minutes or more, or until the sauce is of a good gravy consistency. Wash the shrimp; then in a separate pan, pour in the remaining ½ cup white wine and steam the shrimp for about 5 minutes. Shell shrimp and set aside. Put the previously drained oil in a large skillet and fry 4 slices of bread, turning once to brown on the other side. Next, fry 4 eggs, then place one each on top of the toast slices. Taste the chicken sauce, correct seasoning if needed, and add lemon juice, cognac, if desired, and chopped parsley. Put chicken in the middle of a large serving platter. Cover lightly with the sauce. Arrange the egg-topped toast slices around the chicken, top each egg with a shrimp, and adorn the chicken with any remaining shrimp.

Fegato Contadini

Peasant-Style Liver

For 6

If calves' liver is your pleasure, this very old recipe from Piedmont may well become a favorite.

2 ounces fresh pork fatback
2 cloves garlic
¼ cup chopped parsley
3 onions
4 tablespoons butter
2 pounds calves' liver
1 tablespoon flour
1 cup good red wine
Pepper to taste
½ teaspoon sage
2 teaspoons lemon juice
1 bay leaf
Salt to taste

Chop fatback; crush garlic and parsley together. Slice onions very thin. In a broad skillet, melt the butter and sauté the chopped vegetables until onions are soft. Slice liver thin, then add it to the pan and sprinkle with flour. Mix by gently pulling the liver slices "through" the sautéed pan contents. Add wine, pepper, sage, lemon juice, and bay leaf. Cook 10 minutes (no more) over moderate heat, basting often. When liver is cooked, add salt (never salt liver *before* cooking, it toughens the meat). Remove the bay leaf and serve the liver on a heated platter.

Insalata di Riso Lazzaro

Beatrice's Rice and Shrimp Salad

For 6

Inspired by the superb rice dishes of Piedmont, Beatrice makes this summer salad treat.

¾ pound small shrimp
2 cups sliced carrots and peas, cooked
½ cup blanched mushrooms
Bea's Garlic Salt (see page 31) to taste
4 cups cooked rice
½ green pepper, diced
½ red pepper, diced
¼ cup chopped parsley
½ cup sliced scallions
¾ cup chopped celery
¾ teaspoon sugar
½ teaspoon dry mustard
2 tablespoons wine vinegar
6 tablespoons olive oil

Steam shrimp in small amount of water, covered, for about 2 minutes. Remove from pan, shell, devein, and chill. In the same pan water, heat the sliced carrots, peas, and the mushrooms. Season to taste with garlic salt. Put rice in a large bowl; drain and add the cooked vegetables, diced peppers, chopped parsley, scallions, celery, and cooked shrimp. Adjust seasoning as needed. Toss to combine.

In a small bowl, combine the sugar, mustard, vinegar, and olive oil to make the dressing. Pour over salad, and toss so that each grain of rice is coated. Taste again for seasoning (cold rice and pasta need stronger seasoning than when cooked). Serve in a chilled glass bowl that has been lined with lettuce leaves. Garnish appropriately.

Insalata di Radicchiella

Dandelion Salad

For 4

Dandelion greens have a tart crispness that makes them a salad favorite in many parts of Italy. This recipe is courtesy of Mrs. Mario Barba, whose proud origins stem from Cigliano in the Piedmont region. On the traditional Italian menu, this combination of greens and dressing serves more as a "true" salad as we know it. And, although the vegetables — used cooked or raw — vary with the season, this "truer" and simpler salad is served after the main course to clear the palate.

- 1 pound fresh dandelion greens
- 4 tablespoons olive oil
- 2 tablespoons wine vinegar
- ½ teaspoon salt
- ½ teaspoon pepper
- 3 hard-boiled eggs, quartered
- 1 onion, sliced

Wash dandelion leaves thoroughly, cut in pieces, and let dry on paper toweling. Mix together oil, vinegar, salt, and pepper. Gently toss together the dried salad greens and dressing; top with the quartered eggs and onion slices, and serve.

Torta di Mandorle

Almond Cake

For 10 to 12

A Northern classic, simple and delicious.

- 1 cup almonds
- 2 cups flour
- ¾ cup sugar
- ½ teaspoon cinnamon
- ⅛ teaspoon ground cloves
- 1 cup butter
- 2 eggs, well beaten
- 2 tablespoons amaretto liqueur

Preheat oven to 350°F. Blanch, toast, and chop almonds. Put flour in a mixing bowl; add sugar, cinnamon, and cloves. With electric beater, work butter into dry ingredients until you have a crumbly mass. Add chopped almonds. Stir in eggs and the amaretto. Blend thoroughly. Butter and flour a 10-inch torte pan. Spread batter into pan and bake 45 minutes at 350°F. Remove and allow to cool on rack. Can be eaten plain or you may brush top with a mixture of creamed butter and confectioners' sugar, sprinkled with toasted almonds.

Torta Schiaccianoci

Nutcracker Torte

For 10 to 12

Torta Schiaccianoci *is enjoyed over much of Northern Italy. However, this recipe is Bea's own derivation.*

Cake:

- 1 recipe Genoese Sponge Cake (see page 89)

Make sponge cake. Prepare filling while it cooks.

Filling:

- ⅔ cup sugar
- ¼ cup water
- 4 egg yolks
- 1 cup toasted filberts
- 1½ cups butter

Boil sugar and water, taking care not to let crystals form on sides of the pan. Boil syrup to 236°F. on candy thermometer. Beat yolks in mixer, then pour syrup in a stream onto the yolks while mixer is on low speed. Then beat at medium speed until cool. Reserve a few filberts for garnish, and pulverize the rest in a processor or run through a grinder twice. Break butter into pieces and beat into egg mixture. When batter is thick and smooth, beat in the ground filberts.

Assembly:

- ¼ cup each, Bailey's Irish Cream, Vodka, and Kahlua
- 1½ cups sweetened whipped cream
- Whole filberts (reserved from filling)
- Chocolate curls, for garnish

Cut sponge cake horizontally into 4 equal parts to become "layers." Place first layer on a serving plate, drizzle mixed liqueurs over it, and then spread with ⅓ of the nut-butter cream. Place another layer on top, spread with liqueurs and cream, and repeat until you have the fourth layer on top unadorned. Frost sides and top with whipped cream and decorate edge with the remaining filberts, coarsely chopped, and curls of chocolate. Refrigerate until ready to serve — at least 3 hours.

Torta Gianduia

Hazelnut Torte

For 8 to 10

The Piedmontese passion for hazelnuts (filberts) may well be the result of Swiss influence, but we prefer to think the nuts are so popular simply because they grow in Piedmont and are so singularly delicious. This dessert is a multiphase extravaganza, its only problem being that it disappears too quickly.

Cake Batter:

- ½ cup butter, plus extra for pan and cookie sheet
- ½ cup hazelnuts, plus extra for garnish
- 1¼ cups plus 3 tablespoons sugar
- 1 cup semisweet chocolate bits
- 6 eggs, plus 3 extra yolks
- 1½ cups flour

Preheat oven to 350°F. and butter a 10-inch spring-form pan. Toast hazelnuts and rub off skins. Reserve some nuts for garnish, then put ½ cup skinned nuts in food processor but do not process. Butter a small cookie sheet.

In a small skillet, heat and caramelize 1¼ cups sugar, stirring constantly. When the sugar is brown and completely liquid, pour onto cookie sheet and allow to harden. Pry up with spatula and place this "brittle" in the processor with the hazelnuts. Add the chocolate bits and pulverize the 3 ingredients. Set aside. In the bowl of an electric mixer, put eggs, extra yolks, and remaining 3 tablespoons sugar, and blend at low speed. Put bowl over simmering hot water (as though it were the top part of a double boiler) and continue to beat or whisk the egg mixture until warm to the touch. Return to the mixer base and beat at high speed until triple in volume. Sift flour; fold into egg mix. Melt the ½ cup butter and add to batter along with the chocolate-nut mix. Fold gently so as not to lose volume. Pour the cake batter into spring-form pan and bake 35 to 40 minutes.

Filling:

- 1½ cups heavy cream
- ¾ cup semisweet chocolate bits
- 1 teaspoon vanilla

Heat cream; add chocolate bits. When chocolate has melted, stir well, add the vanilla, and refrigerate. Stir often while cooling. When very cold, beat until stiff.

Assembly:

- ½ cup brandy
- ½ cup maraschino liqueur

Slice cake into 3 horizontal layers. Put the first layer on a serving plate, mix the liqueurs, and spoon ⅓ of the liqueurs over the cake. Next, spread half the chocolate cream filling over the liqueured layer. Next, top with a second layer of cake. Soak this layer with liqueurs and spread with the remaining chocolate cream. Add the third layer of cake and moisten with the remaining liqueurs. Put in refrigerator while you prepare the glazes (below).

Apricot Glaze:

- ⅔ cup apricot jam
- 3 tablespoons sugar

Bring jam and sugar to a boil and allow to cool and thicken for a few minutes. Strain. Remove torte from refrigerator and spread glaze over top and sides. Refrigerate again.

Chocolate Glaze:

- ¾ cup semisweet chocolate bits
- 4 tablespoons butter
- ½ cup very strong *espresso* coffee
- Chocolate curls, for garnish

Melt chocolate with butter; add the coffee. When thin enough, allow to cool slightly and spread over top and around the sides of the torte. Use remaining toasted hazelnuts and chocolate curls to decorate.

Baci di Dama

Hazelnut Cookies — Makes 30 or so

These cookies are known as "Ladies' Kisses." Who wouldn't exchange a quick kiss for one of these chocolate nut delights?

½ pound hazelnuts
2¼ cups flour
1 cup butter
¾ cup confectioners' sugar
½ teaspoon vanilla
½ cup semisweet chocolate bits

Toast nuts at 250°F. for 15 minutes. Remove skins and chop nuts fine. Put in a mixing bowl with flour, butter, ½ cup confectioners' sugar, and vanilla. Mix well. Refrigerate for 1 hour.

Increase oven temperature to 325°. Shape dough into very small balls and place on cookie sheet about 1½ inches apart; flatten slightly and bake for 15 minutes. Remove from sheet and allow cookies to cool. In the top of a double boiler, melt the chocolate bits. Then spread the flat side of the cookie with chocolate, and top with another cookie to make a sandwich. Then dust lightly with remaining confectioners' sugar.

Budino al Rhum

Rum Pudding — For 8 to 10

Lombardy is generally thought of as the home of the rich, chilled pudding desserts, or semi-freddi *as they are called. However, this recipe is Beatrice's version of a dish she first enjoyed as a girl touring in Turin.*

½ pound sweet butter
1¼ cups confectioners' sugar
6 egg yolks
¾ cup rum
½ pint heavy cream
1 cup milk
2 tablespoons granulated sugar
2 packages ladyfinger cookies

Cream butter with confectioners' sugar; beat until light and fluffy. Add egg yolks and pour in ½ cup of rum, a few drops at a time.

Whip the cream and fold in gently. Mix the remaining ¼ cup rum with milk and granulated sugar. Line an 8-inch spring-form pan with ladyfingers soaked in the milk and rum mixture. Pour in half of the rum-egg mixture. Cover with a layer of more soaked lady-fingers and cover that layer with the remaining rum-egg mixture. Top with a last layer of soaked ladyfingers, cover with waxed paper, and refrigerate overnight.

Note: This rum pudding may be iced with a layer of piped whipped cream or a chocolate or fruit glaze. It can be frozen and served as if it were ice cream, or served cold as a *semi-freddo* (for the latter, remove it from the cold about an hour before serving). The choice of liquor may also be varied. The recipe would be excellent with coffee liqueur, amaretto, or any fruit liqueur.

Zabaglione

Creamy Marsala Froth — For 6

Known all over Italy, this flavorful dessert is sometimes spelled without the "gl." Traditionally it has been served as a simple crema (crème) in a lovely sherbet glass. It is also used as a topping for fruit and pastries.

- 6 egg yolks
- 6 tablespoons sugar
- ½ cup Marsala wine

In a double boiler, or in a bowl set over simmering water, beat the yolks with the sugar until they begin to thicken, incorporating as much air into the mixture as you are able. Continue to beat or whisk as you add the Marsala a little bit at a time. The consistency should be that of whipped cream. Serve either warm or cold from the refrigerator with or without crisp cookies (see Index, if you like, for specific cookie suggestions).

Caffè alla Valdostana

Coffee Valle d'Aosta-Style

For 4

A charming ritual in Valle d'Aosta and some villages in Piedmont is that of the *Grolla dell'Amicizia*, the friendship cup. The cup itself may be made of clay or wood and has a wooden cover. It measures about four inches in diameter and has four drinking spouts.

Coffee, along with *grappa* or brandy, is put in the *grolla*, and orange peel and sugar are added. The vessel is brought to the table with the liquid flaming — a sensational sight and scent. The cover is put on to extinguish the flames, and the cup is passed from person to person. What a delightful way to end an evening!

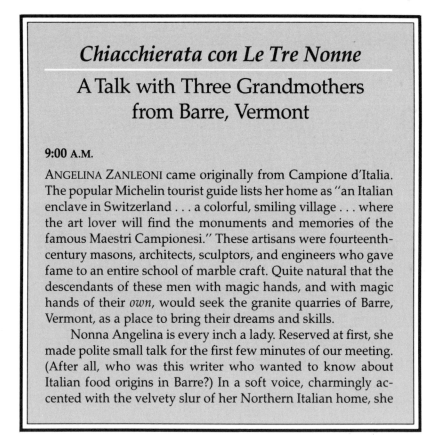

Chiacchierata con Le Tre Nonne

A Talk with Three Grandmothers from Barre, Vermont

9:00 A.M.

ANGELINA ZANLEONI came originally from Campione d'Italia. The popular Michelin tourist guide lists her home as "an Italian enclave in Switzerland . . . a colorful, smiling village . . . where the art lover will find the monuments and memories of the famous Maestri Campionesi." These artisans were fourteenth-century masons, architects, sculptors, and engineers who gave fame to an entire school of marble craft. Quite natural that the descendants of these men with magic hands, and with magic hands of their *own*, would seek the granite quarries of Barre, Vermont, as a place to bring their dreams and skills.

Nonna Angelina is every inch a lady. Reserved at first, she made polite small talk for the first few minutes of our meeting. (After all, who was this writer who wanted to know about Italian food origins in Barre?) In a soft voice, charmingly accented with the velvety slur of her Northern Italian home, she spoke of how her realtor husband (also a city alderman during his lifetime) teased her about never learning to speak English "properly." Then, suddenly warming, she twinkled engagingly when asked about the origins of her famous pasta business.

"Cooking has been a forty-year hobby," she began. "I've always loved the kitchen, always cooked for the pleasure of it . . . and finally" — her eyes smiled for the first time — "it *made* me communicate with people . . . . I *had* to learn English."

After about a half an hour of "verbal cooking," she asked me if I'd like to see her "other" kitchen (in reality, her pasta room). We moved through the spotless house to a large, sunny room behind the primary cooking center. Laid out on drying linens were four different colors of pasta: green, orange, the usual golden beige, and a cocoa-colored pile.

"Cocoa-colored?" I asked.

"I flavor and color it with unsweetened cocoa . . . and that pile with squash, and those with basil. Would you like to try some?"

Before I had a chance to swallow the raw noodle I was munching, into the kitchen she bustled, and within a breathless twenty minutes I had a *Gourmet* magazine plate in front of me invitingly laden with quadricolor pasta and chicken breasts *Zanleoni*. Oh, that every writing assignment should turn out so deliciously!

10:30 A.M.

ANGELA PACETTI, born in Feriolo (near Novara), is a hearty, vital eighty-eight years young. Times were hard in the early 1900s for the young immigrant wives, and the life expectancy of the quarriers was short. There were many widows, enduring and creative women whose primary skills were domestic. What to do to augment the meager disability or survivor's allowance? — the thing they already did magnificently: *cook!*

After Angela's husband fell ill with the lung disease so common to the granite worker, Angela remembers the preparation and stirring of bottomless pots of *polenta*. No easy task for the diminutive lady, keeping 15 or more pounds of the heavy porridge-like delicacy from sticking to the cast-iron pot or becoming lumpy . . . and always remembering to stir in one direction, clockwise. But I should let Angela tell it in her own words:

"The filled pots were too heavy for me to lift . . . so when the *polenta* was ready, the owners came with sons, brothers — any available pair of hands — and took them away. I was 'cheeky' in those days and scolded them to make sure they brought the pots back clean!"

Happily, the local family restaurant owners and the voracious appetites of the Barre stonemasons — plus Angela's own hard work and a little help from her friends — saved the Pacetti house from foreclosure.

12:00 NOON

PACE NICOLINO had a box of photographs already out. She poured fine coffee and tempted me with a plate laden with airy *Pasta Frolla* (see recipes on page 90 and 158). She recalls the second decade of this century, and, as a young girl, how stark and ugly she found her new home in comparison with the beauty of her lakeside (Lago Maggiore) village of Baveno in Piedmont. Here again, it was the granite that sang to her father, the breadwinner. However, Pace grew up surrounded by a loving family, enjoying weekends of picnics in Kelly's Woods, riotous ball games in the field that bordered Main Street, and cooking odors that still evoke salivary reactions today — along with great teasing from Libero, her jovial spouse.

Before I reluctantly bundled up to leave, I tasted what Pace considers "*real* antipasto." Then, clutching the recipe and several family photographs, I made my way back to the Victorian living room of my hosts, the Somainis, a perfect place to make the transition to today's 1980s, sort out my notes, and put down on paper why my head and heart were as full as my belly.

The quarries are still operative, and the cemetery is a quiet showplace of extraordinary examples of the stonecutters' art. Barre, Vermont, is a small New England town with a singular history, and a present still very much alive — in the granite quarries, of course, but also in the legacy of its fragrant, steamy kitchens, and the men and women who found in them both solace and joy . . . the essence of the Italian at table.

PIEDMONT
EMILIA
ROMAGNA
Genoa
TUSCANY
La Spezia
LIGURIAN SEA

Liguria

The Special Wines & Cheeses of *Liguria*

Wines of the Region*

Demi-sec red: *Dolceacqua* (light, and the best red of the region)

Dry whites: *Coronata, Cortese di Liguria, Polcevera, Sarticola, Sciacchetra* (the best white), *Vermentino* (semi-bubbly)

Sweet white: *Sarticola*

*Liguria exports little or no wine.

Cheeses of the Region

Formaggette, Pecorino Liguriano

A tavola rotonda, non si contende del luogo.

At a round table, nobody fights for place!

Thrift and toil, long considered the heart of the Puritan ethic, are also characteristic of the inhabitants of Liguria, the vertical Italian Riviera. Tilling their terraced farms and emptying their handmade nets of the finny treasures of the sea was prime conditioning for the rigors of the New World for those who chose to immigrate. For those fishermen and farmers, there was welcome room, especially in the Northeast.

The origins of the wholesale florists who line Boston's Albany Street can most often be traced to Liguria, the carnation capital of Italy. Other products of this mild and fragrant area are hazelnuts, citrus fruits, green vegetables in abundance, potatoes, herbs, and honey — the product of cottage industry, Ligurian honey is world famous. Here, too, broad-brush strokes of green mark the symmetrical plantings of Bosco grapes in the La Spezia countryside.

Another interesting parallel between this region of Italy and New England is that of their equally busy ports; Boston and Genoa. From the travels and adventures of their seamen, both cities grew intellectually and in matters culinary. Spices, in Boston, and herbs, in Genoa, were introduced to shore-bound cooks from the seagoing galleys: flavorings and preservatives were needed to withstand long periods at sea without refrigeration. As a result, savory recipes evolved on each shore to make use of both the ocean's produce and the special knowledge brought by her sailing men. Homecoming celebrations were another common bond.

Then, as now, Genoa is the home of slow cooking, where *confeto* and *stracotto* are both arts. These elaborate sauces result from hours of careful watching while the fragrant ingredients are allowed to cook down and distill. The sunny olive oil native to Liguria's mountains, when wed to the enormous variety of local spices and herbs that grow in profusion on the same slopes, provides the basis for a cuisine deservedly envied.

Recipes for a number of the Ligurian regional dishes follow. Others for which the region is justly proud include *Burrida,* a spicy fish stew; *Cappon Magro,* a pickled fish salad; *Cima alla Genoese,* featuring beef stuffed with sweetbreads, pork, and fresh peas, served hot or cold; *Gnocchi al Pesto,* potato dumplings in a basil-based sauce; *Riso Arrosto alla Genoese,* an oven-browned timbale of rice, sausage, and vegetables; and *Torta Pasqualina,* a holiday quiche-like dish very similar to the *Imbrogliata di Carciofi* you'll find here.

One of the colorful epicurean extravaganzas for which Liguria is known is the Camogli Fish Fry. It takes place in Genoa, the port city, on the second Sunday in May. Here, the *padellone* (an enormous frying pan 16 feet in diameter) is used to feed reveling fishing families and tourists. Another famous fish festival takes place in June in Lavagna. There, instead of in a mammoth skillet, the fish are baked on huge slabs of slate.

With 205 miles of coastline, it is no wonder that Neptune's influence is so strongly felt in Liguria, but the shelter of the Apennines, a bulwark against the capricious Alpine weather, is equally vital in making Liguria a place of beauty and bounty.

Frittata di Funghi Lazzaro

Mushroom Omelet

For 4 to 6

Ligurian mushrooms are so plentiful and varied they should be considered regional "treasures." This recipe is made all over Italy, but is particularly delicious when made with the earthy-flavored field mushrooms. It was a specialty of Beatrice's Grandmother Nina.

- 1 pound fresh mushrooms
- 1 small onion, sliced
- 2 tablespoons olive oil
- 4 tablespoons butter
- ½ teaspoon Bea's Garlic Salt (see page 31)
- 6 large eggs
- 3 to 4 tablespoons water
- 2 tablespoons chopped parsley

Brush, clean, and slice the mushrooms, and sauté along with the onion in a mixture of the oil and butter. Add garlic salt. Beat the eggs with the water and parsley, and pour over mushrooms and onions. Fry omelet on one side, turn, and fry on other side.

Note: Italian omelets, or *frittate,* are not soft in the center as are the French omelets. The upper side may be cooked by placing the *frittata* under the broiler for a few seconds instead of turning it in the pan.

Imbrogliata di Carciofi

Artichoke Quiche

For 6

A specialty of Savona, this luncheon or light supper dish reminds us that the cuisine of Liguria relies heavily on the backyard vegetable garden.

- 10 small artichokes, fresh or canned
- Juice of 1 lemon
- 4 tablespoons olive oil
- 1 clove garlic
- Salt and pepper to taste
- 4 eggs
- ¼ cup grated Parmesan cheese
- 1 cup half-and-half cream
- ¼ cup dry bread crumbs
- ½ cup Gruyère cheese
- Paprika

If fresh artichokes are used, remove hard leaves and cut off tips. Then cut in half and remove chokes. Only the heart of the artichoke is used. Soak artichoke hearts in the lemon juice and enough water to cover for about 10 minutes. Then blanch in saucepan for about 3 minutes or until just tender, and drain. (Canned artichokes may be used as is.)

Heat olive oil in skillet, sauté garlic, and add artichokes. Cook, covered, until tender. Remove garlic. Season artichokes with salt and pepper.

In a bowl, beat the eggs; add Parmesan cheese, cream, bread crumbs, and Gruyère (Groviera) cheese. Put artichokes in a 9-inch buttered casserole; pour the egg mixture over them, and sprinkle with paprika. Place the casserole in pan of hot water. Bake at 350°F. until "set" when tested with knife.

Liguriun Minestrone col Pesto

Basil-Flavored Vegetable Soup

For 8

Pesto *is the pride of Liguria, and deservedly so. The green sauce is the color of the parasol pines famous throughout Italy. Two versions of this fine sauce may be found immediately following this recipe, and Bea's own version on page 44. We've become quite accustomed to seeing it on fine Northern Italian cookery menus and in the refrigerated cases of specialty food stores. In this section we present two classic ways to enjoy the sauce: stirred into minestrone and served with pasta.*

1 pound fresh shell beans
3 quarts water
2 potatoes, peeled
1 large onion
2 large tomatoes
3 stalks celery
2 zucchini squash
1 head escarole, chopped
1 small cabbage
2 carrots
2 leeks
¼ cup olive oil
1½ cups cooked small pasta
⅔ cup *pesto* (use recipe of choice or good-quality prepared)

Shell, then boil, beans in the 3 quarts of water. Slice the vegetables uniformly. Divide shell beans into 2 parts and purée half. Return purée to the pot with the water and cook for about 2 hours. Add the vegetables and the olive oil. Simmer until the vegetables are just done (they should retain their crunch). Then add the pasta, the other half of the beans, and the *pesto*. Heat the soup for a few minutes over a low flame to warm it through, then serve.

Pesto Genoese Classico

Classic *Pesto*

For 4 to 6

¼ cup pine nuts *(pignoli)*
36 fresh green basil leaves
2 cloves garlic
½ stick (4 tablespoons) butter
Coarse salt to taste
½ cup olive oil
¼ teaspoon pepper
¼ teaspoon sugar
4 tablespoons mixed Parmesan and Sardo cheeses

Toast pine nuts. If using a mortar, crush nuts, basil, and garlic together. Blend in butter, salt, and oil. Add pepper and sugar. Mix with the cheeses.

If using a blender or processor, put all ingredients except the butter into the machine. Soften the butter and add to the purée last. Blend quickly. Use *pesto* at once, or it may be stored in a jar, covered, with a little extra olive oil on top. It also freezes well.

Pesto Louisa Carbone

Basic Sauce

For 4 to 6

This recipe from Bea's friend, Louisa, who lives in Beverly, Massachusetts, is a richer variation on the classical theme.

- ⅓ cup chopped basil
- ½ pound cream cheese
- 1 cup grated Parmesan cheese
- ¼ teaspoon salt
- 2 tablespoons olive oil
- 2 cloves garlic, crushed
- 1 cup heavy cream

Put everything, except cream, in blender or processor. When all is puréed, put into a bowl and gradually blend in heavy cream.

Trenette o Fettuccine col Pesto

Pasta with Basil Sauce

This is the second of the recipes featuring the pesto *Ligurians so enjoy. Again, take your choice of the three* pestos *suggested for the* Ligurian Minestrone col Pesto.

Allowing 1 pound pasta per 6 people, cook *al dente* the amount of pasta twists or noodles you will need. Then, just before serving, stir in the warm *pesto* sauce. Allow 2 or 3 cups sauce for each 1 pound of pasta.

Salsa di Pomodoro Crudo

Raw Tomato Sauce

For 4 to 6

This is an excellent simple Italian sauce widely adaptable to many pasta dishes and one that Bea often uses.

- 6 large ripe tomatoes
- 1 teaspoon salt, or to taste
- ½ cup olive oil
- 3 cloves garlic, crushed
- ⅔ cup chopped basil
- ½ cup chopped parsley
- ½ cup combined grated Romano and Parmesan cheeses
- 1 small mozzarella cheese, diced

Peel, seed, and chop tomatoes; salt well, and put in colander to drain. In a separate bowl, combine olive oil, garlic, basil, and parsley. Then add tomatoes, the grated cheeses, and the mozzarella. Allow to marinate for at least 6 hours at room temperature. Serve over hot pasta with additional cheese on the side.

Ravioli Genoese Racioppi

Ravioli, Genoa-Style

For 6

A treasured recipe of Beatrice's mother.

Pasta:

- 1 recipe Pasta for Filling (see page 36)

Make pasta. Set aside while you prepare filling.

Filling:

- ½ pound breakfast sausage
- 2 pounds cooked spinach
- 1 pound ricotta cheese
- 1 pound cream cheese, softened
- 1 teaspoon Bea's Garlic Salt (see page 31)
- 4 eggs
- 1 cup grated Parmesan cheese
- Dash of nutmeg

To make filling, warm sausage in pan, remove casing, and crumble. Put in bowl with drained, chopped spinach. Add ricotta, cream cheese, garlic salt, eggs, grated cheese, and nutmeg. Mix well. Then set aside.

Assembly:

Roll out pasta into a circle (a small amount at a time, it handles more easily). When dough is no more than ⅛-inch thick, spread half with the filling; fold other half over and seal edges. Using a wooden yardstick, press down at 1½-inch parallels and then press across these parallels to make squares (see sketch). Cut with fluted pasta wheel along pressed lines.

To "mass-produce" the pasta for Ravoli Genoese Racioppi, *fold the unfilled half of a good-sized pasta dough circle over the filled half and use a rule or other blade to mark out rows of ravioli squares; then cut with pasta wheel.*

Boil filled squares in salted water for about 5 minutes. Remove carefully to a buttered bowl and serve with a sauce of your choice. Parmesan cheese is served on the side.

Risotto del Campagnolo

Country-Style Rice

For 4 to 6

This is an ancient Ligurian recipe. Some cooks prefer to use prosciutto in place of the sausage for a more delicate flavor.

- ½ ounce dried Italian mushrooms
- 2 tablespoons olive oil
- 2 tablespoons butter
- ½ cup chopped onion
- 4 sausage links, skinned
- ½ cup fresh peas
- 2 canned artichokes (tender parts only)
- 1½ cups broth
- Salt and pepper to taste
- 1½ cups uncooked rice
- ¼ cup pan juices (from previous roast or stew)
- ¼ cup grated Parmesan cheese

Soak mushrooms in water to cover until soft; chop coarsely. Put oil and butter in saucepan and sauté onion, mushrooms, sausage, peas, and the tender parts of the artichokes. Add broth, and salt and pepper to taste. Set sauce aside.

In a large saucepan, bring 4 cups of water to a boil and add the rice. Cook 8 minutes and drain. Put the rice in a medium-sized casserole with the pan juices and a few tablespoons of water. Add the grated cheese and the sauce. Mix well. Bake in a 375°F. oven for 30 minutes or until rice is cooked and dry and has a crust on top.

Note: When the liquid in the rice is almost absorbed, if desired, ¼ cup white wine and 1 tablespoon of butter may be added.

Cozze (Mitili) Ripiene

Savona Stuffed Mussels

For 4

Imagine sitting on the terrace of your villa in Alassio, the fragrance of basil and the sea enveloping you. In such a setting, this is the *dish to enjoy — the special mussels of the region, stuffed with all manner of delights and served with a bright green sauce.*

- 2½ to 3 pounds fresh mussels
- 3 Italian sweet sausages, skinned
- 4 slices of mozzarella cheese, diced
- ¼ cup olive oil
- ¼ cup butter
- 1 onion, chopped
- 2 tablespoons chopped parsley
- 1 tablespoon fresh basil
- Pinch of oregano
- 1 clove garlic, crushed
- 1 cup dry bread crumbs
- Salt and pepper to taste

Wash mussels and remove the beards. Put them in a broad pan over medium-high heat to allow them to open. Discard any that do not!

Sauté the sausages and cheese in the combined fats, along with the chopped onion, parsley, basil, and oregano. Cook 8 to 10 minutes. Add the crushed garlic and the bread crumbs, mixing well. Adjust seasoning with salt and pepper if necessary. Fill mussel shells (both sides, the half with the mussel and the empty half), and place shells side by side in a baking dish. Make sauce (below) and complete recipe.

Sauce:

- 1 onion, grated
- ¼ cup olive oil
- 1 teaspoon chopped parsley
- 1 teaspoon chopped basil
- 2 tablespoons tomato paste
- 1 tablespoon flour
- ⅔ cup broth (see Note)

Sauté onion in olive oil; add parsley, basil, and tomato paste. Cook for 6 to 8 minutes, then add flour gradually to form a paste. Add the broth and cook 15 minutes more. Strain sauce over mussels in a large baking pan and bake for 15 minutes at 375°F.

Note: After cleaning mussels, if you like, you may open them by steaming them in a cup or two of water. You may then reduce the resulting liquid until you have the ⅔ cup broth necessary for the sauce. However, the mussel broth must be strained to remove any sand or bits of shell. If you prefer, any vegetable or chicken stock may be substituted.

Ciuppin

Fish Stew

For 6

Fish stews are made all over the "Boot," but none is more savory than this pride of the sea. Ciuppin *is Ligurian dialect for* Cioppino.

- 1 onion
- 1 stalk celery
- 1 carrot
- 2 cloves garlic
- ⅓ cup chopped parsley
- ⅓ cup olive oil, plus extra for spreading on bread
- ⅔ cup dry white wine
- 5 ripe tomatoes
- 1 quart water
- 2 to 3 pounds assorted fish
- Salt and pepper to taste
- Sliced bread

Chop onion, celery, carrot, garlic, and parsley (this is best done in a food processor or blender). Put olive oil in a Dutch oven, add all the chopped vegetables, and sauté. When all the water from the vegetables has evaporated, add the white wine and simmer until it has evaporated. Add peeled, seeded tomatoes and water, and cook for 30 minutes over moderate heat. Clean and cut fish into serving chunks. Add firmer fish to vegetables, cook a few minutes, then add remaining fish and continue to cook, seasoning to taste. Brush slices of bread with oil and toast in hot oven.

Put toast in soup bowls and spoon individual servings of mixed fish and broth over top. If the broth is too thin, reduce it by boiling; if too thick, add a little water.

Note: This stew can also be used as a sauce to serve over pasta.

Manzo Soffocato con Funghi

Smothered Beef and Mushrooms

For 6

The word soffocato *might be translated as "braised and sauced." Mamma Racioppi, Beatrice's mother, delighted her family and friends often with this "no frills" meal. Today it takes particularly well to a Crockpot or other slow-cooker, and is delicious served with a salad and a glass of ruby red Chianti.*

- 4 tablespoons olive oil
- 2 tablespoons butter
- 3 to 4 pounds beef bottom round
- ¼ cup parsley
- 1 slice unsmoked bacon
- 1 each onion, carrot, and celery stalk
- Salt and pepper to taste
- 1 cup dry red wine
- 1 cup beef broth
- 1 ounce Italian dried mushrooms
- 1 pound fresh button mushrooms

In a Dutch oven, heat oil and butter. When very hot, add beef and brown on all sides. Add the parsley, bacon, and the vegetables. Sauté with the meat until onion is golden. Season to taste, add the wine and allow to evaporate. Then cover pot and cook over low heat. Turn meat often and moisten with broth as needed. Soak dried mushrooms in water until soft, chop and add to cooking pot with the fresh mushrooms; cover and continue to simmer slowly over low heat until the meat is tender. To serve, put meat on a platter and cover with the mushrooms and sauce.

Fricassea Liguriana

Sautéed Chicken Breasts

For 6

We think of Liguria as a seafood center, as well we might, but this poultry dish is an international winner. As you read along in the recipe you'll see that the coastal Italians were using nouvelle cuisine *techniques long before they were so-named.*

- 2 pounds chicken breasts, boned
- ¼ cup butter
- 1 onion, chopped
- 3 sprigs of parsley
- ¼ cup toasted pine nuts
- 2 cups hot broth (see Note)
- 1 pound peas, shelled
- 2 eggs
- Zest plus juice of ½ lemon

Cut chicken breasts in half. Put butter in a large skillet and sauté the breasts. Set aside. In a blender or processor, purée onion, parsley, pine nuts, and a little broth. Combine with the remaining hot broth, add the peas, and pour over the chicken breasts. Cover and cook until tender; do not overcook. Beat the eggs and lemon zest plus juice with a little of the hot pan juice to "temper." Mix with the rest of the sauce in the pan, remove to a heated platter, and serve over toast points, or with pasta or rice.

Note: A chicken broth is preferable but a vegetable broth will do.

Funghi Ripieni

Stuffed Mushrooms *Cinque Terre*

For 4 to 6

Here is the product of the Ligurian Riviera at its finest: earthy mushrooms filled with herb-flavored stuffing.

- 3 or 4 pieces Italian dried mushrooms
- 12 large fresh mushrooms
- 3 tablespoons butter, plus extra for dribbling
- 2 tablespoons olive oil
- 1 small onion, finely chopped
- 1 clove garlic, crushed
- Salt and pepper to taste
- 1 cup soft bread crumbs
- ½ cup grated Parmesan cheese
- Pinch of marjoram
- 1 teaspoon Bea's Garlic Salt (see page 31), more or less
- ⅔ cup milk
- Fresh basil, for garnish

Soak dried mushrooms using water to cover. Clean fresh mushrooms; remove stems and chop, reserving the caps. In a skillet, melt butter; add oil, chopped onion, garlic, and salt and pepper to taste. Sauté until onions are soft. Chop soaked dried mushrooms and add to skillet with chopped fresh mushroom stems. Cook another 5 minutes. Add the soft bread crumbs, grated cheese, and marjoram. Mix and blend well. Touch the hollow of each fresh mushroom cap with a bit of garlic salt. Fill caps with the stuffing. Mound them high to be sure all the filling is used. Put the milk in the bottom of a medium-sized baking pan. Set the mushrooms in the bottom of the pan, dribbling a little melted butter over the top of each. Bake at 350°F. until mushrooms are tender when tested with a fork. Use a fresh basil leaf for garnish.

Pasta Genoese

Sponge Cake *Génoise*

For 8 to 12

This recipe, made like a French génoise, *has been incorporated magnificently into the multifaceted dessert offerings of the Ligurians and their neighbors.*

- 6 eggs
- 1 cup sugar
- 1 teaspoon vanilla
- 1 cup flour
- ½ cup clarified butter

Preheat the oven to 350°F. Put eggs and sugar in the bowl of an electric mixer. Invert a custard cup in bottom of a large saucepan (this will form a base so that the bottom of the mixing bowl does not sit directly in the water). Fill bottom of saucepan with boiling water, setting bowl on top of cup. Whisk eggs and sugar, and when mixture is warm to the touch, return bowl to mixer and beat at medium speed. Add vanilla. Increase speed until eggs and sugar are tripled in volume. Sift flour, and sift again into egg mix. Fold in flour with a spatula. Dribble clarified butter over mixture and *carefully* mix it in with the spatula – leave no streaks of melted butter. Bake 30 minutes or more.

This will make three 8- or 9-inch layer cakes; one 9- by 13-

inch sheet-pan cake; or one cake baked in a 9-inch spring-form pan. All the pans should be buttered and floured.

Note: To clarify butter, allow it to melt thoroughly over low heat, then let it cool. The milk solids will settle to the bottom and the clear "upper" liquid can be strained into a container and kept indefinitely in the refrigerator.

Torta di Pasta Frolla

Butter Flake Torte

For 6

Frolla *means "flaky," and this Italian classic certainly merits the inter-regional bickering about its true area of origin.*

- 2 cups flour
- ¼ teaspoon baking powder
- ½ cup granulated sugar
- 2 tablespoons lard or shortening
- 1 stick (8 tablespoons) butter
- 2 egg yolks
- Rind of 1 lemon, grated
- Jam, for spreading
- Confectioners' sugar

Preheat oven to 375°F. Put flour, baking powder, and sugar in a mixer bowl. Cut shortening and butter into pieces, and add to mixer bowl. Mix until butter and shortening are the size of peas. Add egg yolks and grated lemon rind. Mix, then with hands, draw ingredients together into a ball. Knead with heel of hand 4 or 5 times. Put dough in plastic bag and let it "relax" for 30 minutes. If dough seems crumbly or a little dry, add a few spoonfuls of water. Roll out dough, and fit it loosely in a 9-inch pan. Weigh dough down by setting another pan, or baking marbles, on top; this prevents dough from puffing up. Bake until golden. Remove from oven and cool.

Spread with jam of your choice. Roll out more dough and cut into strips. Weave a lattice top. Place a long strip around the edge to cover the ends of strips and press down with your fingers to seal. Bake again at 375° until edge is golden. Cool and sprinkle with confectioners' sugar.

SWITZERLAND
TRENTINO ALTO ADIGE
Lake Maggiore
Lake di Como
Lake Iseo
Adda
Lake Garda
Milan
Brescia
Oglio
VENETIA
PIEDMONT
Po
Cremora
Po
EMILIA ROMAGNA

Lombardy

The Special Wines, Cheeses & Sweets of ***Lombardy***

Wines of the Region

Dry reds: *Barbagallo (Barbacarlo), Buttafuoco, Carlo Bottai, Frecciarossa Rosso, Grumello, Inferno, Monsupello, Negri Rosso, Riviera del Garda, Sasella, Villa*

Demi-sec red: *Sangue di Giuda*

Dessert rosé: *Chiaretto del Garda*

Dry whites: *Baron della Corte, Frecciarossa Bianco, Lugana, Pinot Bianco, Zenato*

Dessert whites: *Moscato di Casteggio, Tocai del Garda*

Wines Available in the United States

Dry reds: *Carlo Bottai, Grumello, Monsupello, Negri*

Dry whites: *Baron della Corte, Lugana, Pinot Bianco, Zenato*

Dry sparkling: *Bellavista, Franciacorta Brut*

Cheeses of the Region

Bagoss, Bitto, Caprini, Crescenza, Fiorone, Gorgonzola, Grana, Groviera, Magri, Mascarpone, Panerone, Provolone Lombardo, Robiolini, Robiolo, Stracchino, Taleggio

Special Sweets

Colomba Pasquale, Cremona Nougat, Panettone

Forte è l'acetato di vin dolce.

Sweet wine makes sharp vinegar.

Lombardy is like a huge mixed bouquet of flowers, some cultivated and some randomly picked from the wild. Samuel Chamberlain called it a "blend of the brash and the beautiful."

The cross-country skier, hiker, fall fisherman — all outdoors folk, it seems, scan a Lombardian menu and order a steaming bowl of *minestrone*. The Lombardian would swell with pride. "We were the *first* to put together the hearty soup, and we make it the proper way — *with rice*," he would say. Whether the boast is historically accurate or not, these Northern provinces (from the picturesque lakes and valleys, formed long ago by glaciers, to the verdant plains of the Po) occupy a premium position in the food archives of the world.

The Brianza district is the grazing land of some of Italy's choicest cattle. Half of the livestock is destined for the tables of the nation as beef; the rest forms the dairy herds whose creamy product is the base ingredient for that gold and blue glory — Gorgonzola. Lush pastures of fodder, wheat, and maize are delineated by the swaying sentinel poplars and, closer to the ground and peculiar to this region, mulberry bushes, for Lombardy is also the center of Italy's famed silk industry.

The subject of cheese must not be abandoned, however, by the mere inclusion of Gorgonzola. A Lucullan feast of just Lombardian cheeses could be prepared from the local dairy products. Paired with some of the finest fruits in Europe, or coupled with sweet butter on a slice of the local crisp-crusted bread, reach for your wineglass and sigh with surfeited senses. This is surely a table set in Paradise!

The cheeses highlighted on our regional title page have bred a unique type of investment banking. Eight "suburban branches" (as we would call them in the United States) of the largest bank of the area have *cheese vaults*. Here the dairy product is held as security for the following year's production. In the interim, the cheeses are maintained at the correct temperature and humidity, and treasured exactly as if they were gold bullion.

The agricultural prominence of maize and corn explains the relatively small importance paid to pasta in the Lombardian kitchen. This is *risotto* and *polenta* country.

Polenta has a special history. It is said to be an evolution of the early Roman soldiers' field ration. The coarse corn grain was boiled into a porridgelike consistency, and either eaten hot or allowed to cool and then cut into portable squares to be eaten on the move.

If we stop to consider that the nine provinces of Lombardy cover a land mass no larger than that of the state of New Hampshire, it is quite extraordinary that so much natural bounty is concentrated there. But the blessings multiply: Milan, like Boston, is a hub city, an international market for export and import, and a metropolis with a naturally expansive attitude about food.

Only a very few of the culinary treasures of Lombardy have escaped this book. The rest you will find here — everything from the traditional *Minestrone alla Milanese* and *Risotto alla Milanese* to the perhaps lesser-known *Peperonata,* a sautéed mix of peppers and other vegetables, *Tinca Carpionata,* a marinated fish, and of course, the *Mostarda di Frutta* (fruit mustard) for which the region is so well known.

From the downy texture of a holiday *panettone* (a sweet bread) to the culinary caress of velvety *mascarpone* (a cream cheese); from the silken-clad Continental ladies who sparkle at La Scala to their elegantly tailored industrialist spouses, Lombardy is a coffer of varied riches, ready to be discovered and savored.

Busecca Matta

Sliced Omelet Pasta with Sauce

For 4

These are actually thin slices of omelet masquerading as pasta — a Lombardian gift to any menu.

- 3 tablespoons olive oil
- 6 eggs, beaten
- 3 tablespoons butter
- 1 medium onion, chopped
- 1 slice prosciutto or boiled ham
- Several sage leaves
- 5 fresh tomatoes or 1 can plum tomatoes, strained
- Salt and pepper to taste
- Grated Parmesan cheese, for sprinkling

In a small crêpe pan, heat olive oil. Pour in a small amount of beaten egg — just enough to cover the bottom of the pan. Flip when cooked on one side. When both sides are cooked, slide omelet onto plate. Continue this procedure until all the egg mixture has been made into thin omelets. Roll each omelet into a tube and slice it, crosswise, into thin noodle-like strips.

In another larger skillet, melt the butter and sauté the onion, ham, and sage together. When onion begins to color slightly, add strained tomatoes, and salt and pepper. Let simmer for 10 to 15 minutes. Add the egg "noodles" and heat quickly through. Serve sprinkled with Parmesan cheese.

Variations:
Mushrooms, celery, carrots, or peas may be added to sauce. Cheese may be mixed into the egg batter and the omelet "noodles" may be used in broth.

Uova ai Nidi di Spinaci

Eggs in Spinach Nests

For 6

A specialty of Bea's Aunt Mary.

- 3 pounds spinach, cooked and chopped
- 2 tablespoons olive oil
- ½ cup butter, melted
- Bea's Garlic Salt (see page 31) to taste
- 6 eggs, plus 1 yolk
- ½ cup grated Parmesan cheese
- Salt and pepper to taste
- 1 tomato, thinly sliced
- Chopped parsley, for sprinkling

Prepare spinach. In a frying pan, put olive oil, 3 tablespoons butter, and garlic salt to taste; add spinach and simmer lightly. Remove from heat; add egg yolk and ¼ cup grated Parmesan. Mix well. Mound spinach in 6 nest-like portions in a buttered shallow baking dish (make an indentation in each spinach mound to form the nest). Put an egg in each nest, and sprinkle with a little salt and pepper. Cover each egg with a slice of tomato. Sprinkle with chopped parsley and the rest of the grated cheese. Dribble remaining melted butter over each nest and bake in a 350°F. oven until egg white has coagulated, about 8 to 10 minutes. Serve hot from baking dish at the table.

Minestrone alla Milanese

Classic Minestrone from Milan

For 6 to 8

Because this dish is so internationally well known, the exact translation from an Italian cookbook of the early 1900s follows. We feel the method is unnecessarily complicated and have successfully made the dish by sautéing all the vegetables together first, adding the pasta and basil last (the herb loses flavor through long exposure to heat), and then topping the whole shebang with cheese — and brazenly serving it as the genuine article. Regarding it as a great way to clean out the refrigerator also helps justify the time input!

- 2 stalks celery
- 2 carrots
- 2 zucchini squash
- 1 pound fresh tomatoes
- 3 potatoes
- 1 thick slice unsmoked bacon
- 3 sprigs parsley
- 2 onions
- 1 large clove garlic
- ¼ cup olive oil
- 3 tablespoons butter
- 4 sage leaves
- 1 large piece pork rind
- 1 pound fresh shell beans
- 3 quarts water
- 2 cups fresh peas
- ½ small cabbage
- 1 cup rice or small pasta
- ⅓ cup chopped basil
- Salt and pepper to taste
- Grated Parmesan cheese, for topping

Slice celery, carrots, and zucchini thin. Peel, seed, and squeeze tomatoes; then chop coarsely. Peel and dice potatoes. Grind bacon, parsley, onions, and garlic, and sauté in oil and butter in a large soup kettle. Add sage, pork rind, and the mix of prepared vegetables. Add shell beans and 3 quarts water. Boil over moderate heat for about 2 hours. Add peas and the cabbage *leaves* (discard the hard core). Add rice or pasta, and basil. Continue to cook for about 5 minutes. Season to taste and serve hot with a topping of grated Parmesan cheese.

Note: If more liquid is needed, add stock or bouillon.

Crema di Asparagi Milanese

Cream of Asparagus Soup

For 4 to 6

There is a time in early spring in Lombardy when the children sell bunches of reed-thin asparagus, clutching and waving the stalks as if they were the first wildflowers. Those bunches are what make this memorable soup!

- 2 pounds thin asparagus
- 1 stick (8 tablespoons) butter
- 1 cup flour
- 1½ quarts milk, warmed
- 1½ quarts chicken broth
- Salt to taste
- 3 egg yolks, beaten
- ½ cup grated Parmesan cheese
- ½ cup heavy cream
- Dash of nutmeg and white pepper
- Toasted croutons, for garnish

Cut asparagus into tips and then into 1-inch pieces, discarding the very woody and bitter parts. Put tips aside. In a large soup kettle, melt half of the butter, then add the flour and mix well. Then add the warm milk, whisking to prevent lumps. Cook the tougher parts of the asparagus in the chicken broth for flavor, discard the asparagus pieces, and strain the broth. Add strained broth to milk mixture, whisking energetically to avoid lumps. Add asparagus tips. Simmer for 1 hour, stirring often; do not allow to boil. Salt to taste. Put mixture through blender or processor and strain. In a tureen, add egg yolks, the remaining butter, Parmesan cheese, and heavy cream to the hot soup, whisking well. Season with nutmeg and white pepper and serve with croutons.

Spezie Lombardina

Lombardian Spice Mix

This is the special spice mixture used all over Lombardy. Housewives prepare it in batches and keep it tightly covered in jars to age. It is good to have handy in the kitchen, and gives food a delightful fragrance and flavor. Lombardian cooks use it frequently in soups and in various pasta and main dishes.

To make the spice mix, combine well 2 teaspoons ground cloves, 2 teaspoons white pepper, 2 teaspoons ground bay leaves, 7 teaspoons ground cumin, 7 teaspoons ground nutmeg, 3½ teaspoons basil, and 3½ teaspoons thyme. Grind the ingredients together thoroughly with a mortar and pestle or in food processor. Strain through a fine sieve or cheesecloth and keep in a tightly covered jar until needed. *Makes about ½ cup.*

Casônsèi

Ravioli, Brescian-Style — For 6

The Lombardian town of Brescia is sometimes called "The Lioness" because of the bravery of her defense against the Austrians in 1849. Could her good men have been fueled by these hearty ravioli?

Pasta:

1 recipe Pasta for Filling (see page 36)

Make pasta as directed. Roll out thin (to ⅛-inch thick or less). With a fluted wheel, cut into 4- by 6-inch rectangles. Set aside while you prepare the filling.

Filling:

- 1 cup milk, or more if needed
- 1 cup fresh bread crumbs
- 1 pound sausage
- 1 cup grated Parmesan cheese

Mix milk with bread crumbs. Remove skin from the sausage and crumble the meat. Add grated cheese and continue to blend until the mass is the consistency of thick, cooked oatmeal (add a little more milk if it's *too* thick).

Put a spoonful of the filling in the center of each square; fold long side of pasta over filling, seal edges well, and curve (see sketch). Boil pasta gently in salted water to *al dente*. Serve with a sauce of preference.

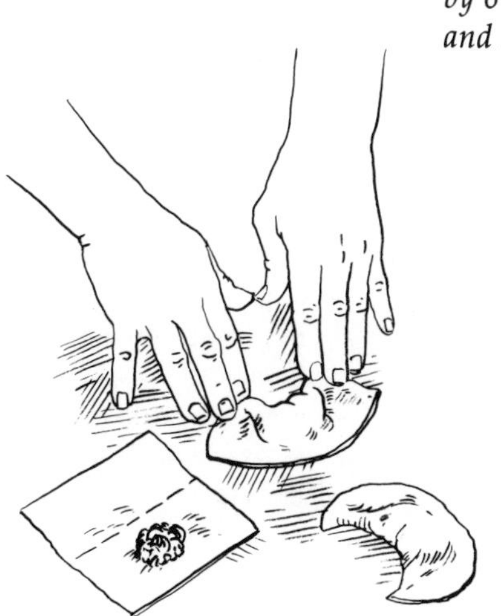

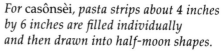

For casônsèi, *pasta strips about 4 inches by 6 inches are filled individually and then drawn into half-moon shapes.*

Gnocchi Zanleoni

For 6

Made in the fashion of Campioni d'Italia, the tiny Lombardian province surrounded by Switzerland, this is a superb gnocchi, *quite different from that of other regions. Compare it and see. It gets its name from the Zanleonis of Barre, Vermont, who gave us the recipe.*

- 4 pounds white potatoes
- Flour (amount varies with cooked potato measure; see below)
- 2 whole eggs
- 1 cup dry, plain bread crumbs
- Salt to taste

Cook, peel, and mash the potatoes. Then measure them into a large measuring cup. Calculate *half* the cooked potato measure and use that as the amount of flour to be used (if the mashed potatoes measure out to 6 cups, for example, use 3 cups of flour). Then set aside about ¼ of the flour, to be used for flouring the board and in case the dough is a bit "thin." Mix potatoes, eggs, bread crumbs, flour, and salt to taste. Work the mixture in a large bowl for about 5 minutes or until the dough is smooth but still a bit sticky. Cover and let rest for 15 to 20 minutes.

When ready to roll out, uncover dough and divide into several manageable mounds. Flour a board and divide each dough

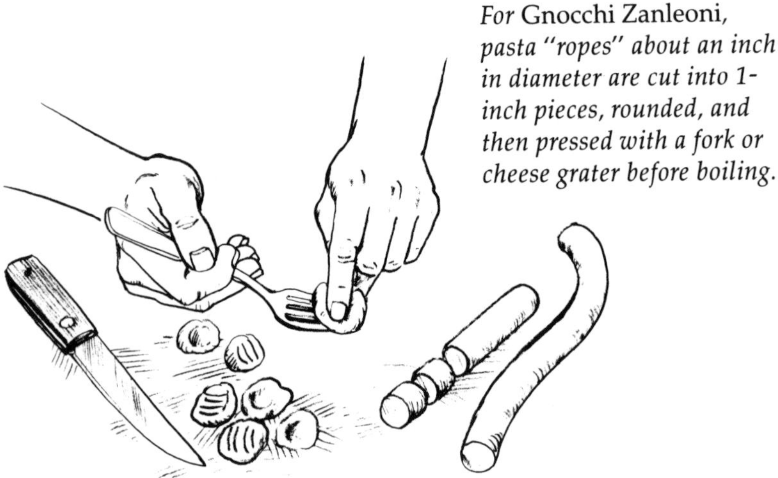

For Gnocchi Zanleoni, *pasta "ropes" about an inch in diameter are cut into 1-inch pieces, rounded, and then pressed with a fork or cheese grater before boiling.*

mound into several balls. Roll the dough out into ropelike shapes about an inch in diameter. Then cut the "ropes" into 1-inch lengths. Score the "ropes" with a fork or *gnocchi* board and indent the lengths with your finger (see sketch). Place on cookie sheet and freeze. As serving time approaches, cook *gnocchi* in boiling, salted water for about 5 minutes, stirring gently from time to time with a wooden spoon. Drain and serve with butter and cheese or with a sauce of your preference.

Risotto alla Milanese

Rice, Milan-Style

For 6

With all the bustling activity that marks Milan as the industrial center of Italy, every predinner hour will find half of the cooks in the city preparing this old Patrician dish. Arborio rice originates in Lombardy and can be obtained at Italian specialty shops. If necessary, plain raw rice — preferably the short-grain kind — can be substituted.

- 1 cup butter
- 4 tablespoons bone marrow
- 1 onion, chopped
- 2 cups Arborio rice
- 5 cups chicken or beef broth
- ¼ teaspoon saffron
- Salt and pepper to taste
- ⅓ cup grated Parmesan cheese

Melt ½ cup of the butter in large saucepan. Add the marrow and onion and cook 15 minutes without allowing onion to brown; then remove onion. Add the rice all at once and toast in butter, stirring constantly to coat all the grains and also to keep the rice from overbrowning. Add a soup ladle of broth, stir and continue to add more broth until it is absorbed, reserving ½ cup. Moisten the saffron in the remaining ½ cup broth and stir into rice. Add the remaining butter and freshly ground pepper and salt to taste. (The amount of salt needed — if any — depends upon how salty the broth was; taste carefully so as not to overdo.) Then add the Parmesan cheese and serve.

Tinca in Carpione

Marinated Freshwater Fish

For 6

Also known as Tinca Carpionata, *this unusual way of preparing fish can be used to fine advantage incorporating the leftovers from a fish fry. It is a superb way to handle North American regional freshwater fish, such as catfish, and may be served as either a main course or an appetizer.*

- 2 pounds fish fillets
- 1/3 cup flour
- 4 tablespoons butter
- 4 tablespoons olive oil
- 1 shallot or mild onion, chopped
- 1/2 cup dry vermouth
- 1/2 cup white wine
- 1 clove garlic, crushed
- Rind of 1 lemon, grated
- Salt and pepper to taste
- Lemon rounds and parsley, for garnish

Wash and dry fish fillets. Put flour into plastic bag and, one by one, drop fillets into flour, shaking bag to coat well. Heat butter and oil in skillet and sauté shallot or onion until transparent. Fry each fillet on one side until golden, then turn and cook until second side is lightly brown and fish is white but not yet flaky. Remove to paper towels to drain. Mix vermouth, wine, crushed garlic, and lemon rind in a flattish bowl. Turn fish fillets in the liquid, cover with plastic wrap, and refrigerate. Allow from 6 hours to overnight for the fish to flavor in the marinade. Adjust seasoning if necessary. Remove to a plate and garnish with lemon rounds and parsley.

Osso Buco Milanese

Sautéed Veal Shank, Milanese-Style

For 6

The old Lombardian cookbooks give the recipe for this delicate veal dish as is, served with the concentrated flavor of the pan juices. Most modern cookbooks indicate that it should be served with gremolata, *a sauce made of garlic, parsley, lemon or orange rind, and even (in some writings) an anchovy or two. Because the purpose of this book is to emphasize a "pure" cuisine, we will give you the old recipe and, as an addendum, give you the ingredients for a* gremolata *(or* gremolada*). For this recipe, ask your butcher to cut six 2-inch-thick slices of veal shank (across the bone).*

- 2 cloves garlic
- 2 tablespoons olive oil
- ½ cup butter
- ½ cup flour
- 6 slices veal shank
- 1 onion, chopped
- 1 carrot, chopped
- 1 stalk celery, chopped
- 1 sprig sage
- 1 sprig rosemary
- 1 cup dry white wine
- 2 tablespoons tomato paste
- 1 cup beef broth, or more as needed
- ¼ cup chopped parsley

In a large skillet, sauté 1 clove garlic in oil and butter. When clove is golden, discard. Flour the veal and sauté each piece, turning until nicely browned all over. Remove to a plate. Put chopped vegetables and herbs in the skillet and sauté until vegetable liquid has evaporated. Return veal shanks to skillet, pour in the wine, and let the liquid evaporate over high heat. Add tomato paste and broth. Add more broth during cooking if needed to keep meat moist. Cook over low heat for 1 hour or more (see Note). Remove meat to a platter. Scrape together pan juices, crush and add remaining clove of garlic and a little broth to deglaze pan. Pour this mixture over veal shanks and serve garnished with chopped parsley.

Note: This dish may be finished in a baking dish in a 375°F. oven with the bones standing upright in the sauce and covered with aluminum foil.

Gremolata Sauce

- 1 clove garlic, crushed
- 2 tablespoons butter
- 1 teaspoon grated citrus rind
- 1 anchovy (optional)

Mash and mix all ingredients with the pan juices of the *Osso Buco*. Serve with chopped parsley garnish.

Cotolette Milanese

Veal Milanese

For 6

The pride of Lombardy. For ease in understanding a menu in Milan, keep in mind that cotòlette *is boneless and that* costolette *(note the "s") has a small bone. This recipe is fried in butter with a small amount of olive oil to prevent burning.*

- 12 slices veal (about ¼-inch thick)
- 1 teaspoon Bea's Garlic Salt (see page 31)
- 1½ cups dry bread crumbs
- ½ cup grated Parmesan cheese
- 3 eggs
- 2 tablespoons water
- ⅔ cup butter
- 2 tablespoons olive oil
- Lemon wedges for garnish
- Parsley, for garnish

Pound veal slices with flat side of cleaver or kitchen mallet. Nip edges of cutlets to prevent curling while cooking. Mix garlic salt with bread crumbs and cheese. Dip each cutlet in crumb mixture to coat each side. Lightly beat eggs and water together. Dip cutlets into egg mixture and again into crumb-cheese mixture. Let cutlets rest before frying. In skillet, melt butter; add olive oil. When hot, fry each cutlet 3 or 4 minutes on each side until golden. Arrange on platter, garnish with parsley and lemon wedges.

Peperonata

Pickled Sweet Peppers

For 6

This combination is served either hot or cold and is an excellent accompaniment to roasts and cold meats. The vinegar helps to preserve the bright red and green of the dish.

- 2 to 2½ pounds large green peppers
- 1½ pounds ripe tomatoes
- 5 onions, sliced
- ½ teaspoon salt
- ¼ cup olive oil
- ½ cup wine vinegar

Wash peppers and cut into ½-inch strips. Peel and seed tomatoes, squeeze out excess juice, and chop coarsely. In a large skillet, sauté the vegetables with the salt in the oil, covered, for about an hour. Add the wine vinegar and cook for a few minutes more, allowing most of the moisture to evaporate. Serve hot or cold.

Mostarda di Frutta

Cremona Fruit Mustard

Cremona is the home of this special mixture, which combines the piquancy of fine English mustard with the opulent sweetness of the Italian fruit basket. Departing from the *Savor di Frutta* of Emilia Romagna (see page 152) the Cremona recipe adds dried mustard to taste — approximately two tablespoons mustard for each quart of *Savor.* In Lombardy, it comes to table with everything from sausages to boiled meats and is also enjoyed simply spread on fresh, crusty bread along with a glass of the local wine.

Torta Paradiso

Heavenly Torte — For 8 to 12

"Opulent" is an adjective often used when speaking of the cuisine of Lombardy. Strange use of the word to describe food? Not really!

- 1 cup butter
- 1¼ cups granulated sugar
- ½ cup confectioners' sugar, plus extra for topping
- 1 teaspoon vanilla
- 3 eggs, separated, plus 5 yolks
- 2¼ cups flour

Preheat oven to 350°F. In a mixing bowl, beat butter, then add the granulated and confectioners' sugar, vanilla, and egg yolks, incorporating one yolk at a time so that each is well mixed before adding the next. Mix in the flour. Beat the egg whites until peaks form, then carefully fold into batter. Butter and flour a 9-inch spring-form pan. Bake for 40 to 45 minutes, testing after 40 minutes. If the tester comes out clean, indicating cake is done, remove cake from oven and let it cool. When cool, remove cake from spring-form pan onto a serving plate, and shake confectioners' sugar over top.

Tirami Su Torte

Mocha Fluff Torte — For 8 to 12

Tirami Su *means a "pick me up," and we cannot imagine any greater psychic energizer than this sinfully delicious dessert. Beatrice has added a few flourishes of her own to this venerable regional recipe.*

Cake:

1 recipe Genoese Sponge Cake (see page 89)

Make a Genoese Sponge Cake in a 10- by 15-inch pan. Cut the cake horizontally into 3 equal layers.

Filling:

3 egg yolks
¼ cup sugar
2 large packages (8 ounces each) cream cheese, softened
1 cup sour cream
½ teaspoon vanilla
2 tablespoons brandy

Beat egg yolks with sugar in a bowl set over hot water until sugar has dissolved. Remove from heat; set bowl in cold water. Add softened cream cheese along with the sour cream, vanilla, and brandy to the cooled egg mixture. Whip until light and creamy.

Assembly:

⅓ cup strong regular or *espresso* coffee, sweetened to taste
½ cup brandy

Put ⅓ of the cake on a serving platter. Soak cake with ⅓ of a mix of the coffee and brandy. Spread with half of the cream cheese mixture. Put a second layer of cake on top and repeat the process, then place the third layer on top and soak with the remaining coffee mix.

Icing:

¾ cup semisweet chocolate bits
3 tablespoons butter
⅓ cup *espresso* coffee, sweetened to taste
3 cups heavy cream, sweetened and beaten stiff

Melt chocolate with butter. Add *espresso* and beat until of spreading consistency. Spread icing over top of torte, glazing thinly. Decorate with whipped cream piped from pastry tube in a 1-inch garland around the top edge of the torte. Finish icing the sides of the cake with the remainder of the whipped cream.

Note: The original recipe for this torte calls for Italian mascarpone cheese instead of the cream cheese given here. Because the mascarpone is not always available, cream cheese blended with sour cream is suggested as a suitable substitute.

Fave dei Morti

Almond Cookies

Makes 3 to 4 dozen

A somewhat imponderable name for a sweet, this translates literally to "Beans of the Dead." A specialty of Milan and environs.

- 1½ cups almonds
- ¼ cup butter
- ¾ cup granulated sugar
- 2 eggs
- ¼ cup pine nuts
- Zest of 1 lemon
- 1 tablespoon amaretto
- 1½ cups flour
- ½ teaspoon cinnamon

Preheat oven to 350°F. Blanch, dry, and coarsely chop almonds. Cream butter and sugar together; add eggs, nuts, lemon zest, amaretto, flour, and cinnamon. Blend together to make a soft dough. Roll dough out to a ¾-inch thickness. Cut into pieces 1½ inches long by about ¾-inch wide. Make an indentation across the top of each cookie by pressing down slightly with your index and second fingers. Place on a buttered sheet pan. Bake 25 to 30 minutes. Cool.

Dolci di Crema e Nocciole

Nut Cream Tarts

Makes about 15

Sweets made with nuts are a specialty of the North. This tart is rooted in the Old World, but improved by Beatrice's special touch.

- 1½ cups filberts (hazelnuts)
- 1 cup sweet butter
- 1¼ cups confectioners' sugar
- 2 egg yolks
- ½ teaspoon vanilla
- 15 crisp, oblong butter cookies
- 1 package ladyfingers, cut in halves crosswise
- ¼ cup Nocino or Frangelico liqueur
- 2 cups semisweet chocolate bits

Preheat oven to 300°F. Toast filberts, stirring often so they do not burn. Remove from oven to a clean cloth, and rub together to remove skins. Reserve 15 whole nuts for topping. Finely grind the rest in a food processor. Cream butter, then add sugar and egg yolks, beating until smooth, light, and fluffy. Add vanilla and the ground nuts. Put mixture into a pastry tube with a ¼-inch tip. Put butter cookies on rack. Dip ladyfinger halves into the liqueur and place one half on top of each cookie. Pipe the nut cream around and up over the cookies, ending in a little peak in the center. Place a toasted filbert on top. Repeat same process for all cookies, then refrigerate to harden.

Melt chocolate in top of a double boiler. Put cookie rack over a sheet of waxed paper and place cookies on rack. Quickly spoon the melted chocolate over each pastry, covering it completely. Allow to cool, then serve.

Tirami Su — Copa Mascarpone

Creamy Cheese Fluffs

For 4

A classic Lombardian dessert similar to the Tirami Su Torte *given earlier on page 106.*

- 3 eggs, separated
- 2 tablespoons confectioners' sugar
- ½ pound mascarpone cheese
- 3 tablespoons rum
- ⅓ cup small semisweet chocolate bits
- 8 vanilla cookies
- ½ cup *espresso* coffee
- Chocolate curls or cocoa, and a cherry, for garnish

Beat yolks with sugar until sugar is dissolved. Add mascarpone or cream cheese and beat until light and creamy. Add rum. Beat egg whites and gently fold them into the mascarpone or cream cheese mixture. Add chocolate bits. Dip half of cookie in *espresso* coffee. Put 2 cookies cone fashion, with the wet ends down, in a parfait cup; repeat for remaining cookies and pour in cream filling. Refrigerate for several hours and serve very cold, each decorated with chocolate curls or cocoa powder and perhaps a cherry.

Note: If mascarpone is unavailable, substitute three (3-ounce) packages of cream cheese blended with ½ cup sour cream.

Budino di Milano Tassinari

Milanese Pudding

For 10 to 12

One wonders if the Milanese eat so well because they are industrious or vice versa. But with sweet, distinctive desserts like this, who really cares?

- 1 1/4 cups sugar
- 1/4 cup cornstarch
- 2/3 cup flour
- 4 eggs, separated
- 1 teaspoon lemon zest
- 1/2 teaspoon salt
- 1 quart milk, heated
- 1/2 cup rum or brandy
- 1 cup heavy cream, whipped
- 1 cup toasted almonds, chopped

Mix 1/2 cup sugar with cornstarch and flour. With whisk, beat 4 egg yolks, lemon zest, and salt until blended and smooth. Add the quart of hot milk little by little. Pour mixture into a double boiler and cook, stirring constantly until it thickens. Remove from stove, cover, and refrigerate. When cool, add 1/4 cup rum or brandy and blend. Beat egg whites until stiff, fold into cooked mixture, and set aside. Caramelize remaining 3/4 cup sugar. Pour it into a tube pan or a 9-inch round baking pan, moving the pan so that the caramel coats the bottom and up about 1 inch on the sides. (Handle pan with care, as this can give you a nasty burn.) Then pour the set-aside cooked mixture into the baking pan and cover with foil. Set pan in a larger pan of hot water over burner. Cook over very low heat for 2 hours. Remove from heat and cool. Refrigerate until ready to serve.

When serving time comes, invert pudding and turn out onto a serving dish. Liquefy the hardened caramel on the bottom of the pan by putting it over low heat. When melted, pour the caramel over pudding, along with the remaining rum or brandy. Before serving, top each slice with a dollop of whipped cream and a sprinkling of chopped, toasted almonds.

Trentino–Alto Adige

The Special Wines & Cheeses of

Trentino–Alto Adige

Wines of the Region

Dry reds: *Lago di Caldaro, Marzemino, Merlot Trentino, Santa Maddalena, Terlaner, Teròldego*

Dessert rosé: *Casteller*

Dry whites: *Istituto di San Michele, Pinot Chardonnay, Terlaner*

Demi-sec whites: *Riesling Italico, Riesling Renano, Traminer*

Dessert whites: *Fratelli Pedrotti, Moscato Giallo, Vin Santo Ambrato*

Wines Available in the United States

Dry red: *Teròldego*

Dry whites: *Istituto di San Michele, Pinot Chardonnay*

Sweet whites: *Fratelli Pedrotti, Moscato*

Dry sparkling: *Brut Champenoise, Ferrari*

Cheeses of the Region

Cioncada, Formaggio Magro, Formaggio Stravecchio Carnico, Pestolato, Vézzena

Senza bacco e cerere, venere trema per il freddo.

Without wine and bread, love remains cold.

The inhabitants of this Northern region of Italy look out at their respective surroundings through eyes as blue as the sky that frames the silhouettes of the jagged Dolomite mountains. The Austrian influence is not only genetic — it adds flavor to the language and the kitchens of this singular countryside.

In the late 1800s it was not easy for these proud mountain folk who felt completely Italian but were constantly buffeted by Teutonic influences. Their regional dialects (completely unintelligible to anyone not from their own villages) only served to reinforce the need for a separate identity in their bicultural world. These dialects also served as a common defensive idiom for their nomadic business dealings.

Although Trento and Bolzano are this region's chief towns, the small town of Pinzolo is well known as the home base of an important fraternity of craftsmen — the grinders and sharpeners of the world. For more than a century this trade community has had its roots in this region's Rendena Valley. The proper honing of the housewives', chefs', and other food personnel's vital kitchen tools was considered an art, and the men of Pinzolo and its neighboring hamlets traveled the byroads and markets of Europe plying their artisanry. It was a hard and lonely life for the *moleta* (grinder) and his apprentice; competition was fierce, and while the *maestro* worked at his stone, the boy would scout the labyrinthine cobble and dirt streets, drumming up trade with his clanging bell. A part of the repertoire were bird whistles, shouted bits of ribald verse, and — of course — the occasional scuffle with a competitor's "advance man." Sixteen hours a day were the norm, at the end of which the exhausted pair would gulp a meager meal and bed down in a stable or friendly haystack. The men usually returned to the village in the early spring, just in time to repair the winter's ravages, to do the spring planting, and to make the acquaintance of the newest offspring, born while they were distantly plying their trade.

The driving force behind the first great migration to the United States from Trentino–Alto Adige was the same as that for much of the rest of the country: a starving economy and dreams of better things in America. There were no volcanic eruptions or cholera epidemics in the region, but the Trentinos and Bolzanos were compelled by another impetus, the omnipresent shadow of the feuding and shifting Austro-Hungarian empire. The Italians were considered, if they were thought about at all, as a mindless mass occupying a territory under dispute, and whose future was of very little importance to the titled players.

The Boston suburbs of Somerville, Medford, and parts of Brockton became the haven of opportunity for the small group of immigrants from the banks of the region's foaming Sarca River. The Binellis, Maffeis, Maestranzis, Povinellis, Maganzinis, Pollis, and Collinas came to New England with their *argagns* (wheelbarrow-mounted grinding stones). Testimony to the hardiness of this small group is patriarch Valentino Maganzini, the entrepreneurial force behind the Medford Grinding Company, which sharpens utensils for not only New England's hotels, restaurants, and serious cooks, but for a national clientele. Nonno Valentino is eighty-three; his health is good, his memory phenomenal, and his appetite prodigious. The recipe for *polenta* included here is one of his family recipes to be found in these pages.

The sad fact about the cuisine of this area is that, because of its Germanic influence and content, many Italian cookbooks tend to ignore and exclude its hearty specialties entirely! Some of these include *Piatto Elefante* ("Elephant Platter"), a mammoth food offering combining a dozen vegetables and a half dozen meats, which legend tells us was concocted to honor King Solomon; *Speck*, smoked fatback; *Gnocchi di Magro*, distinct from other Italian *gnocchi* in that they are made from wholewheat and rye flours; *Gulasch*, the classic meat dish transliterated from the Bohemian; *Crauti*, sauerkraut *alla Italiana*; and *Merano*, a dark coarse-grained bread.

The *polenta* of this region, like the *gnocchi*, is made with a dark-colored grain similar to our buckwheat or whole-grained wheat. The combination of zesty sausages, sauerkraut, dumplings, and the pastry of the Tyrol adds dimension to the local specialties. Imagine the steamy fragrance of bits of veal with sauerkraut and *polenta*. Wonderful! While the number of dishes may be small, their unique cross-cultural ingredients make them well worth their inclusion . . . and your experimentation.

Zuppa di Carne

Northern Beef Soup

For 6

A soup to come home to when the Alpine winds howl around one's ears. The longer it cooks, the better it tastes.

- 1 pound beef chuck or round
- 2 onions
- 4 tablespoons butter
- 1 tablespoon olive oil
- 1 clove garlic, crushed
- 8 cups water
- 1 pound potatoes
- ½ cup dry white wine
- 1 tablespoon flour
- 5 beef bouillon cubes
- 12 caraway seeds (optional)
- Seasoning to taste

Cube beef into bite-sized pieces; chop onions and melt butter with the oil in a soup pot. Brown meat; add onions, garlic clove, and 4 cups of the water. Peel and dice the potatoes, add to meat with the wine, and continue cooking. Sprinkle with the flour and stir until flour is absorbed. Dissolve the bouillon cubes in the remaining 4 cups water and add, along with the caraway seeds if desired. Simmer for at least 1 hour and season to taste.

Canederli Eugenia

Eugenia's Dumplings

For 4

A staple of Trentino–Adige, reflecting the German influence on the local cuisine. Shared by Eugenia Maganzini.

- 3 quarts broth
- 3 bouillon cubes
- ½ loaf stale bread
- 1 cup milk, or more if needed
- 4 eggs
- 2 cloves garlic, crushed
- 3 to 4 sausages, skinned and crumbled
- ½ cup ground leftover meat
- Freshly ground pepper to taste
- ¼ cup chopped parsley
- ⅓ cup grated Parmesan cheese, plus more for garnish
- ¼ cup finely chopped celery (optional)
- Flour, for rolling

Put broth in a large pot on the stove, fortifying it with the bouillon cubes. Soak the bread in milk for an hour or so, adding more milk if needed to soak bread thoroughly. In a large bowl, put soaked bread, eggs, crushed garlic, sausage, and ground leftover meat. Add pepper, parsley, Parmesan cheese, and celery if desired. Blend well with the hands and form into balls the size of Ping-Pong balls (makes about 12). Roll the balls in flour and drop gently into the boiling broth; cook for about 20 minutes or until the dumplings are all floating on top of the broth. Fill soup bowls with the broth, divide the dumplings among the bowls, cover with Parmesan cheese, and serve.

Polenta Maganzini

Wood-Stove *Polenta* For many

One of the great difficulties, albeit charms, of writing a regional cookbook with roots in the past is that the best documentation is a verbal one. Mouth-to-mouth communication is done in two ways. First you listen *to the "how," and then you* taste *it. There are several* polenta *recipes to be found in these pages, but because this one typifies the loving cooperation of the many people with whom Beatrice and I worked on this book, I am going to try faithfully to reconstruct the "original" recipe; then I will give you "equivalents."*

Eugenia Maganzini comments that her father-in-law, Nonno Valentino, feels the only *way to make* polenta *is over a charcoal stove: "Genia" feels that it can be done quite efficiently over gas, but "electric is no good!"*

Native Recipe	*Equivalents*
A big pot of water	1 gallon water
Salt	Salt to taste
5 or 6 handfuls coarse cornmeal	$2\frac{2}{3}$ cups stone-ground cornmeal

The Native Recipe instructions are detailed: "Bring the covered pot to a boil; add the salt. Begin to pour in the cornmeal slowly, stirring constantly in one direction. When all the rough flour is in the water . . . WITHOUT LUMPS . . . go and set the table." This allows about 5 minutes for the water to return to a boil. Then, to continue with the "native" instructions, "Plan to stay with this. . . . Keep stirring with a strong wooden spoon until a crust begins to form around the edges. Don't let the crust frighten you . . . that's all right! It means the *polenta* is cooked."

How long were we stirring this golden grain that gets heavier with each sweep of the spoon? For 30 to 45 minutes — it depends on the *polenta*. It seems to have a mind of its own!

Manzo alla Vecchia Trento

Beef "The Old Way"

For 6 to 8

The old ways are often the best ways. This dish has been found on Trentino tables for hundreds of years. In the original recipe the herb and spice amounts were not indicated; they were left to the cook's judgment and family preference. However, here Bea offers a little guidance; feel free to adjust to your own taste.

- 3 to 4 onions, finely chopped
- 1 slice pork fat
- 4 tablespoons butter
- 4 tablespoons vinegar
- 2 to 3 pounds beef, tied
- 3 sprigs rosemary
- 1 clove garlic, left whole
- Rind of 1 lemon, grated
- ½ cup milk or more as needed
- Salt as needed
- Pepper to taste

Cook onions and pork fat together, with the butter, until onions are transparent. Sprinkle with vinegar and let it evaporate. Add meat, rosemary, garlic clove, and lemon rind. Let brown. Add ½ cup milk and salt, as needed. Cover and simmer over low heat for 3 hours, adding additional milk if too dry. Stir occasionally. Remove garlic and rosemary and serve hot. Slice and pour sauce over sliced meat.

Note: This is a splendid slow-cooker recipe.

Lucanica coi Crauti

Sausage with Kraut For 4

How Germanic can the Italian kitchen be? Here is a classic example of the very best of culinary "infiltration." This dish is served with polenta, *golden and steamy.*

2 ounces unsmoked bacon
2 pounds sauerkraut
1 cup broth of choice
¼ cup white wine
1 pound pork sausage
1 teaspoon caraway seeds (optional)
2 tart apples, sliced

Chop bacon and sauté. Rinse sauerkraut and cook for 2 to 3 hours with broth and wine. When kraut is half-cooked, add the bacon, sausage, caraway seeds, and the apples, and continue cooking until all is just tender.

Note: For a truly gala dish, use a good domestic champagne instead of the white wine, and buy a mild kielbasa-type sausage (Plumrose makes a good one, not too smoky or too salty).

Garretto di Maiale

Pork Shin For 4

This recipe may also be made with a veal shin, cooked in the same manner.

1 pork shin (3 to 4 pounds)
1 clove garlic, thinly sliced
2 sprigs rosemary
¼ cup butter
1 cup white wine
Salt and pepper to taste

Lard pork shin (make slits in meat and insert) with sliced garlic and rosemary. Melt the butter in a Dutch oven and brown the meat. Pour the wine over the browned meat. Place in a baking pan in the oven. Cook at 325°F. for about 2 hours or until meat thermometer inserted in fleshy part (not touching bone) registers 190°. Make a light gravy with the pan juices, seasoning as needed, and serve with pasta.

Strudel di Manzo

Meat Strudel

For 6

Here is a classic melding of the Northern border cultures — a party dish par excellence that can be made in advance and served either hot or cold. If you prefer, frozen phyllo dough may be substituted for the pastry.

Pastry:

2½ cups flour
1 egg
¼ cup butter, softened
½ teaspoon sugar
1 teaspoon salt
Tepid water

Put flour on a bread or pastry board, making a well in the center. Add egg, softened butter, sugar, and salt. Mix, stirring with a fork to incorporate all of the flour. Add enough tepid water to make a soft dough. Slap dough against the board several times to push out any trapped air. Knead until elastic. Put dough in a bowl, cover, and let rest for 15 minutes. On a floured cloth, roll out dough very, very thin into a rectangle about 8 inches wide.

Filling:

2 firm apples
3 cups ground leftover meats
2 tablespoons meat juice or gravy
⅓ cup pine nuts
1 egg, beaten
1 tablespoon milk
4 tablespoons butter, melted

Peel and slice apples very thin. Add chopped meat, meat juice, and pine nuts. Blend in the beaten egg and milk. Mix well. Spread filling on pastry, rolling it up as you go. Pinch ends and curve roll into a large arc. Brush with melted butter and bake for 1 hour in a 375°F. oven until top crust is golden.

Torta di Castagne

Sweet Chestnut Torte For 10

All of the Northern border regions relish the chestnut. Although it is often eaten unsweetened in a variety of ways, used as if it were a vegetable, here it makes a superb dessert torte worthy of your most special guests.

- ⅔ cup butter
- ¾ cup granulated sugar
- ¾ cup flour, sifted
- ½ pound Chestnut Purée (see recipe below)
- 9 eggs, separated
- 1½ teaspoons vanilla
- 2 cups heavy cream (lightly sweetened if desired)
- 10 marrons glacés, chopped (optional)

Preheat oven to 350°F. Cream butter and add sugar until mixture is light and fluffy. Combine flour with purée, and add to butter and sugar, a small amount at a time. Incorporate beaten egg yolks, little by little, and add vanilla. Beat egg whites until they form stiff peaks, then fold into chestnut mixture with a very light hand. Pour batter into a buttered and floured 9-inch spring-form pan. Bake 45 minutes or more. Test with toothpick. When done, remove cake from oven and set on a rack to cool. Beat whipping cream well (sweeten it with confectioners' sugar if you desire) and refrigerate. When cake is cool, cut horizontally into 2 layers and spread bottom layer with chilled whipped cream. Put on top layer, ice with additional whipped cream, and garnish, if desired, with chopped marrons glacés.

Chestnut Purée

Boil 1 pound shelled chestnuts for 1 hour in half milk and half water to cover. When tender, drain, skin, and put in glass container of your blender or processor. Add 1 tablespoon butter and 3 tablespoons heavy cream; purée. If you wish a sweet purée, add a bit of sugar and cinnamon.

Note: If you prefer, chestnut purée may be purchased in all gourmet specialty shops.

Torta di Fragole

Strawberry Torte

For 6 to 8

An international favorite. Who can resist the siren song of a luscious red and white strawberry shortcake alla Italiana?

- 1 sponge cake (½ recipe for Genoese Sponge Cake on page 89)
- 1 quart strawberries, plus several perfect berries for garnish
- ⅓ cup confectioners' sugar, plus extra for sweetening whipping cream
- ⅓ cup maraschino liqueur
- 1½ cups whipping cream

Preheat oven to 350°F. Make sponge cake and bake in a 9-inch tube pan. When done, cut a paper-thin slice off the top to remove crust. Wash strawberries very well and crush them with sugar and 2 tablespoons of the maraschino liqueur. Soak top of sponge cake with remaining liqueur, then spread with crushed berries. Whip cream until very stiff and sweeten with remaining sugar. Top strawberries with whipped cream. Decorate with whole berries and refrigerate until ready to serve.

Emilia Romagna

The Special Wines, Liqueurs & Cheeses of
Emilia Romagna

Wines of the Region

Dry red: *Sangiovese*

Sparkling dry reds: *Lambrusco di Castelvetro, Lambrusco di Sorbara*

Sparkling demi-sweet reds: *Lambrusco Grasparossa, Lambrusco Salamino, Lambrusco di Sorbara*

Dry whites: *Albana, Trebbiano di Romagna*

Sweet whites: *Albana, Bianco di Scandiano*

Liqueurs of note

Nocino (walnut), *Sassolino* (star anise flavor)

Wines Available in the United States

Dry reds: *Lambrusco, Gutturnio, Sangiovese di Romagna, Rosso Armentano*

Sweet red: *Lambrusco Dolce*

Dry whites: *Trebbiano di Romagna, Albana di Romagna*

Dry sparkling: *Pinot Spumante*

Cheeses of the Region

Parmigiano reggiano (the most noteworthy), *Pecorino, Provolone piacentino, Ravigiolo, Robiola, Soliole*

Casa mia, per piccina che tu sia, tu mi pari una badia.

My home, however tiny you may be, you seem a Paradise to me.

As the "cradle" of Bea Lazzaro's culinary genius, Emilia Romagna is now inextricably interwoven with New England, which has been the performance site of that genius for more than seventy years.

If you were to superimpose a map of the region upon a map of Massachusetts, a startling similarity would be apparent. Let's exchange the Adriatic for the Atlantic, and then go west on each map to view ancient mountains: in the old country, the Ligurian Apennines, and here, our own green Berkshires.

As another play in our geographic charade, the famous *Via Emilia* (Emilian Way) in its East/West course might be compared to the Boston Post Road, the latter lacking the antiquity and history, but both having been trade arteries, and in their flower, the backbones of important commerce. Today, both are congested and noisy in places, but still in use and much a part of the regions they dissect.

The immigrants to New England from this area came well nurtured from the source of gourmet Italian cuisine, appropriately named *La Grassa* or "The Abundance." They were a hardy, "hearty" group, as life-loving as the New Englanders were austere, as round as their new neighbors were spare. What interesting things these two peoples had to interchange. The cultural sharing and transfusion were not always easy, but the greatest lever for beginning comprehension is a shared interest, and what more nonthreatening subject between strangers than our great common human need — food.

La Cucina Bolognese is everywhere accepted as being rich, both in the number of recipes and in their content. Much of this deserved fame (or infamy, as your dietary philosophy dictates) comes from the use of butter and unsmoked bacon (fatback), along with olive oil. And still another sin against today's all-important slenderness is the *sfoglia,* that airy layering of transparent sheets of pasta, which are the beginning of an exquisitely tempting inventory — *cappelletti, tortellini, pappardelle, lasagne,* and so many more.

The Adriatic is less saline than the Atlantic because it is fed with clear water run-off from Alpine streams. A great assortment of finny and shell fish make their homes in its welcoming tides, and here again we have comparisons. Ravenna might be compared to Gloucester. Both are active fishing centers and both supply the means with which their respective peoples make their fine fish dishes. Happily, all of the authentic fish recipes found in these pages are adaptable to the catch of the North Atlantic, now available in most corners of the United States much of the time.

In Emilia Romagna, eel is a particular specialty of Comacchio and Ravenna, with several different species considered particular delicacies. This, too, is a shared interest: many American fishmongers also sell eel. Various other specialties of the region have enriched our New World tables. Modena's famed Balsamic vinegar is available in most fine food stores. Mortadella, the illustrious forebear of our popular deli treat, bologna, and *zampone,* a stuffed pig's-foot creation sporting hoof and all, are also available, if only in ethnic *salumerie* or Bea's kitchen.

Other specialties include *Zuppa di Pesce,* a fish soup, and pastas in all manner of shapes and with all manner of stuffings, from chicken parts and pork, to prosciutto and squash. *Cotechino* is a sausage dish eaten with lentils. Veal is done in many ways, breaded and filled with cheese, prosciutto, and tomatoes, and stuffed in rolls. *Passatelli in Brodo* is a renowned dumpling and broth dish, while *Risotto alle Vongole* features rice with clams. And this only begins to scratch the surface: you'll find recipes for some of these and many others following.

The true Emilian kitchen also includes a rarity of fresh, regional breads: the Ferrarese fantastically shaped loaves; the bread from Bologna, with its odd little four-cornered forms; the unleavened *piade* (a sort of Italian "pita" pocket). The list is long and hardly describable; here the eyes and the taste buds must do the communicating.

A hungry sage once remarked that the tables of Emilia Romagna are intended for large, happy families with many friends. So it is there, and so it is here at *Casa Lazzaro,* food for sharing — a cottage craft to give joy to the world!

Pane Bolognese

Bolognese Bread Makes 16 four-inch rolls, or 3 large or 8 small loaves

Perhaps the very best bread in all of Italy. Beatrice is a consummate bread baker, and she attributes her success to long kneading. This task is less arduous nowadays, thanks to all of our new kitchen "toys," but this bread must still be hand-kneaded for at least 20 minutes. This recipe can be made up in small or large loaves and in both small and large rolls — we're making rolls here.

- 1 (2-ounce) yeast cake (see Note) or 2 packages dried yeast
- 7 to 8 cups bread flour
- 2 cups warm water (90 to 110°F.)
- 2 teaspoons sugar
- 4 tablespoons lard, softened
- 1 teaspoon salt
- Egg white, for brushing crust

Proof a small piece of the yeast to make sure it is active. (To do this, use 2 tablespoons warm water and a pinch of sugar; stir in crumbled yeast and let sit for 5 minutes. If there is foaming action, you know your yeast is "live.")

Put 5 cups of the flour in a large bowl. Make a well, and put in the yeast, warm water, and sugar. Incorporate some flour into the yeast liquid. Let it form a sponge. Add remaining flour. Add softened lard and salt; blend to form a firm mass. Knead well for several minutes and beat with the rolling pin (actually bang down on the ball of dough) several times. Continue to knead until you have a very smooth, pliable dough. Then let rise until doubled in bulk in a warm (110°F.) oven. Remove from oven and punch down. Break off pieces of dough and let them rest about 10 minutes. When ready, roll pieces into "ropes" 8 inches long and about 1¼ inches in diameter. Make a loose single knot in the center of each "rope." Slash tops with a razor (see sketch). Let pieces rise again 30 minutes or more.

Preheat oven to 375°F. Place a pan of water in oven for moisture. Place "loaflets" on a baking sheet and brush with water and egg white. During baking, brush bread again with water and egg white (this makes the crust crunchy). Bake for 30 minutes or until roll tops are golden.

Note: Since nowadays supermarket cake yeast more frequently comes in smaller (3/5 ounce) packages, don't let this "1 cake" fool you. Bea, however, still uses the larger cakes; she buys them in a local bakery.

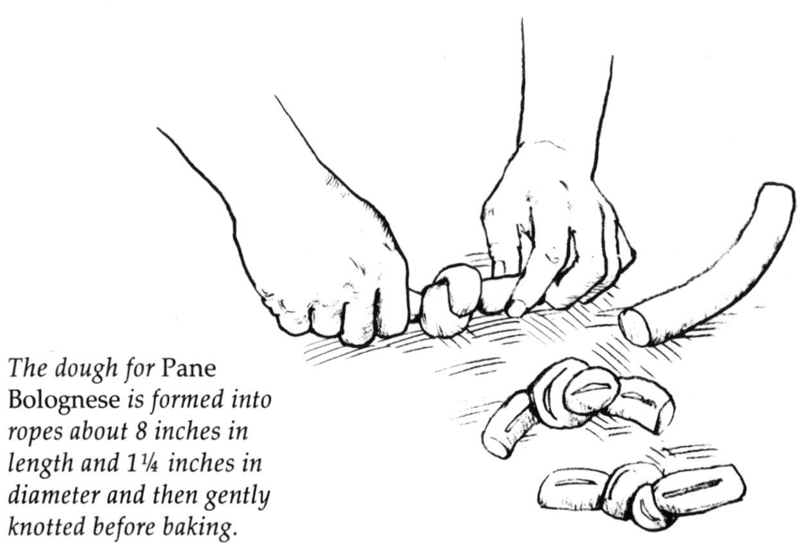

The dough for Pane Bolognese *is formed into ropes about 8 inches in length and 1¼ inches in diameter and then gently knotted before baking.*

Gnocchi al Prosciutto

Prosciutto Bread

Makes two 9-inch loaves

If bread is our staff of life, then prosciutto must surely occupy much the same importance in the Italian kitchen. Here the two products are wed in a most savory fashion.

Make recipe for Bolognese Bread (see above), kneading in a half pound of finely chopped prosciutto. When well kneaded, make flat, 9-inch rounds and let rise for about 20 minutes in a warm, draft-free place. Then bake at 400°F. for 30 minutes.

Minestra di Fagioli con Taglierini

Pasta and Bean Soup

For 6

Bea's grandmother made this rich soup four or five times a year, starting when the fresh, young shell beans came to market in late September. It is her personal version of the area's traditional soup.

Pasta:

1 recipe Classic 3-Egg Pasta (see page 36)

Make pasta. Set aside while you prepare the soup.

Soup:

- 1½ pounds fresh shell beans
- 1 onion, finely chopped
- 3 quarts water
- 3 cloves garlic chopped
- ½ (6-ounce) can tomato paste
- ½ cup chopped parsley
- 4 tablespoons butter
- ⅓ cup olive oil
- Bea's Garlic Salt to taste (see page 31)
- Grated Parmesan cheese, for topping (optional)

Boil beans and onion in salted water to cover. When cooked, drain and reserve liquid. Purée beans and onion in a processor or food mill. Add bean water to purée and simmer slowly. In a small skillet, sauté the garlic, tomato paste and parsley in a mix of the butter and oil. Season with garlic salt to taste. Add water (about ¾ cup) as the sauce condenses. Pour sauce into soup kettle with the bean "soup" and simmer another 30 minutes. Add pasta cooked *al dente*, and serve.

Note: This is a thin soup; you may wish to sprinkle each portion with a grating of Parmesan cheese for extra "zip."

Zuppa Imperiale Lazzaro

Imperial Soup — For 6 to 8

This delicate soup is a natural for cold winter evenings. These pasta "first cousins" make a royal addition to a clear brodo *(consommé).*

- 4 eggs
- ½ stick (4 tablespoons) butter, melted
- 1 cup grated Parmesan (or Romano) cheese
- ¼ cup semolina or cracked wheat
- 1½ to 2 quarts broth (preferably chicken)

Beat the ingredients except the broth together. Spread on a jellyroll sheet to a thickness of about ⅛-inch. Bake at 375°F. until butter foams up and dough becomes golden in color, about 10 to 15 minutes. Remove from oven and allow to cool. Flip out onto a board and cut into ½-inch squares. Drop into a pot of broth and bring to a boil. Cover and banish to the back of the stove until ready to reheat for use.

Passatelli della Nonna Nina

Grandmother's Soup "Boosters" — For 6 to 8

Another variation on the "good things that Italian families float around in their chicken broth."

- ½ stick (4 tablespoons) butter, melted
- 3 cups bread crumbs
- 1½ cups grated Parmesan cheese
- 2 eggs
- Sprinkling of nutmeg
- Salt and pepper to taste

Mix the ingredients together until you have a hard mass. Put the mass through a meat grinder and drop the "beads" into a boiling broth of your choice. After liquid returns to a boil, cover and put on back of the stove for later reheating.

Salsa di Pomodoro Lazzaro

Basic Tomato Sauce

For 4 to 6

By popular vote, the tomato would probably be elected as the most indispensable vegetable in Italy. Here is the basic, ruby-red tomato sauce — a sauce that has as many variations as there are changes in New England weather.

- 2 pounds tomatoes (canned or fresh)
- 1/4 cup olive oil
- 1 medium onion, chopped
- 1 stalk celery
- 4 to 5 fresh basil leaves
- 1 carrot
- 1/2 (6-ounce) can tomato paste
- 2 tablespoons butter
- Salt and pepper to taste

Chop tomatoes and put in a large saucepan with the olive oil. Add the onion, celery, basil leaves, carrot, and tomato paste. Cook over moderate heat, covered, for 30 to 40 minutes. Remove lid and continue cooking for another hour, stirring occasionally. When sauce seems the right consistency, strain through a coarse strainer, stir in the butter, and season to taste with salt and pepper. Use when ready or save for another day. It keeps well in the refrigerator and freezes superbly.

Note: This sauce adapts beautifully to your own inventive genius and actually improves with an infusion of leftover whatevers! Add sautéed hamburger meat, sausages, mushrooms, green pepper bits, or whatever else you have on hand.

Salsa di Gorgonzola

Gorgonzola Cheese Sauce

Makes about 2 cups

A superbly creamy sauce traditionally served with fettuccine.

- 1 stick (8 tablespoons) butter
- 4 ounces Gorgonzola cheese
- 1 cup heavy cream

In a heavy saucepan, melt butter. Add cheese, stirring until thoroughly blended. Add heavy cream in sufficient amounts to thin the sauce to the desired consistency.

Salsa di Noci Lazzaro

Walnut Sauce

Makes about 2 cups

- 1 cup walnuts, plus extra for garnish
- 2 tablespoons olive oil
- 3 tablespoons butter
- 1 small package (3 ounces) cream cheese
- 3 sprigs parsley
- 3 tablespoons ricotta cheese
- 2 tablespoons milk
- Salt and pepper to taste

Put all the ingredients in a blender or food processor and process until it is a smooth purée, but not too thick. If necessary, add a bit more milk. Serve over fettuccine or a similar pasta, and garnish with a few whole nuts.

Note: An elegant and expensive variation may be made by substituting pine nuts for the walnuts. But make sure that you garnish with a few of the whole nuts before serving, so that everyone will know how caringly extravagant you are!

La Famosissima Salsa Bolognese Lazzaro

Bolognese Meat Sauce

Makes 6 cups

Even the most frequent traveler to Bologna would have difficulty finding a better version of this famous sauce of Emilia Romagna. Here is Beatrice's genius in full flower!

- 1 ounce dried Italian mushrooms
- 5 tablespoons butter
- 2 slices unsmoked bacon
- 1 onion
- 1 stalk celery
- 1 carrot
- 1½ pounds ground beef
- ½ pound ground pork
- ½ cup dry white wine
- 1 chicken liver, chopped
- ½ (6-ounce) can tomato paste
- ⅛ teaspoon nutmeg
- 1 teaspoon poultry seasoning
- 1 teaspoon garlic salt
- 1 cup light cream
- Flour, for sprinkling
- 1 to 1½ cups broth

Soak mushrooms in hot water to cover; chop when soft. Melt butter in skillet. Process (or grind) the bacon and the vegetables. Sauté until soft. Add beef, pork, and drained mushrooms. Fry until water has evaporated and the mixture sizzles. Add wine and allow it to evaporate. Add chicken liver; cook 5 minutes. Stir in tomato paste and cook 5 minutes more. Add nutmeg, poultry seasoning, and garlic salt. Add cream and stir. Sprinkle flour over the sauce and stir gently. Add 1 cup of the broth, cover, and cook for 2 hours over low flame, stirring occasionally and adding more broth if necessary. Let settle and skim fat from surface; the sauce should be dark and thick. This sauce freezes well.

Note: Sauce can also be made without the pork; the flavor is different, but still quite delicious.

Besciamella Lazzaro

Béchamel Sauce

Makes scant 3 cups

With the addition of the egg yolks, Beatrice challenges the sauce purists and deliciously treads the line between Mornay *and the classic* Balsamella, *as it was once called in most of Italy.*

- 6 tablespoons butter
- 6 tablespoons flour
- 2½ cups milk, warmed
- White pepper to taste
- ¼ teaspoon nutmeg
- 2 egg yolks, well beaten

Melt butter in saucepan, lower heat, and stir in flour, taking care that it does not brown. Add the warmed milk to the flour mixture very gradually, whisking constantly. Season with pepper and nutmeg. Put beaten egg yolks in a bowl, pour in a little of the sauce, and whisk to "temper." Then slowly add to the sauce, stirring continually. Remove from heat and use immediately. This sauce does not "hold" or keep well. If you try to refrigerate excess, it will become gluey and refuse all attempts at reconstitution.

Note: If you are using this sauce for layering lasagne, add ½ cup of grated Parmesan or cut a small amount of Gruyère cheese into the sauce before adding the egg yolks. This will give a more pronounced flavor.

Salsa Agrodolce di Talignano

Sweet and Sour Sauce — Makes about 1 cup

This savory sauce, native to Emilia Romagna, gives flavor to the plain boiled-meat (Bollito Misto) *dish so enjoyed by the Reggiani.*

- 2 cloves garlic
- 1 bunch parsley, finely chopped
- 2 tablespoons olive oil
- 1 tablespoon flour
- 2 tablespoons sugar
- 2 tablespoons vinegar, preferably Balsamic
- ½ cup water
- 2 tablespoons tomato paste
- Salt and pepper to taste

Crush garlic and mix with finely chopped parsley. Sauté in olive oil; *do not allow garlic to brown.* When pieces of the garlic begin to rise to the surface, stir in flour and sugar; mix well and add the vinegar and water. Stir in the tomato paste and allow to cook for a few minutes until flavors are well blended. Season to taste.

Salsa di Salsicce Lazzaro

Beatrice's Sausage Sauces — For 6

Sausage in Italy is almost as universally admired as is the hot dog in this country. Here are two variations of sausage-based toppings for pasta, vegetables, or egg dishes.

Sausage Sauce 1:

- 1 onion, finely chopped
- 1 tablespoon olive oil
- 2 tablespoons butter
- ½ pound breakfast sausage
- ½ (6-ounce) can tomato paste
- ¼ cup water
- ½ pint light cream
- Bea's Garlic Salt (see page 31)

Sauté the onion until soft in the olive oil and butter. Skin the sausage and add to the pan, mashing with a fork. Fry over medium heat for a few minutes and then stir in the tomato paste. Cook for a few minutes and add the water. Allow to thicken. Stir in the light cream and season with garlic salt to taste.

Sausage Sauce 2: Ragù

- ½ stick (4 tablespoons) butter
- 1 small onion, chopped
- 1 clove garlic, crushed
- 1 pound Italian sausage, skinned
- 1 pound ripe tomatoes, peeled and seeded
- 1 bay leaf
- ⅓ cup white wine

Melt butter in saucepan; sauté onion and garlic. Add sausage. Allow meat to brown slightly, breaking it into pieces with fork. Add the tomatoes (if using canned, drain well) and bay leaf. Cook for 20 minutes to allow flavors to blend. Add wine; let evaporate while simmering. Then cook another 30 minutes over low flame, covered. Remove bay leaf before serving.

Spaghetti Nonna Nina Tassinari

Spaghetti with Mushrooms and Cream

For 6

This is a recipe from Renazzo made by Beatrice's grandmother. It is one of those exquisitely simple dishes that evokes fond smiles in Beatrice's family and many happy gustatory memories.

- 3 ounces dried Italian mushrooms
- ¾ cup hot water
- 3 tablespoons olive oil
- 3 tablespoons butter
- 1 small onion, chopped
- 1 teaspoon Bea's Garlic Salt (see page 31)
- ⅔ (6-ounce) can tomato paste
- ½ cup broth or bouillon
- 1 pound spaghetti or fettuccine
- 1 cup heavy cream
- Grated Parmesan cheese, for topping

Soak mushrooms in hot water. When soft, drain and chop, reserving the liquid. Heat oil and butter in a saucepan; add onion and garlic salt. Sauté until onion is soft and transparent. Add mushrooms and stir 2 to 3 minutes. Add tomato paste; stir and cook for 5 minutes. Add mushroom liquid and broth, and continue cooking until medium thick.

Cook spaghetti or fettuccine *al dente* in salted water. Drain and place in a deep bowl. Bring sauce to simmering point, add the heavy cream, and stir well. *Do not allow to boil.* Pour over pasta and serve with grated Parmesan cheese.

Tortellini Beatrice Lazzaro

For 6

This is the dish that brought the authors together in the Benotti kitchen — the recipe that "started it all"! Tortellini *usually begins with circles, but Bea begins with squares.*

Filling:

- 1½ pounds lean pork, cut into 2- to 3-inch chunks
- ½ stick butter (4 tablespoons)
- 1 small onion, peeled
- 1 teaspoon Bea's Garlic Salt (see page 31)
- 4 eggs
- 1½ cups grated Parmesan
- ½ teaspoon ground nutmeg
- Small pinch of cloves
- ½ teaspoon cinnamon

To make filling, sauté pork in butter and add whole peeled onion. Cook slowly so that meat does not crisp and get dry. Grind (or process) cooked meat; add garlic salt. Put in a bowl and add eggs, cheese, pan juices, and spices. Mix with hands to blend thoroughly. Cover and refrigerate.

Pasta:

- 1 recipe Classic 4-Egg Pasta (see page 36)
- 1½ to 2 quarts broth

Make pasta and roll out thin. Then cut into 1½-inch squares. Place small amount of filling on each square. Pinch opposite corners to form triangles; seal edges well. Take 2 points (on fold of triangle); "twist through" (see sketch) and press together firmly. Allow to dry on a cloth and then cook in 1½ to 2 quarts broth for about 5 minutes. Serve dressed with butter, heavy cream, and grated cheese; plain in chicken broth, or accompanied by a light tomato sauce.

To make tortellini, *the ends of the filled pasta packets are held together by twisting them together around a finger.*

Maccheroni alla Bolognese

Baked Macaroni, Bologna-Style

For 4

Note the similarities in the seasonings of this classic Bolognese recipe with others from the same region.

- 4 tablespoons butter
- ½ pound ground meat
- 1 carrot
- 1 onion
- 1 stalk celery
- 1 slice unsmoked bacon
- 2 whole cloves
- Salt and pepper to taste
- 2 chicken livers, chopped
- 1 tablespoon flour
- ½ cup broth
- 1 pound rigatoni
- Grated Parmesan cheese, for topping

In a skillet, melt butter and add meat, vegetables, and bacon. Add the cloves, salt, and pepper. Sauté until moisture has evaporated and the meat begins to sizzle. Add the chopped chicken livers and cook for 2 minutes. Sprinkle flour over mixture and stir. Add the broth.

In a large pot of salted water, boil the rigatoni *al dente,* then drain and place in a deep bowl. Spoon the sauce over the pasta and serve with grated Parmesan cheese.

Cappellacci con la Zucca

Squash-Filled Pasta "Hats"

For 7 to 8

This is Beatrice's recipe for a specialty of Ferrara. It is enjoyed during the Lenten season because of its golden vegetable filling, and is also served traditionally on Christmas Eve.

Pasta:

1 recipe Pasta for Filling (see page 36)

Make pasta. Roll out and cut into 3-inch squares.

Filling:

- 2 to 3 pounds butternut squash
- 1/3 cup butter, melted
- 2 eggs, beaten
- 1/2 cup grated Parmesan cheese, plus extra for garnish
- 1/4 teaspoon nutmeg
- 1/3 cup dry, fine bread crumbs
- Salt and pepper to taste

To make filling, steam butternut (or other yellow winter squash); mash and mix with the melted butter. Blend in the beaten eggs with the rest of the ingredients, and season to taste.

Assembly:

Fill pasta squares with a spoonful of the filling. Bring opposite ends (on the fold) together and down, pressing them together with your finger (see sketch for *tortellini* on page 137). Allow to dry on a clean cloth.

Boil the *cappellacci* in salted water *al dente*, and remove with a slotted spoon to a buttered serving bowl. Serve with grated cheese and a simple tomato sauce or melted butter mixed with heavy sweet cream.

Note: These "hats" are excellent with sausage, tomato, and cream sauce.

Fettuccine Bolognese Lazzaro

For 4

Several things are constant in the cuisine of Emilia Romagna. This is only one example of the many recipes using some of these constants: fresh tomatoes or tomato paste, chicken livers as flavor heighteners, and the omnipresent soffritto *(sautéed onion, carrot, and celery base).*

Pasta:

1 recipe Classic 2-Egg Pasta (see page 36)

Make pasta. Cut noodles ½-inch wide.

Sauce:

- 4 pieces dried Italian mushrooms
- Liver, giblets, and heart of 1 chicken
- 1 slice unsmoked bacon
- 1 small onion
- 1 clove garlic
- 1 pound fresh tomatoes, peeled, seeded, and chopped
- 3 tablespoons butter
- ½ cup dry white wine
- 1 cup chicken broth, more or less

To make sauce, soak mushrooms in hot water until soft; drain, and chop. Chop chicken parts together. Chop bacon with the onion and sauté with the garlic clove. When the clove begins to brown, remove and discard. Add the mushrooms and the tomatoes.

In another skillet, put half the butter and sauté the chicken parts, adding the white wine in small amounts at a time; let evaporate. Moisten with broth; cover the pan and let simmer for 45 minutes, adding broth as necessary. Add the mushroom-tomato sauce to chicken-liver sauce. Cook until oil surfaces.

Assembly:

- Salt and pepper to taste
- Grated pecorino or Parmesan cheese, for garnish

Boil the fettuccine in salted water *al dente*, drain, and put in serving dish. Spoon half the sauce over the pasta and toss lightly. Spoon the other half on top with the remaining butter. Season with salt and pepper, and garnish with a liberal grating of cheese.

Tortellini di Natale

Christmas Filled Pasta — Makes approximately 300 pieces

The Grignaffini family in Wellesley observes holidays with the culinary gusto that is so much a part of their food culture. This recipe originated in the mountainous Bella Gamba (Parma) area in the Emilia Romagna region, and has been handed down from Joseph Grignaffini's grandmother.

Filling:

- 2 packages (10 ounces each) spinach or Swiss chard
- 1 small package (3 ounces) cream cheese
- 1 pint ricotta cheese
- 2 cups fine bread crumbs
- 2 cups grated Parmesan cheese
- 1 teaspoon ground nutmeg
- 2 eggs
- Salt and pepper to taste

To prepare filling, cook spinach or Swiss chard until tender. Drain, cool enough to handle, then squeeze out surplus water. Chop and put into a large bowl. Add all filling ingredients and mix together thoroughly; mixture should be soft but easy to handle. Put in refrigerator while making pasta.

Pasta:

- 4 cups all-purpose flour
- 4 eggs
- 6 tablespoons cold water
- Olive oil, for coating

Prepare pasta as follows: Mix all ingredients (except oil) together until dough is easily handled and can be rolled. Roll dough into a ball, coat lightly with olive oil, then put in a bowl, cover, and let set for 10 minutes. Roll out a small piece at a time, making strips about 3 inches wide and 24 inches long. This will make about 18 strips. (If pasta machine is used, roll out to No. 1.) Spoon filling (about the size of a gum ball) along the center of each strip, fold pasta over, and press edges together. With the edge of your hand, separate each mound and cut with a ravioli cutter; size of ravioli should be no larger than 1½ inches by 1½ inches. Place on waxed paper on a cookie sheet; don't let ravioli touch each other. Place cookie sheet in the freezer when full; it will take approximately 15 minutes to quick-freeze them. When frozen enough not to stick together, put ravioli into 5 zip-lock freezer bags (each bag holding about 60 ravioli, enough to serve 6 to 8 people).

Cooking in Brodo (with broth):

Empty bag of frozen ravioli into 1 quart of boiling chicken broth. Cook for approximately 15 minutes or until done. Sprinkle with Parmesan cheese and enjoy.

Cooking in Sauce:

Cook in boiling salted water until done, drain, and place in a bowl or casserole in layers with your favorite tomato-meat sauce. *Mangia bene!*

Pasticcio Verde al Forno Lazzaro

Baked Green Lasagne

For 6

A Bolognese holiday specialty well worth the effort!

Pasta:

1 recipe Green Spinach 2-Egg Pasta (see page 36).

Make pasta and roll out by hand or machine. Cut into strips 4 inches wide and an inch less than the length of your baking dish. Let dry on cloth toweling. Boil 2 or 3 strips at a time in salted water to which you've added a spoonful of oil (to prevent pasta from sticking). Drain, rinse under cold water, and spread again on a clean cloth until ready to assemble.

Sauce 1: Meat Sauce

½ pound ground pork
1 pound ground beef
1 thin slice prosciutto
1 onion
1 carrot
1 stalk celery
¼ cup butter
1 slice unsmoked bacon
½ teaspoon sage
¼ teaspoon nutmeg
½ teaspoon rosemary
1 tablespoon flour
2 tablespoons tomato paste
1 cup broth (chicken preferred)
1 chicken liver, chopped
½ cup cream
¾ cup grated Parmesan cheese
Salt and pepper to taste

Chop pork, beef, and prosciutto together. Coarsely chop the onion, carrot, and celery. In a broad skillet, melt butter and add the bacon and vegetables. Add meats, herbs and spices, and continue sautéing until meats begin to sizzle. Add flour. Add tomato paste; after a few minutes, add the broth. Cook over low heat for 1 hour, stirring occasionally and adding more broth if necessary. Add chopped chicken liver and cook 5 more minutes. Add cream and season. Sauce should be heavy with meat and juicy.

Sauce 2: Besciamella

Prepare as for recipe on page 133.

Assembly:

¾ cup grated Parmesan cheese
Butter, for dotting

Spread some Meat Sauce on the bottom of a 9- by 13-inch baking pan and lay in strips of pasta to cover the pan. Spread more Meat Sauce over pasta, sprinkle with grated cheese and spread with a layer of *Besciamella*. Repeat procedure until all pasta is used. Over top pasta layer, spread a thin layer of the *Besciamella*, then sprinkle with a generous portion of grated cheese and dot with butter. Put in lower third of a preheated 400°F. oven and cook for about 30 minutes. Let it set before serving.

Note: This recipe can also be made with the plain Classic 2-Egg Pasta. It's best made a little ahead, then refrigerated a while before baking.

Gnocchi Fritti della Nonna Nina

Grandmother Nina's Fried Dough — Makes about 40

This is one of those basic recipes whose results allow the cook a great deal of "play." These fried squares may be sugared and eaten as a sweet, or they are equally tasty salted and served as appetizers or between-meal snacks.

2 cups flour
2 tablespoons lard, softened
1 egg
½ teaspoon baking powder
½ cup milk, or more as needed
½ teaspoon salt
Fat, for frying

Put flour on board, make a well, and put the lard, egg, baking powder, milk, and salt in the center. Mix well with a fork, and knead for a few minutes. This is a soft dough; you may wish to add a bit more milk. Put dough in a plastic bag and refrigerate for 1½ to 2 hours. Then roll it out, cut into small squares (about 2 inches), and score with fork to make a corrugated design. Fry in hot oil until golden on both sides.

Aragosta Lazzaro

Lobster Lazzaro

For 4 to 6

A truly elegant way to eat lobster — all the taste excitement and none of the mess!

Sauce:

- 4 tablespoons butter
- 1 small onion, chopped
- 1 small carrot, chopped
- 1 tablespoon chopped parsley
- 1 bay leaf
- ½ teaspoon Bea's Garlic Salt (see page 31)
- ½ teaspoon pepper
- 1 cup tomato purée
- ¾ cup broth (fish stock preferred)

To make sauce, put butter, onion, and carrot in a saucepan and sauté. Add parsley, bay leaf, garlic salt, and pepper. Cook until vegetables are soft and have separated from butter. Add tomato purée and stir, cooking for 6 to 7 minutes. Add broth and simmer slowly until sauce is of a good "gravy" consistency.

Lobster:

- 3 lobsters (1 pound each)
- ⅓ cup olive oil
- Salt and pepper to taste
- ½ cup white wine
- ⅓ cup brandy
- 1 cup light cream
- ⅓ cup butter, softened

The lobster should be cut up uncooked. (You may use ready-cooked lobster meat if you prefer.) Split each lobster in half. Remove the vein in the tail section, remove sack under the head, and break off the "knuckles." Remove the green "tomalley" and reserve. Remove all the lobster meat you are able. Cut tail sections and claw meat into bite-sized pieces.

In a large saucepan, heat the olive oil. When hot, add the lobster and heat through. Spoon out oil. Add salt, pepper, and the wine, and allow to evaporate. Pour in brandy and flame. Add the tomalley, mixing it with the prepared sauce, light cream, and softened butter. Cook together for 20 minutes over a tiny flame. Pour into serving bowl and serve with rice or buttered noodles.

Note: "Tomalley" is actually the liver of the lobster. It is the creamy green substance that is found in the third of the body cavity nearest the head. It is considered a delicacy and in some fish stores may be bought by the pound at prices that rival imported caviar. Served as a dip or on crackers, it is Neptune's answer to *foie gras.*

Vongole "Testa di Marmo"

Stuffed Quahaugs

For 6

Beatrice's recipe for the wonderful clams that her grandsons bring home from the beach.

12 large clams
¾ cup butter
¼ cup olive oil
2 cloves garlic, crushed
¼ cup chopped parsley
2 cups cracker crumbs (coarse)
½ teaspoon freshly ground pepper
4 slices stale (but not dry) bread
Paprika, for sprinkling

Remove clams from shells, reserving 12 shells. Wash shells and clams under running water to remove all traces of sand. Chop clams; do not grind or process. Put chopped clams in a bowl. In a small pan, melt butter; add oil and crushed garlic. Sauté a few minutes but do not let garlic brown. When white garlic particles surface, remove pan from heat. In the bowl with the clams, pour in all but ¼ cup of the sautéed garlic-oil-butter mix, parsley, 1½ cups of the cracker crumbs, and freshly ground pepper. Mix well and stuff the shells using all this filling.

Remove crusts from the bread; discard. Grind the decrusted bread coarsely. Mix bread crumbs, remaining cracker crumbs, and the reserved ¼ cup garlic-oil-butter mix; blend well and top each stuffed clam. Sprinkle with paprika. Put on baking sheet, and bake at 400°F. for 20 to 25 minutes.

Lumache alla Piacentina

Christmas Snails

For 4

Piacenza boasts a very ancient past. This recipe is also from long ago, but is still enjoyed today as it was then. As eel is the regional Christmas delicacy in the Abruzzi, snails are in this twelfth-century city.

- 2/3 cup butter
- 2 tablespoons olive oil
- 1/2 onion, finely chopped or grated
- 1 tablespoon tomato paste
- 1/4 cup water, or more as needed
- Salt and pepper to taste
- Pinch of nutmeg
- 1 large clove garlic, crushed
- 1/2 cup chopped parsley
- 1 sage leaf
- 1 bay leaf
- 2 tablespoons dry white wine
- 3 dozen snails

In a pan, put butter, olive oil, onion, tomato paste, water, salt, pepper, nutmeg, crushed garlic, chopped parsley, sage, and bay leaf. Cook for 20 minutes. Add white wine; let evaporate. Add snails; cook 15 minutes more. If sauce seems dry, add more water. Remove the bay leaf before serving.

Costolettes — alla Parmigiana, Bolognese e Modenese

Veal Cutlets (Scallops) Three Ways

For 6 to 8

The region of Emilia Romagna, particularly Bologna (the center of "rich" cuisine), offers the cook a wide choice of modus operandi *for everyone's favorite veal dish! Here are three versions. Begin each with the following first step.*

- 1 1/2 cups bread crumbs
- 1/2 cup grated Parmesan cheese (omit for *Modenese*)
- 2 eggs, beaten with 2 tablespoons water
- 1/2 teaspoon Bea's Garlic Salt (see page 31)
- 8 slices baby veal
- 1 stick (8 tablespoons) butter
- 2 tablespoons olive oil

Mix bread crumbs and the grated cheese. Beat eggs and water together with garlic salt. Dip veal in crumbs, then in egg mixture, and again in crumbs. Melt butter with oil in a large skillet and brown the cutlets on both sides over moderate heat.

Alla Parmigiana:

Add 8 slices of *soft* Parmesan cheese or a thick coating of grated Parmesan.

2 cups Basic Tomato Sauce (see page 131)

On a rimmed cookie sheet, place the cutlets as prepared above; cover each with a slice of the soft or grated Parmesan and the tomato sauce. Dot with butter. Cover cookie sheet loosely with a sheet of aluminum foil and place in a hot (450°F.) oven until the cheese melts, about 10 minutes. Serve immediately.

Alla Bolognese:

Add 8 thin slices of prosciutto

1 cup shredded Swiss cheese

½ cup melted butter.

Put browned cutlets on a sheet pan. Top each with a slice of prosciutto and a mound of cheese. Cover pan with aluminum foil and place in a medium oven until cheese melts, about 10 minutes. Pour melted butter over all and serve at once.

Alla Modenese:

Add 8 thin slices prosciutto

8 thin slices of Groviera or Fontina cheese

Follow instructions for the preceding two cutlet styles (omitting the Parmesan cheese).

Arrosto di Maiale alla Reggiana

Emilian Roast Pork

For 6 to 8

Here is a classic example of the natural cook's "license." The list of ingredients is the traditional one, as listed in the old cookbooks of the region. The method is Beatrice's grandmother's.

- Pork loin (3 to 4 pounds)
- ¾ cup olive oil
- 1 tablespoon fresh rosemary
- 4 or 5 juniper berries, cracked
- 2 cloves garlic, crushed
- 2 tablespoons wine vinegar
- 1 teaspoon Bea's Garlic Salt (see page 31)
- 2 cups of milk, or more as needed

Bone the loin and tie into a long roll. Make a marinade of the oil, rosemary, juniper berries, garlic, vinegar, and garlic salt. Marinate the meat overnight in a Dutch oven.

The next day, put the meat, still in the marinade, over low heat and cook slowly for about 30 minutes. Heat the milk, pour over the meat, and continue cooking for another hour, or until the meat is tender, adding more milk if needed. Raise the heat and brown the meat well on all sides, then degrease the pan juices. Slice the pork, not too thin, and serve with the degreased pan gravy, adjusting the seasoning as desired.

Bistecca Lazzaro

Steak Lazzaro

For 4

Exotic in flavor, yet easy to prepare.

- 4 beef strip steaks
- 1 stick (8 tablespoons) butter
- ½ teaspoon Bea's Garlic Salt (see page 31)
- 1 teaspoon green peppercorns
- 2 tablespoons brandy
- ⅓ cup sweet cream

Broil or pan-fry steaks, rare to medium. In a skillet, melt butter and "warm" the garlic salt; do not allow it to brown. Add the green peppercorns. Warm the brandy slightly and add to pan; ignite it and let it burn out. Add cream. Cook for 2 or 3 minutes. Put steaks into pan, turning them once in the sauce. Place steaks on a heated platter, pour the sauce over them, and serve at once.

Pollo Cacciatore Indimenticable

Unforgettable Chicken *Cacciatore*

For 4

Cacciatore *is a universally popular way to prepare fowl, meats, and even seafood. Beatrice's touches of cream and "love" make this dish truly as represented in the recipe's name.*

- ¼ cup olive oil
- 3 tablespoons butter
- Flour, for dusting
- 1 frying chicken
- 1 onion
- ½ cup white wine
- 2 tablespoons Balsamic vinegar
- 1 clove garlic
- ½ teaspoon Bea's Garlic Salt (see page 31)
- 1 large can (28 ounces) tomatoes
- 1 pound mushrooms, coarsely chopped
- ½ cup heavy cream
- ½ cup tomato purée
- 3 tablespoons chopped parsley

Put olive oil and butter in a large skillet. Put flour in a medium-sized plastic bag. Cut chicken into serving pieces and remove the skin. Wash and dry. Put pieces in bag with flour, and shake well to thoroughly coat chicken. Sauté half of the onion with the dark meat pieces for about 20 minutes. Add the white meat. When golden, add white wine and vinegar and let evaporate. Crush the garlic clove into the pan, stir in the garlic salt, and add the canned tomatoes. Continue to cook until the chicken is tender; meanwhile gently sauté mushrooms. Mix the heavy cream with the tomato purée and blend into the pan juices. Add in the parsley and mushrooms. Put chicken on heated platter and pour on the sauce. Serve with plain or buttered pasta, rice, or potatoes, or something to soak up every last drop of sauce!

Ali di Pollo Parmigiana Lois

Chicken Wings Parmesan For 6

Beatrice's daughter-in-law Lois is a fine cook in her own right. This recipe of hers is a favorite of the entire Lazzaro family.

4 pounds chicken wings
¾ cup butter
1½ cups grated Parmesan cheese
4 tablespoons chopped parsley
1 tablespoon fresh rosemary (or 1 teaspoon dried)
1 tablespoon fresh sage (or 1 teaspoon dried)
2 teaspoons paprika
Salt and pepper to taste

Cut tips off chicken wings (freeze and keep them for soup). Cut through the wing joint. Melt the butter. Mix the grated cheese and seasonings together. Dip the "straightened" wings first in the melted butter and then roll them in the seasonings. Put on a sheet pan and bake 1 hour in a 375°F. oven, turning them frequently until they are golden and crisp on all sides.

Note: Lois serves these as an entrée or as an appetizer. They are *great* finger food!

Frizon con Salsiccia

Sausage-Vegetable Sauté For 4

Italian sausages are enjoyed the world over, both for their taste and for their versatility. Doubling the enjoyment is the fact that they are usually quite reasonably priced and made with natural ingredients. Here is a great suggestion for a Sunday night supper.

1 pound fresh tomatoes
1 sweet green pepper
2 pounds mild onions
4 potatoes
2 pounds sausages
4 tablespoons combined oil and butter
Salt and pepper to taste
Grated cheese, for garnish (optional)

Peel the tomatoes, remove the seeds, and chop. Cut the green pepper into slices, discarding the seeds. Slice onions, peel and quarter the potatoes, and remove the skin from the sausages. Cut each sausage into 4 parts. Heat oil and butter together in a skillet, and add all ingredients and sauté over low heat for about 1 hour. Add salt and pepper to taste. You may also garnish with grated cheese if desired.

Note: Italian sausages come in two different forms: "SWEET," flavored with fennel, and "HOT," which can be well-laced with cayenne and/or hot chili peppers. The flavors of the Italian sausage vary from region to region, cook to cook, or, in the case of the commercial product, brand to brand. Experiment and find your own preference.

Salsa Fredda di Giovanni Cevolani

Chef Giovanni Cevolani's Dressing

Ample for 6

Chef Cevolani was Elena Benotti's father, and in a sense this book is the result of his special legacy of love and respect for the kitchen arts and those who practice them. He taught his daughter Elena, and Elena introduced Bea and me to each other. This dressing is excellent just as is over a bed of lettuce; delicious mixed into a vegetable salad; a tasty side dish for cold meat, poultry, and fish; and can also be used as a barbecue marinade.

- 1 Bermuda onion, sliced thin
- ½ cup olive oil
- 2 red peppers, cut into julienne strips
- 2 green peppers
- 1 pound small white mushrooms
- 1 clove garlic, crushed
- Salt and pepper to taste
- ¼ teaspoon dry mustard
- 1 teaspoon sugar
- ½ cup white vinegar, mixed with water to make ¾ cup

Put Bermuda onion in a pan with olive oil, and sauté over moderate heat. Add peppers and continue cooking for 5 to 8 minutes. Then add mushrooms, crushed garlic, salt and pepper, dry mustard, and sugar. Add white vinegar–water mixture. Mix well and refrigerate.

Savor di Frutta

Fruit Conserve

Makes approximately 3 quarts

A wonderful way to perfume your house for days. Cook up a batch of this typically Emilian preserve. It is also multipurposed: use it as a side dish with meats and poultry (much as you might use a spiced peach or cranberry sauce), or to fill dessert ravioli *(see page 156) or* tortelli, *or simply in inviting spoonfuls to quiet a ravening sweet tooth!*

- 4 apples, peeled and chopped
- 4 pears, peeled and chopped
- 1 cup pitted dates, chopped
- 1 cup dried apricots
- 1 medium can (10 ounces) unsweetened pineapple
- ¼ pound chopped citron
- 1 cup pitted prunes, chopped
- 1 cup golden raisins
- 2 cups grape jelly
- Rind of 1 orange, grated
- Rind of 1 lemon, grated
- ½ cup walnuts
- ½ cup filberts or almonds
- ¼ cup brandy

Put all the fruits in a saucepan with the grape jelly. Add the grated orange and lemon peel. Cook over a tiny flame, stirring often to prevent scorching. The cooking time is lengthy; the desired result is a very thick "marmalade" consistency. When thick, add the nuts and the brandy, blending them well. When cool, put into plastic containers and cover well. This savory keeps for several weeks in the refrigerator and also freezes well.

Fronde di Felce in Casuolo

Fiddleheads Somaini

For 6

Fiddleheads, so named because of the similarity of their shape to the curve of a violin's scroll, are to be found in damp, wooded areas and along brooks and rivers in the spring. Because these fern fronds become bitter as they mature, Bob Somaini — our Barre, Vermont, friend who gave us this recipe — suggests they be picked "young" and used immediately. They can be frozen if they are blanched first.

- 1½ pounds fiddleheads
- ½ pound bacon
- 2 tablespoons finely chopped parsley
- 1 medium onion, minced
- 2 cloves garlic
- 1½ cups grated white Cheddar cheese

Blanch fiddleheads in boiling water for several minutes. Fry bacon until crisp, reserving some of the strained grease. In a well-buttered medium-sized casserole, place half of the fiddleheads and cover with 1 tablespoon of parsley, minced onion, and 1 clove of garlic either minced or crushed and spread about. Add half of the crisp bacon. Repeat the process, topping the casserole with the grated strong white Cheddar. Drizzle some of the strained bacon drippings over the top, adding a bit of melted butter if it looks too dry. Cover and bake in a 350°F. oven until hot, removing the cover for the last few minutes to allow the cheese to brown slightly. Serve at once.

Note: This same recipe works well for broccoli or green beans.

A Chiacchierata on Beginnings

The Grandparents Tassinari's Grocery Store

In 1881, Peter Tassinari, Beatrice Lazzaro's grandfather, came to the United States from Renazzo, in the province of Ferrara. He was twenty-three years old. In 1883, he opened a small grocery store in the booming shoe-industry community of Lynn, north of Boston. It was to Lynn also that he brought Anna (Nina) Fornaciari Tassinari (a petite dynamo who hailed from the same village in Italy) and their two children. Beatrice's mother, Augusta, was the third-born, and the first to be born in the United States.

The hard-earned proceeds from the produce and grocery store fed the stomachs and the dreams of the family, but the store's destiny was not to be fulfilled in Lynn. One sultry day, Nina, pregnant with one of the nine young ones to bear Tassinari's name (seven survived), shivered in the throes of an ugly premonition: something was wrong at the store! *Was Pietro hurt? Had there been an accident, another theft?*

Her feeling of foreboding was uncanny: the store was being held up *again* — her husband facing danger, the merchandise being looted, and the day's cash receipts being wrested from them. Lynn, in those days, was rough on the small business owners, and Peter and Nina decided to move farther north. The year: 1887.

They found a two-story building in Salem, Massachusetts, and established both their residence and business at 152 Essex Street. The new store prospered, filling Peter with enthusiasm for a second venture, a coal and wood yard, which he started in 1895.

Unfortunately, the combination of burgeoning family needs, difficult economic conditions, and capital overextension forced Peter Tassinari into bankruptcy in 1901. With classic pride, Peter's urgency then was to rebuild the produce store so he could repay his debts and continue to support his family. A New York furrier, a Mr. Goldman, recently arrived in Salem, upon hearing of the Tassinari store's closing, gave Peter the money necessary to reopen. It was a good investment: the loan was repaid with interest and every debt made good.

Beatrice tells the story of her grandmother's part in the family's solvency. Once, when a large bill was due ($350 in those days was a very large bill indeed!), Nonna Nina, responding to Peter's worry, dug out a dusty Chianti bottle from the back of the family wine cupboard, counted out the money in a crumpled variety of small bills, grinned conspiratorially, and pushed the few remaining bank notes back into her unusual savings "kitty."

"She was a *smart* one," reminisces Bea.

The time came when Peter Tassinari yearned to *own* the frame building that had been both home and workplace for the family. Where to get a down payment? A lifetime resident and town eminence named Pingree sent Peter to see the local banker.

"I want to own my building," Peter blurted, and then, when asked the price, "No matter the price, I don't have any savings to put down. I could only pay you monthly from the store."

"You don't need a down payment," the banker told him. "If Mr. Pingree speaks for you, that's guarantee enough for this bank!"

In those days, as indeed it still is, the Salem-Marblehead area was a summer vacation haven for the wealthy from all over the United States. The store's customers included the Marshall Fields, the Henry Fricks, Miss Eleanor Sears, the Beveridges, the Lilys (Lily Paper Products), and a long list of the advantaged residents of the coves and rocky outlooks from Lynn to Halibut Point. The shopping *modus operandi* of those days was to send a list (compiled by "Cook") with the chauffeur. So, at times, there were three or four Pierce Arrows, Bentleys, and Rolls lining the street in front of the Tassinari store, their liveried chauffeurs chatting and smoking with their polished boots resting on the elegant chromed bumpers.

As it happened, Beatrice's Aunts Mary and Florence often took note of the usual, and unusual, Spencerian addenda to some of the weekly lists. One of their favorites: "If there is anything else you think we might like, please add it to the order," written with full confidence that only the best and the freshest would be sent.

These were the roots of the tradition that is, today, Beatrice Tassinari Lazzaro's kitchen.

Ravioli Dolci

Fruit-Filled Dessert Ravioli

Makes about 20

These ravioli were a Christmas specialty of Bea's grandmother.

- 4 cups flour
- 3 eggs
- 4 tablespoons softened butter, plus 4 tablespoons firm for dotting
- ½ tablespoon salt
- 2 tablespoons sugar, plus extra for sprinkling
- 1 scant teaspoon baking soda
- Oil, for frying (optional)
- 1 cup *Savor di Frutta* (see page 152)

Sift flour onto a pastry board, and make a well. Put eggs, soft butter, salt, 2 tablespoons sugar, and baking soda into the well. Begin to beat and incorporate the flour. Mix well, knead only a few minutes, then cover and let rest. Roll the dough out onto a floured board and shape it into a ¼-inch-thick rectangle. Dot ⅔ of the rectangle with remaining 4 tablespoons butter. Fold the plain remaining third of dough over the middle third, and the last third with butter over the folded dough. Cover and let it rest a few minutes. Roll out again, ⅛-inch thick. Cut strips 4 inches long by 2½ inches wide. In the center of each strip, put a spoonful of *Savor di Frutta* or other cooked fruit and nuts. Moisten edges of dough with water, fold edges over and seal thoroughly. Fry in hot oil until golden or bake in 375°F. oven until nicely browned. Sprinkle with granulated sugar and serve.

Note: Fruit marmalades also make tasty fillings for these sweet dessert ravioli.

Torta di Mele

Apple Tart

For 8 to 12

Because Ferrara and its environs present perfect growing conditions for several different kinds of apples, for both eating and for cooking, it is quite natural that it should be famous for its apple tarts. This recipe is a classic from the region. We must add, however, that the Tuscans (borrowing the fruit from neighbors, perhaps) also make a superb tart.

3 eggs
½ cup sugar
1 cup cake flour
1 teaspoon baking powder
Rind of 1 lemon, grated
4 tablespoons soft butter, plus 2 tablespoons firm for dotting
2 to 3 tablespoons milk
3 pounds apples, peeled and thinly sliced
½ teaspoon cinnamon

Beat the eggs and ¼ cup sugar until creamy (about 7 to 8 minutes). Fold in the flour and baking powder a small amount at a time. Also gently fold in the lemon rind, soft butter, and milk. Butter and flour a torte pan or a 9-inch spring-form pan. Put all the dough in the pan, pat over bottom and build up the sides prettily. Place the apples symmetrically over the dough. Mix the remaining ¼ cup sugar with the cinnamon and sprinkle over the apples. Dot surface with butter. Bake at 350°F. for about 45 minutes, or until apples are slightly browned.

Note: The Tuscan version soaks the apples in a mixture of a shot of whiskey with 3 tablespoons of sugar. The tart is then covered with a lattice of pastry and baked.

Bonissima

Emilian Nut Tart

For 8

The name means "very good," and this specialty from Modena certainly is!

Pasta Frolla Emiliana (Sweet Pastry Dough):

- 1 cup plus 2 tablespoons butter
- 2½ cups cake flour
- ½ cup granulated sugar
- 3 egg yolks
- Rind from 1 lemon, grated
- Salt to taste

Measure butter and put in freezer so that it is very hard; then cut into pea-sized pieces. When butter is ready, put flour on board; make a well, drop in butter pieces, and work with the flour. Add sugar, egg yolks, lemon peel, and salt. Mix together to form a soft dough. Knead 6 or 7 times, pushing with heel of hand. Shape into a ball and set aside to relax dough.

Filling:

- 1½ cups walnuts
- 1 cup honey
- ¼ cup rum

Preheat oven to 350°F. Drop nuts into boiling water for 1 minute; drain and chop. Then put in saucepan and add honey and rum. Mix thoroughly with a wooden spoon. Taste and, if wanted, add a little more rum.

Assembly:

Using *Pasta Frolla*, roll out dough-like pie crust, reserving enough for a separate dough circle. Transfer crust to 8- or 9-inch pie plate, extending sides up about 1 inch. Pour in filling. Draw edges of crust back over filling and moisten with water. Cover with circle of dough (see sketch), and bake in moderate 350°F. oven until golden on top and bottom. Cool and cover with a chocolate glaze (see recipe on page 69).

The bottom crust for bonissima *is cut large enough to allow an extra inch to stand above the pie plate. The pie is then filled and covered with the top crust; the overage from the bottom crust is then pulled back over the top crust to seal the pie.*

Ciambella Zia Meri

Renazzo Cake Ring

For 12 or more

In Emilia Romagna, one can always tell the approach of a Feast Day by the heavenly perfume of the many ciambelle *being prepared in every local oven.*

- 1 cup butter, plus 2 tablespoons soft butter for spreading
- 1 cup sugar
- 4 eggs
- 4½ cups cake flour
- 4 teaspoons baking powder
- ½ teaspoon salt
- ¼ cup milk
- 1½ teaspoons vanilla
- Rind of 1 lemon, grated
- Granulated sugar, for sprinkling

Preheat oven to 350°F. Cream 1 cup butter and sugar. Add eggs and beat together. Add flour, baking powder, and salt sifted together. Add milk, vanilla, and grated lemon rind. Put a very small round bowl in the center of a prepared 10-inch round buttered and floured pan, open side down. Put dough around outside of bowl to form a ring. Spread soft butter on top of cake and sprinkle with granulated sugar. Bake 30 minutes or more until golden.

Zuppa Inglese Lazzaro

Beatrice's Italian Trifle

For 10

A classic dessert of Emilia Romagna, made for all Feast Days and ceremonies.

Sponge Cake:

- 6 eggs
- 1 cup sugar
- 2 tablespoons warm water
- 1 teaspoon vanilla
- 1 cup all-purpose flour
- ½ teaspoon baking powder

Preheat oven to 350°F. Place a mixing bowl in a pan filled with hot water. Whisk eggs and sugar until they are warm to the touch. Add the warm water and vanilla, whisking continually. Sift flour and baking powder, and add to the egg mixture, folding in gently. Pour into three 9-inch layer-cake pans. Bake for 30 to 35 minutes, or until layers spring back with gentle finger pressure.

Filling:

- Simple Syrup (see below)
- 1 quart milk
- 1 cup sugar
- 1 tablespoon cornstarch
- 6 tablespoons flour
- ¼ teaspoon salt
- 4 extra-large egg yolks
- 1½ teaspoons vanilla
- ½ cup butter
- 2 ounces semisweet chocolate, coarsely chopped
- ¾ cup white rum
- 2 tablespoons maraschino liqueur

Make the Simple Syrup by heating together ½ cup sugar and ¼ cup water. Then set aside.

Heat milk, but do not boil. Mix 1 cup sugar, cornstarch, flour, and salt. Add warm milk, a little at a time, whisking constantly. Cook over low flame until it comes to a boil, mixture thickens, and there is no "raw flour" taste. Stir in egg yolks, and cook a few minutes more. Add vanilla and cool. Cream butter and blend with the cooled custard mixture. Divide the custard into 2 parts, adding the chocolate pieces to 1 part. Mix the rum and maraschino liqueur with the Simple Syrup.

Assembly:

- 1 cup apricot marmalade, for spreading
- 2 cups sweetened heavy cream, whipped, for topping.

Place 1 sponge layer on serving plate and soak with mixed liquors. Spread a thin coating of apricot marmalade over top. Pour cooled plain vanilla custard over that. Cover with a second layer of cake. Soak with liquor, coat with marmalade, and pour cooked *chocolate* custard over second layer. Cover with third layer of sponge cake; soak with remaining liquor and another spreading of apricot jam. Cover and freeze. When ready to use, cover the top and sides with whipped cream piped from a pastry tube and decorate. (Candied cherries, drained and dried canned sliced peaches, mandarin slices, and curls of chocolate are all appropriate. You can be as wildly creative as you like.)

Pan di Natale

Christmas Bread

For 8 to 12

A Christmas specialty of Bologna.

- ¾ cup honey
- ½ cup sugar
- 2 teaspoons baking soda
- 2⅛ cups cake flour
- ⅞ cup boiling water
- ½ cup golden seedless raisins
- ¾ cup almonds, blanched
- ½ cup citron, chopped
- ¼ cup pine nuts (*pignoli*)
- 4 ounces semisweet chocolate bits
- ½ teaspoon combined grated lemon and orange peel
- ½ cup chopped candied cherries (red and green)
- ½ cup dried apricots, chopped

Preheat oven to 350°F. In a saucepan, put the honey, sugar, and baking soda. Mix well. Then add flour a little at a time and mix well again. Over this, pour the boiling water, mixing thoroughly. Add raisins, almonds, citron, pine nuts, chocolate bits, lemon and orange peel, candied cherries, and apricots. Butter well two 8-inch pans. Fill with batter and bake 30 to 40 minutes, testing with a toothpick.

Note: The measurements for this recipe may seem odd. This is because the recipe is translated from its original metric form. Remember that 1/8 cup is equal to 2 tablespoons.

Budino al Caffè

Adele's Coffee Pudding

For 8

This recipe was given to Bea in Renazzo by Signorina Adele.

- 2 whole eggs, plus 4 egg yolks
- 1/4 cup sugar, plus 1 cup for caramel
- 1 teaspoon vanilla
- 1 can evaporated milk
- Pinch of salt
- 1 cup *espresso* coffee
- Fresh milk to complete quart measure
- 1/3 cup brandy
- Whipped cream, for topping
- Toasted chopped almonds, for topping

In a bowl, put whole eggs, extra yolks, 1/4 cup sugar, and vanilla. Heat just to mix. Add the canned milk, salt, and coffee. Pour this into a quart container. Bring the measure to a full quart with fresh milk or cream.

Caramelize remaining 1 cup sugar over low to medium heat until melted. Preheat oven to 325°F. Pour caramel into a 4- by 8-inch loaf pan, tipping pan to coat all sides and bottom. (Careful: many cooks get burned during this maneuver!) Pour in the custard mix, and set loaf pan in a larger pan of hot water that is already sitting in the oven. Bake until firm (about 60 minutes or more). Refrigerate overnight. Then invert onto a serving dish. Add a little water to the baking pan. Put pan over low heat to melt the hardened caramel. Mix in the brandy. Pour sauce over pudding, and serve with whipped cream and toasted chopped almonds.

Bea's Note: This custard was concocted by Adele during World War II when canned milk was given out to stretch the supply of fresh milk.

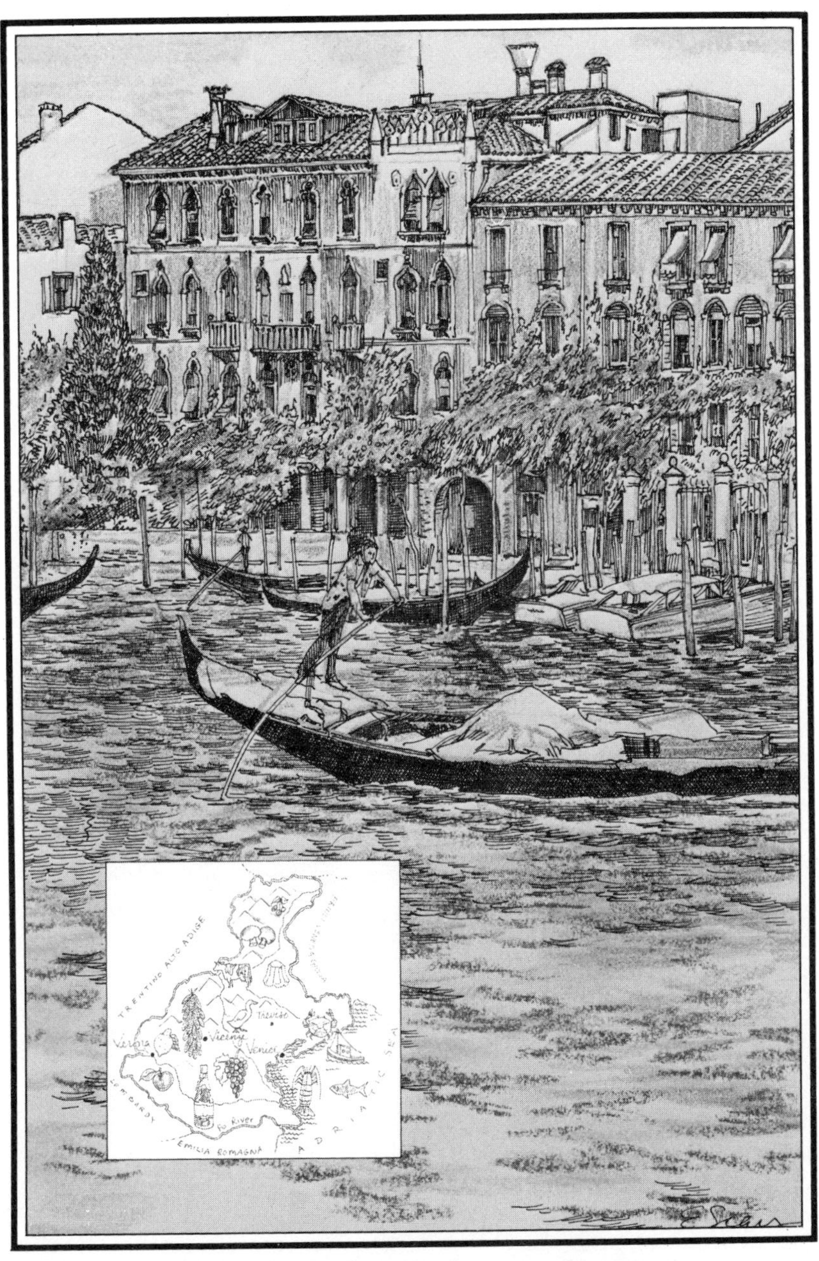

Venetia/Venice

The Special Wines & Cheeses of

Venetia/Venice

Wines of the Region

Dry reds: *Barbarano, Bardolino, Bertrani, Breganze, Cabernet di Treviso, Cabernet Franc, Merlot del Piave, Quintarelli, Raboso Friulano (di Piave), Recioto Amarone, Rubino della Marca, Tocai di Lison, Valpantena, Valpolicella*

Dry whites: *Barbarano Bianco, Breganza Bianco, Gambellara, Pieropan, Soave*

Demi-sec white: *Prosecco di Conegliano*

Dessert whites: *Pieropan, Prosecco* (sparkling)

Wines Available in the United States

Dry reds: *Bertrani Classico Superiore, Quintarelli, Valpolicella Classico, Valpolicella "Secco"*

Dry whites: *Pieropan, Soave "Calvarino"*

Dessert wines: *Maculam, Pieropan, Recioto di Soave, Torcolate*

Dry sparkling: *Venegazzù Brut Champenoise*

Cheeses of the Region

Asiago, Morlacco (salty), *Sigher* (a goat cheese), *Spress* (a goat cheese), *Tosela*

Morire a Venetia è morire felice.

To die in Venice is to die happy.

Venetia lies in the northeastern portion of the Po Valley. It abuts Emilia Romagna to the south, Lombardy to the east, Trentino–Alto Adige to the northeast, and Friuli–Venetia Giulia to the west. At its crown sit high mountains, which soon give way to smaller hills, and then gradually to lowlands that stretch down to the sea and to Venice, the fabled "Canal City." The Venetian region boasts other vibrant towns — Padua, Verona, Vicenza, and Treviso among them — but it is Venice that so often commands our attention.

It is difficult to describe the city of Venice and its environs. When you are there it is a magical state of being. When you are far away it is a state of mind, with a rich inventory of yearnings. If you are among the blessed, the inventory may be fattened with memories — memories of sunny days, misty nights, and unforgettable dining.

Venice "The Opulent": water-traversed, a treasure chest of art and history — a city that needs no introduction to the reader. Even the armchair traveler has volumes within easy reach from which to choose which of her facets to explore. How singular that, for all her universal fame, Venice is almost an "embarrassment of riches" to her nearby country neighbors.

The contrast of living and eating so close to the home site of the Doges' extravagances merits a special mention. The Venetian kitchens of Verona, Vicenza, Treviso, Padua, and other neighboring towns produce an honest blend of simplicity and fine flavor. Condiments there are kept to a reasonable minimum (with the exception of the famed spicy *soffritto*). The feeling seems to be that their home-grown, home-prepared dishes have a tasty nobility all their own. They are happy to leave the pretensions to the canaled Queen in their midst!

Uncomplicated fare is prepared from the gleanings of each carefully tilled property. This land gives generously to its caring tenders, and the tables are a glorious reflection of the almost ever-present sun and the waters of the surrounding rivers: the Po, the Garda, the Livenza, the Tagliamento, and the Mincio.

Green is everywhere — surely Cézanne had Italian blood! Each day's harvest is a "still life": the delicate golden green of the celery from Agordo; the deeper tones of the fresh, young peas destined for *Risi e Bisi*; Treviso's lavender, long-leaved chicory; and — not to be forgotten — the sweetheart rose of the salad bowl, *radicchio*. With the variety of terrain — rugged mountainous to crystalline lake shore; the serene Adriatic to the valley views of the Dolomites — everything is here to complete our canvas. Even the covering cloth with which to counterpoint our display is a Venetian labor of love — the world-famous Venetian lace fashioned on the islands of Burano, Torvello, and Chioggi. The final touch? A Murano decanter with its matching glasses, glowing like a ruby or other gemstone, ready for our pleasure. That which is most sumptuous may belong to the city, but *all* of Venetia worships the artistic — and what greater proof of creativity than a delicious repast?

Among the dishes special to this region are *Pasta e Fagioli*, a bean soup; *Fégato alla Veneziana*, liver and onions with a touch of wine; *Baccalà alla Vicentina*, a dried cod dish unlike any other; *Risi e Bisi*, rice and peas; and *Pollo alla Padovana*, a delicious chicken concoction with leeks, cabbage, and cheese. Following here you'll find recipes for several of these Venetian delights — and more besides!

Paparele e Figadini

Noodles with Chicken Livers

For 4

A specialty of Venice, economical and a true taste treat.

- 1 pound chicken livers
- 2 tablespoons butter
- 1 pound of fettuccine (made as given in the rule on pages 38 through 42, or purchased)
- 2 quarts of chicken broth
- Salt and pepper to taste
- Grated Parmesan cheese, for topping

Clean chicken livers, drain, and sauté in butter. Boil the noodles in the chicken broth *al dente*; drain and spoon over the chicken livers. Season to taste and top with ample grated Parmesan cheese.

Note: Use bouillon if broth is not available.

Fiori Fritti

Flower Fritters

For 4

The culinary use of flowers has only recently become quite the rage in our society, although the Europeans have been enjoying this for centuries. Here is a classic Venetian dish prepared with two different kinds of blossoms — a golden accompaniment to a special feast.

- 1 pound squash flowers
- 1 pound acacia blossoms
- ¾ cup cake flour
- 1 tablespoon plus 2 cups light oil (olive and vegetable)
- ⅔ cup water
- Salt or sugar, as wanted

Pick flowers on a dry, sunny day (if they are damp or wilted, the fritters will suffer). Shake the blossoms well to remove dust and check them for "inhabitants." (They really should not be rinsed, but if you feel strongly about this, rinse them quickly under a light spray and then fold them gently into a linen towel.)

In a mixing bowl, put the flour, making a well in the center. Pour the 1 tablespoon oil into the well and slowly add the water, mixing until you have a batter the consistency of heavy cream. Then add the salt.

Put 2 to 3 inches of remaining oil into a deep frying pan and heat just under the smoking point, about 365°F. Dip flowers into the batter, turning them gently to thoroughly coat them, and drop them, a few at a time, into the hot oil. They will puff and turn golden. Remove them at once with a perforated spoon and drain on paper towels. Sprinkle with salt (if using as a vegetable) or sugar (if they are to be an exotic dessert).

Risi e Bisi

Rice and Peas For 4

In Venice, a city that might well be the center of all that is baroque, this classically simple dish appears on every menu. But as with every other beautiful thing, it is presented like a jeweled tiara — the bright green peas floating amongst the snowy grains of local rice.

4 tablespoons butter
2 tablespoons olive oil
1 small onion, chopped
½ cup celery, chopped
2 ounces prosciutto, chopped
5 to 6 sprigs parsley, chopped
1½ cups rice
2½ quarts broth (chicken or vegetable stock preferred)
1 package (10 ounces) frozen peas or 2½ pounds fresh peas, shelled
Salt and pepper to taste
½ cup grated Parmesan cheese

Put 2 tablespoons butter, olive oil, chopped onion, and celery in saucepan. Sauté until onion and celery are soft. Add prosciutto and parsley. Cook a few minutes more. Add rice, cooking and stirring until rice has absorbed oil and butter. Add 2 quarts of broth and peas. Cook until rice is tender. Add more broth if necessary. Season with salt and pepper to taste. Add remaining butter and 4 tablespoons of the grated Parmesan cheese. Mix well. The final product is a dense soup.

Canestrelli di Piazzali

Scallops, Venetian-Style For 4

1½ pounds sea scallops
½ cup white vermouth
2 cups flour
Vegetable oil, for frying
Salt to taste
Lemon wedges, for garnish
Whole cloves, for garnish
3 sprigs parsley
2 sprigs mint

Wash and rinse scallops (the large sea scallops are preferable). Dip into vermouth, then shake and dip into flour. Put oil in a heavy saucepan; bring to a high heat and gently drop the scallops in. Allow scallops a few minutes to brown slightly, then remove to paper towels. Salt to taste and serve with clove-studded lemon wedges. Finely chop together the parsley and mint (the flavors should mingle completely), and sprinkle over the scallops. Serve at once.

Fettuccine al Mare Marta

Marta's Seafood Fettuccine

For 4 to 6

Another seafood specialty of Marta la Rosa, Beatrice's daughter.

- 3 pounds mussels
- ½ pound small shrimp
- ½ cup butter
- 2 tablespoons olive oil
- 2 cloves garlic, crushed
- ½ pound small scallops
- ⅓ cup dry Marsala wine
- ¼ cup brandy
- 1 cup heavy cream
- 3 teaspoons chopped parsley
- Pinch of dried oregano
- 1½ pounds fettuccine, cooked *al dente*
- Grated Parmesan cheese, for topping

Wash mussels very well (it is important to get all the slime off). Put, with water to cover, in a broad pan. Cover tightly and cook over high heat until shells open. Reserve ½ cup mussel broth. Shuck mussels, and put in a bowl. Shell and devein shrimp. Melt butter; add olive oil and crushed garlic cloves; do not brown the garlic. Add shrimp and scallops, and cook until shrimp are pink. Add mussels and reserved liquid. Pour in wine and allow to evaporate. Add brandy and flame. Pour in heavy cream; simmer below boiling point for a few minutes, then add parsley and oregano. Pour sauce over drained fettuccine, reserving some of the shellfish for the top dressing. Shake cheese lightly over the top, add reserved shellfish, and serve immediately.

Pollo alla Padovana

Chicken, Padova-Style

For 4 to 6

A specialty that might have been enjoyed by Shakespeare in one of the merry cafés on the Piazza Cavour in Padua.

- 1/3 cup butter
- 1 slice unsmoked bacon
- 2 leeks, chopped
- 1/4 cup chopped parsley
- 2 cloves garlic
- 1 frying chicken (2 1/2 to 3 pounds)
- 1/2 cup dry vermouth
- 1/2 cabbage, sliced
- 2 stalks celery, sliced
- 1 1/2 cups fresh peas
- Bea's Garlic Salt to taste (see page 31)
- 1/4 teaspoon each ground cinnamon and cloves
- 1 quart chicken stock
- 1 cup raw rice
- 1/2 cup grated Parmesan cheese
- Strips sweet red pepper (optional)
- Strips artichoke heart (optional)

In a broad skillet, melt butter and render with the bacon. Add leeks, parsley, and crushed garlic (*soffritto* basics); remove bacon, and sauté. Clean and wash chicken and cut into individual servings. Put chicken into skillet skin side down; allow to brown. Turn over and let cook for about 30 minutes, moving it frequently so that it does not burn on the bottom. Add vermouth and let evaporate. Add sliced vegetables and peas. Season with garlic salt, cinnamon, and cloves. Cook very slowly, covered. When vegetables are almost tender, add the stock. Allow to cook together for 10 minutes, then add the rice. Simmer until rice is tender but firm, about 15 to 20 minutes. Spoon into a serving dish, and sprinkle with Parmesan cheese. If desired, garnish with strips of sweet red pepper and artichoke hearts. Serve steaming hot.

Pâté di Fegato con Salsa Dolce

Liver Pâté with Sweet Sauce

For 8

Not all liver in Venice is pan-fried. Here is a delicious variation that exemplifies the "fine Italian hand" with a touch of sweet.

- 2 tablespoons olive oil
- 3 tablespoons butter, plus more as needed
- ⅓ cup chopped parsley
- 4 to 5 onions, thinly sliced
- 1½ pounds calves' liver, thinly sliced
- ¼ cup broth or bouillon
- ¼ cup ripe olives, pitted and chopped
- Salt and pepper to taste

Place fats in a skillet. When they begin to sizzle, add parsley and onions. Mix well and cover. Cook over a tiny flame for 1 hour (onions must not brown). Add liver slices, raise heat, and turn meat. Add broth or bouillon. Cook 5 minutes and remove from heat. Place entire contents of pan into a blender or food processor. Weigh the resulting purée and add an equal amount of butter. Blend the two thoroughly. Add chopped olives, season to taste, and mix well. Put pâté in a mold and refrigerate. As the time to serve approaches, make sauce (below) and serve as suggested.

Sauce:

- 2 tablespoons lemon juice
- 2 tablespoons black cherry preserves
- 2 sage leaves, bruised
- 3 tablespoons brandy

Put lemon juice, cherry preserves, and sage leaves in a small saucepan; heat and allow flavors to blend. Warm brandy, add to the sauce, and flame. Unmold liver pâté, and serve with toast points and with the sauce on the side.

Pandoro di Verona

Veronese Sweet Bread

Makes 2 to 3 loaves

Poetically named "Golden Bread," one can imagine Romeo and Juliet enjoying the airy texture of this specialty of their Verona.

- 2 packages (two scant tablespoons) dry yeast
- ¼ cup warm milk
- 5½ cups all-purpose flour
- ⅔ cup granulated sugar
- 1 cup sweet butter, or more as needed
- 3 whole eggs, plus 4 yolks
- 1½ teaspoons vanilla, plus extra for frosting
- ½ cup confectioners' sugar, for frosting

Dissolve yeast in warm milk. Allow to proof with 1 cup flour, 1 tablespoon granulated sugar, and ¼ cup warm milk. When bubbly, add the remaining 4½ cups flour, remaining granulated sugar, 4 tablespoons butter, whole eggs, extra yolks, and vanilla. Work this batter by hand, by beating, or by using the dough hook of the mixer until you have a smooth batter. Then let rise until doubled in bulk. Dust breadboard with flour and place dough on board. Roll out; on ⅔ of the dough put dots of remaining butter. Fold the unbuttered third over the middle third, then the last third over the rest. Continue to dot with butter and flap by thirds. The process is the same as for puff pastry.

Gather the dough, handling gently, and divide into 2 or 3 parts. Butter and flour 2 or 3 tall (2-pound) coffee cans. Place a roll of dough in each can and let rise in a warm, draft-free place until *more* than doubled in bulk. Heat oven to 375°F. Then bake 45 to 60 minutes. When removed from pans, brush with sweet butter and roll in vanilla-flavored confectioners' sugar.

Friuli–Venetia Giulia

The Special Wines & Cheeses of *Friuli–Venetia Giulia*

Wines of the Region

Dry reds: *Merlot, Plozner, Refosco* (robust)

Dry whites: *Chardonnay, Collio, Jermann, Plozner, Tocai del Collio, Tocai Friulano*

Demi-sec whites: *Pinot Grigio, Sauvignon*

Dessert white: *Verduzzo*

Wines Available in the United States

Dry reds: *Merlot, Plozner, Refosco*

Dry whites: *Chardonnay, Jermann, Pinot Bianco, Pinot Grigio, Plozner*

Dessert wines: *Fratelli Turlan, Picolit*

Cheeses of the Region

Liptauer, Montasio, Morlacco, Pecorino, Puina

Chi la vuole cotta e chi la vuole cruda.

Some like it hot, and some like it cold!

A succession of invasions in ancient times and the political footballing of this century have made Friuli–Venetia Giulia a polyglot region. "Ladino" is spoken on the Yugoslav border, a Germanic dialect in the North, and Italian elsewhere, or as the second language. These forces have also created a polyfaceted cuisine, somewhat less rich than one would imagine.

The *focolar* (hearthstone) is as much the soul of the Friuli household as were the huge open fireplaces of this country's early settlers. They have other things in common, too — a love for the homely, for burnished copper and pewter, and for earthenware pots and pitchers, as well as strong ties to church and family.

A travel brochure describes the cookery as "vigorous," with great emphasis on patience, authenticity, and old-fashioned flavors. Country cuisine requires time to prepare, and eating is often the most pleasurable ritual of rural folks' days.

Although the Friuli–Venetia Giulia region could be richer in natural food resources, the marriage here of the seasonings of the "Mitteleuropean" kitchens to those of the North and East have given an added piquancy to the more usual garlic and onions of the national menu. Open windows of the region waft the tantalizing aroma of paprika, cumin, horseradish, poppyseeds, and cinnamon over the landscape.

Polenta and rice stretch the region's slender food budgets. Pork and game are staples, along with the gabbling turkeys everywhere in evidence. There is also a munificence of special vegetable dishes. Asparagus and spinach rotate importance with *radicchio rosso* (the slightly tart red lettuce of relatively recent fame here in America's fine restaurants and greengrocers'), *radicchietto verde* (a small, delicate green lettuce), *topinambur* (a tuber from Gorizia that tastes much like an artichoke), and from Carnia, *brovada,* an interesting dish made from turnips mashed with the grape skin residue that's left after wine pressing.

Not surprisingly, this is sausage country, and the sausages here are superb! Among them are a superior salami; Carso's justly famous specialty, the small smoked *sauri* (a first cousin to the oven-baked version from Trieste); and *luganeghe, soppresse,* and the robust *museto,* a base for many of the leguminous soups. San Daniele is renowned for another Italian pork specialty — prosciutto.

Other of the region's special dishes include *Brodetto,* a local bouillabaisse; *Cotoletta alla Viennese,* a Viennese-style veal chop; *Luganica,* a long, thin sausage; *Gulasch,* much like the goulash we all know; *Pressnitz,* a strudel-like pastry; and *Strucolo,* a filled cake roll. Strangely enough, in this section of Italy, *risotti* (rice dishes) and *polente* (or *polenta*) outstrip the nationally beloved pasta in popularity.

Trieste is really the chief culinary center of the region, embodying a truly international table springing from its diverse influences (Slavic, Greek, Hungarian, and even the early Byzantine), together with some excellent specialties of its own. These, quite naturally, because of Trieste's location, are fish and seafood based.

Because the historical roots of the food of Friuli are so fragmented, it is difficult to categorize them, but when one reaches the closing course of the area's meals, regardless of origin, here is genuine excitement. The desserts are rich, varied, and inventive. Candied and dried fruits, liqueurs (particularly a fine prune brandy), nuts, spices, and chocolate are lovingly included or wrapped in airy pastry, to be devoured happily by the local folk and enthusiastic visitors.

If a sweet tooth is your bent, you can be content here forever, with a *cappuccino,* a slice of *ciambella,* and a view of the unrippled Adriatic.

Us in Funghet

Eggs with Mushrooms in Sauce

For 8

Not surprising from an area that treasures its gifts from the soil and sea, this recipe incorporates dried and fresh mushrooms. The latter would vary according to the season and what the fields might offer. A note from Beatrice mentions that this is considered too "humble" a dish to be served to guests. As a result, its fine flavor is rarely enjoyed outside the village homes.

8 eggs
Salt and pepper to taste
¼ cup chopped parsley
2 tablespoons olive oil
4 tablespoons butter
1 clove garlic
1 ounce dried Italian mushrooms
1 pound fresh mushrooms
3 fresh tomatoes
Cooked *polenta*

Simmer eggs for 20 minutes (do not hard-boil); cool, shell, and cut in half lengthwise. Season eggs with salt, pepper, and chopped parsley. In a skillet, put oil, butter, and garlic. Fry garlic clove until golden, then remove. Soak dried mushrooms in warm water until soft; drain, and chop with fresh mushrooms; add to skillet. Peel, seed, and chop tomatoes and add to mushrooms; simmer 10 to 15 minutes. Pour some of the sauce in a serving dish, and put egg halves on top. Spoon remaining sauce over eggs and serve with fried or fresh *polenta*.

Jota o Jote

Sauerkraut Soup For 6

A specialty of Trieste. This thick soup is one that warrants eating with a knife and fork.

2 cups dried shell beans
2 quarts water
1 pound pork shoulder, cut into small pieces
2 tablespoons olive oil
4 tablespoons butter
1 onion
2 cloves garlic
5 fresh sage leaves or 1 tablespoon dried
5 sprigs fresh parsley
2 ounces smoked bacon
1 pound sauerkraut
1 tablespoon flour
½ cup yellow cornmeal
Salt to taste

Soak beans overnight in a large pot; drain and refill pot with unsalted water. Add the pork pieces along with the bone. In a skillet, melt olive oil and butter together. In a food processor or grinder, finely chop the onion, garlic, sage, parsley, and bacon. Sauté in fats for a few minutes, then add the sauerkraut and cook another 10 minutes over a low flame to allow the flavors to "marry." Sprinkle flour over vegetables, little by little, stirring constantly to avoid lumps. Add this mixture to the soup pot and cook over a low flame. Mix yellow cornmeal with water to moisten and add, a little at a time, to the simmering soup. Salt to taste. The soup can sit over a low flame indefinitely, but consider it cooked when the cornmeal is no longer "grainy" to the taste. Serve soup piping hot.

Polenta Pasticciata

Polenta Casserole For 8

A rib-hugging supper for your favorite "outdoorsman." The special cold of the Friulan Dolomites inspired this dish.

Polenta:

1 recipe *polenta* (see page 58)

Make *polenta.* Allow to cool and slice into ½-inch-thick pieces. Place close together in a buttered deep baking dish.

Sauce:

- ⅔ cup butter
- 1 pound sweet Italian sausages, skinned
- 1 pound ground pork
- Salt and pepper to taste
- 1 ounce dried Italian mushrooms
- 1 tablespoon tomato paste
- Grated Parmesan cheese

Put ½ cup of the butter into a frying pan and sauté the skinned sausages and the ground pork. Season with salt and pepper. Soak mushrooms in hot water to cover. When soft, add chopped mushrooms to meats along with the tomato paste. Sauté. Add water from mushrooms. Cook mixture for about 1 hour over a very low flame, stirring occasionally and adding water so that it does not dry out. In a 2½- or 3-quart casserole, pour sauce over *polenta,* add grated cheese, and repeat another layer. Dot top with remaining butter and bake at 375°F. for 30 minutes.

Lasagne coi Semi di Papavero

Poppyseed Wide Noodles — For 6

A Friulan specialty. The Austrian influence provides a subtle, sweet flavor that helped make this a favorite in Trieste at the turn of the century.

- 1 recipe Lasagne dough (see pages 38 through 42)
- ½ cup browned butter
- 2 tablespoons poppyseeds
- 2 tablespoons sugar

Prepare lasagne dough per recipe and cut into ½-inch strips. Boil pasta in salted water *al dente.* Drain, and toss in a serving bowl with the browned butter and the poppyseeds crushed together with the sugar.

Risotto di Scampi

Rice with Shrimp

For 6

The bright pink of the shrimp and the tomato-kissed rice are perfect companions to an ocean view.

- 2 pounds shrimp
- ½ cup flour
- 3 tablespoons olive oil
- 3 onions, sliced thin
- ⅔ (6-ounce) can tomato paste
- 1 quart water or fish stock, or more as needed
- Juice of ½ lemon
- 1½ cups uncooked rice
- 3 tablespoons butter
- ⅓ cup chopped parsley
- Salt and pepper to taste

Wash shrimp, remove shells, devein, and dip in flour. Fry quickly in hot oil (do not overcook), drain on paper toweling, and set aside. In the same pan, add onions and tomato paste that has been diluted with a spoonful of the fish stock or water. Simmer slowly for 30 minutes. Add shrimp and lemon juice, stir, remove from heat, and cover. Put rice in a 4-quart saucepan. Cover with the stock or water, bring to a boil, and reduce heat. Keep adding liquid in small amounts as necessary, stirring frequently, until rice is cooked *al dente* and all liquid is absorbed. Remove from heat; add butter and parsley, and season to taste. Mix shrimp with its sauce into the rice, reserving a few of the more perfect shrimp to use as garnish.

Gulasch Triestino

Goulash, Trieste-Style — For 6

Italian goulash? Remember that Trieste abuts Yugoslavia, and that the Italian cook is covetous and quick to know a good thing when he or she tastes it!

- 1 slice fresh pork fat
- 2 pounds beef (sirloin tips, bottom round, or chuck)
- 1 pound onions
- Salt and pepper to taste
- 1 cup red wine
- 1 tablespoon paprika
- 2 bay leaves
- ½ tablespoon rosemary
- ½ tablespoon marjoram
- 1 can (6 ounces) tomato paste
- ¾ cup warm water
- Juice of 1 lemon

Render pork fat. Brown meat in fat and add sliced onions. Season to taste with salt and pepper and cook over medium-high heat, stirring frequently. Add wine and allow it to evaporate. Add paprika, bay leaves, rosemary, and marjoram (roll the herbs between your palms to release their flavor). Skim off fat. Lower heat and add the can of tomato paste. Stir and sauté mixture for 3 to 4 minutes; add warm water. Cover and cook slowly for 1 to 1½ hours or until sauce has thickened. Add lemon juice and mix well. Remove meat and place in a serving bowl. Strain juices over meat and serve.

Strucolo

Cheese Pastry

For 8 to 10

The dessert pride of Trieste.

Pasta:

- 2½ cups cake flour
- ⅔ cup butter, softened
- 2 tablespoons warm water

Make a well of the flour on a pastry board; incorporate the butter and water. Mix and knead dough, adding more water if necessary. Put into a bowl, cover, and let dough relax for 1 hour.

Filling:

- 2 cups fresh ricotta cheese
- 3 ounces cream cheese
- 6 tablespoons butter, melted
- ⅓ cup granulated sugar
- ¼ cup fine bread crumbs
- Rind of 1 lemon, grated
- 1 teaspoon vanilla

Put all ingredients into mixing bowl and mix well. Set aside.

Assembly:

- 1 egg yolk, to brush dough

On a floured pastry board, roll out dough into a rectangle shape. Beat the egg yolk and use some to brush over pastry. Spread all the filling evenly over the dough. Roll up and pinch edges. Place roll in a buttered 10-inch spring-form pan; brush top with remaining egg yolk, and bake at 350°F. until golden — 45 minutes or more.

Gubana

Rolled and Filled Coffee Cake

For 8 to 10

In this superb pastry we find the perfect melding of the Venetian, Slavic, and Middle European cultures. It is a specialty of the towns of Gorizia and Carnia.

Dough: Step 1

1 package (scant tablespoon) dry yeast
¼ cup milk, warmed
4 tablespoons flour
1 tablespoon granulated sugar

Mix all the ingredients; set aside and allow to "sponge."

Dough: Step 2

4 cups flour
⅔ cup butter, melted
½ cup granulated sugar
½ teaspoon salt
Rind of 1 lemon, grated

Put flour in a mixing bowl, making a well in the center. Add melted butter, sugar, salt, and lemon rind. Add the yeast "sponge." Mix and work in the flour, forming a soft dough. (If dough seems dry, add a little more milk.) Beat dough with a rolling pin or stick to remove air bubbles. Knead until light. Put into a bowl, cover, and let rise. Make filling (below).

Filling:

¾ cup candied fruits, coarsely chopped
2 slices drained canned pineapple, chopped
1 cup walnuts, coarsely chopped
½ cup semisweet chocolate bits, chopped slightly
⅔ cup golden raisins
⅓ cup sweet wine
⅓ cup pine nuts
1 teaspoon each lemon and orange rinds
⅛ teaspoon cloves
½ teaspoon cinnamon
¾ cup confectioners' sugar
2 eggs, separated

Preheat oven to 375°F. In a bowl, combine fruits, walnuts, and chocolate bits. Add raisins, wine, pine nuts, lemon and orange rinds, spices, confectioners' sugar, and 1 egg yolk. Mix thoroughly. Beat egg whites until they form peaks and fold into the fruit mixture.

Assembly:

- 1/8 cup (2 tablespoons) butter, melted
- Granulated sugar

Roll dough out into a large circle about 1/4-inch thick. Brush with most of the melted butter. Then spread the dough with the prepared filling and roll it up carefully, sealing the ends. Butter a large round baking tin or sheet pan. Coil the roll and put into pan. Beat the remaining egg yolk with the leftover melted butter and granulated sugar. Spread over roll and bake for 45 to 50 minutes.

EMILIA ROMAGNA
Carrara
Lucca
Florence
Pisa
Siena
UMBRIA
OMBRONE
capraia Island
Elba
LATIUM

Tuscany

The Special Wines & Cheeses of ***Tuscany***

Wines of the Region

The Home of Chianti: *Classico, Colli Aretini, Colli Fiorentini, Colline Pisane, Rufina, Colli Senesi, Montalbano* (all dry)

Other dry reds: *Brunello di Montalcino, Vino Nobile di Montepulciano*

Sweet red: *Aleatico di Portoferraio* (specialty of the Island of Elba)

Dry whites: *Arbia, Bianco Vergine dei Colli Aretini, Procanico*

Demi-sec whites: *Candia, Moscato d'Elba*

Wines Available in the United States

Dry reds: *Biondi Santi, Boscarelli, Brunello di Montalcino, Chianti Classico, Chianti Classico Riserva, Costanti, Lilliano, Monte Vertine, Vino Nobile di Montepulciano*

Dry whites: *Antinori, Falchini, Galestro, Vernaccia di San Gimignano*

Dry sparkling: *Antinori, Methode Champenoise, Nature Brut*

Cheeses of the Region

Baccellone, Caciotta Toscana, Marzolino, Pecorino (a hard cheese made from sheep's milk), *Raviggiolo*

Per un grano di sale si perde la minestra.

An extra grain of salt can spoil the soup.

The first impression that one receives as a traveler in Tuscany is that of "order": orderly kitchen gardens, neat farmhouses and orchards (planted geometrically, with espaliered grapevines separating the precisely measured distances between fruit trees), and the curving symmetry of poplar-lined driveways.

Most history students know that Florence — the showcase for Giotto, Michelangelo, and Botticelli — is primarily a Renaissance city, but how many of us are able to define Pisa and Lucca as Romanesque, or Siena as Gothic? Then too, precisely because this region houses so many priceless art treasures, few of us have time to savor her simpler attractions.

For example, Siena boasts a splendid wine museum and library for the serious student of the grape (Tuscany is the home of Chianti); Pisa, besides its fabled tower, offers the thermal spa of Uliveto, minutes away from the center of town (one of nine major Tuscan resorts that feature healing waters); and Capraia, sister island to the famous Elba, is a haven for the nature lover — the home and breeding ground of the Tyrrhenian seal.

But speaking to "simpler attractions," what of the food? It is refined and tasteful, an accompanying hymn to the restrained taste of her people. The local fare offers plain grilled meats, grains, vegetables, and an abundance of mellow cheeses, but few "sauced" dishes. The Tuscan cook's larder includes, along with her treasury of fresh produce, herbs gathered at the doorstep — marjoram, juniper, tarragon, thyme, and rosemary, all used to enhance the flavor of the excellent pork, kid, and game, and often the fish and seafood from Tuscany's coastal waters. This is the kind of "no frills" cooking all of us understand. Fragrant soups and home-baked breads are other enthusiasms we can share with the Tuscans. But, our greatest bond is probably a mutual passion for those noble members of the legume family — beans. Italians from other provinces have dubbed the Tuscans *mangiafagioli* (bean eaters, a denomination not always complimentary). As important as Boston Baked Beans are to New England's national culinary image, so too are the *fave* of Tuscany — from Carrara to Florence to Orbetello, beans are eaten daily . . . cold, hot, whole, mashed; in soup, and in salad.

But beans are not the only Tuscan food specialty — far from it. Others include *Cacciuco*, the local bouillabaisse; *Cee*, delicately flavored eel; *Bistecca alla Fiorentina*, giant broiled T-bone; *Salamini*, *Coppe*, and *Buristo*, three special sausages; *Pappardelle alla Lepre*, pasta sauced with hare, kidneys, and herbs; and *Castagnacci*, a baked chestnut cake

To satisfy one's hunger for beauty *or* bread, Tuscany has the perfect menu.

Pane Toscano

Tuscan Bread

Makes 2 loaves

Tuscany is one of the few Italian regions where pasta is not a primary food source. Instead, homemade bread, almost always made without salt, is the staff of the honest diet of the Tuscan countryside.

- 2 cups warm water
- 1 yeast cake (1¼ ounces) (see Note) or 2 packages dried
- 2 teaspoons sugar
- 4 cups white flour
- 2 tablespoons lard, softened
- 1½ cups wholewheat flour
- ½ cup coarse cornmeal

In a large bowl, put water, yeast, and sugar. Mix and allow to proof. Beat in 2 cups of the white flour and cut in the lard (you may do this with an electric beater or processor). Continue to beat for at least 3 minutes, and add the wholewheat flour until well mixed and smooth. Put dough on board with remaining white flour, knead well, turning every third beat — "push with the heel of the right hand, push with the heel of the left, and turn." Add more flour if the dough seems sticky. Place in a greased bowl, turn once to grease both sides of the ball, cover, and let rise in a warm, draft-free place until doubled in bulk.

Preheat oven to 375°F. Put pan of boiling water on bottom rack of oven. Punch down, and shape dough into 2 round loaves. Sprinkle sheet pan with cornmeal, put loaves on sheet, and let rise until doubled again. Bake for 45 to 60 minutes, brushing tops with water several times during the baking (this makes the crusts extra crispy).

Note: This is an old recipe; chances are you won't find a yeast cake just this size. Today they often come in smaller (3/5-ounce) packages, though bakeries and some markets do carry the larger cakes. Be sure to use enough.

Ziti Fiorentina d'Oreste

For 6

This is a recipe that Bea secured after charming the owner of Oreste's Restaurant in Piazza Santo Spirito, Florence.

- 1½ pounds ziti, cooked *al dente*
- 4 cups Beatrice's Sausage Sauce (see recipe on page 134)
- 2 cups grated Parmesan cheese
- 6 ounces Groviera or Swiss cheese, sliced
- 2 cups *Besciamella* (see recipe on page 133)
- A few twists of grated nutmeg

Drain ziti, return to a large pan, and toss with a small amount of the Sausage Sauce. In a well-buttered 2- to 2½-quart casserole, put a layer of ziti, cover with Sausage Sauce, sprinkle with grated cheese, then top with thin slices of the Groviera or Swiss. Add a little more sauce and continue layering in this fashion. When layering is complete, pour the *Besciamella* sauce over the top, sprinkle with nutmeg, and bake for 20 minutes in a 375°F. oven.

Note: Bel Paese cheese may be used in place of the Swiss-type cheese.

Pappardelle alla Lepre

Pasta with Rabbit Sauce

For 6

This dish is a favorite all over Tuscany, but particularly in Arezzo and Valdarno. The rich, dark brown of the sauce is an exquisite counterpoint to the wide, homemade noodles.

Sauce:

½ cup olive oil
¾ cup butter
1 rabbit, cleaned and quartered
Salt and pepper to taste
1 onion, chopped
1 carrot, chopped
1 bunch parsley, chopped
1 celery stalk, chopped
1 bay leaf
¼ teaspoon thyme
1 slice unsmoked bacon
1½ tablespoons flour
1 cup red wine
2 cups broth

In a large skillet with a cover, melt olive oil and ½ cup butter together and add rabbit. Cover and cook slowly and allow rabbit juices to begin to flow. Pour off excess liquid. Add salt and pepper. In a separate skillet, sauté the chopped vegetables, herbs, and bacon together for several minutes. Then remove bacon rind and bay leaf and add sautéed vegetables to rabbit. Sprinkle flour over all, and continue to cook, allowing liquid to reduce and meat to brown. Add wine and continue cooking until it has evaporated. Add broth. Cook for about 1½ hours over a tiny flame. Add remaining butter to sauce. Remove meat from the bones and stir well into the sauce. Check seasoning. Meanwhile, make the pasta.

Pasta:

1 recipe Classic 3-Egg Pasta (see page 36)
1 cup grated Parmesan cheese, for topping

Make pasta, roll it out, and proceed as for noodles (see page 42 for rule), cutting into strips ¾-inch wide. Boil, *al dente*, in salted water. Drain. Then spoon on prepared rabbit sauce. Serve with grated Parmesan cheese.

Pastasciutta alla Fornaia

Pasta, Leghorn-Style

For 4

Leghorn (Livorno, *as they call it in Italy*) *is one of Italy's busiest ports. Perhaps that's why this uncooked "instant" sauce is so popular.*

- 1 pound spaghetti or linguine
- 1 cup walnut meats
- 1 to 1¼ cups Sardo or Parmesan cheese, plus extra for topping
- ⅓ cup olive oil
- 1 cup fresh basil leaves
- Salt to taste

Cook pasta *al dente.* Then, in the food processor or blender, fine-chop the remaining ingredients to make the sauce. Pour over prepared pasta and serve with extra cheese.

Torta di Riso Delcarte

Rice Tarts

For 6

Rice tarts are made all over Italy. Not only are they tasty, they are also a marvelous way to use up leftover plain white rice. This recipe is one of several from Lena Delcarte.

- ¾ cup raw rice (or 1½ to 2 cups leftover cooked)
- ½ stick (4 tablespoons) butter
- 2 teaspoons salt
- Pepper to taste
- 6 eggs
- 1½ quarts milk
- ¼ teaspoon nutmeg
- ½ cup Romano cheese
- ¾ cup fine bread crumbs

Steam and drain rice (if using leftover rice, this step is obviously not necessary). Melt butter and mix all ingredients except the bread crumbs in a large mixing bowl. Grease generously a 9- by 13-inch baking dish and coat with bread crumbs, pressing down on the crumbs with the back of a large spoon. Pour milk–rice mixture carefully over the crumbs. Bake at 350°F. for 50 to 60 minutes. Allow to cool slightly and cut into serving squares.

Note: This is also delicious served cold.

Gnocchi di Ricotta Lazzaro

Cheese *Gnocchi* For 4

If you count yourself among the gnocchi *"noneaters," try this version of Beatrice's before you take your final vow.*

1 pound ricotta cheese
1 egg
1 teaspoon salt
½ cup grated pecorino and Parmesan cheese
1 "ricotta container" flour (heaping)
¼ cup butter, melted

In a bowl, mix all ingredients together with your hands until you have a dough that "holds together." Cover and let rest for 5 minutes. Turn out onto a floured board and knead until smooth. Roll the dough into ¾-inch-thick "ropes" of manageable length; cut into ½-inch pieces. Press with two fingers and roll on board or cheese grater. Cook in boiling salted water for about 5 minutes; drain and serve with the sauce of your choice.

Note: One way to serve this *gnocchi* is to put it in a baking pan, cover it with *Besciamella* (see recipe on page 133) and grated cheese, and bake it in a 375°F. oven until the top is golden. It's delicious!

To freeze ahead, put uncooked *gnocchi* on a floured cookie sheet. Place in freezer. When *gnocchi* are frozen solid, put them into a plastic bag, tie securely, and place back in freezer.

Bistecca alla Fiorentina

Florentine Steak For 4

Perhaps the most famous steaks in the world. The fact that they come from the renowned white Chianina cattle certainly must have something to do with their fame among the epicurean élite.

4 T-bone steaks, cut 1¼ inches thick
Salt and pepper to taste
4 dollops butter

Do not salt steaks before cooking. Grill steaks over hot fire; turn only once, carefully, with a spatula so as not to pierce the flesh and allow the juices to escape. For the result you want, there should be burned grill marks on both sides of the meat, with the meat itself charred on the outside and rare in the middle. Remove from the grill, sprinkle with salt and freshly ground pepper, and place a dollop of butter on each steak. Serve immediately.

Bistecca alla Cacciatora

Hunter's-Style Steak

For 4

"Alla cacciatora" *is a well-known phrase to most of us. It conjures up a deep, red sauce loaded with mushrooms and herbs. It is prepared in many regions of Italy, the most familiar version being this one from Tuscany. It is also made in Sicily with the unusual addition of eggplant slices. The sauce takes equally well to meat or fowl.*

4 boneless beef steaks, cut ¾-inch thick
Flour, for dusting
Olive oil, for frying

Flour the steaks and fry quickly in olive oil until done to your taste. Remove from skillet. Make *Salsa* (below) and serve.

Salsa Cacciatora:

⅓ cup olive oil
1 onion, chopped
1 teaspoon Bea's Garlic Salt (see page 31)
1 ounce dried mushrooms
1 cup dry red wine
½ pound fresh mushrooms, chopped
2 large ripe tomatoes or ⅓ (6-ounce) can tomato paste

In a meat skillet, add olive oil and sauté the onion with garlic salt until golden. Soak dried mushrooms in warm water until soft; drain and chop. Add wine to skillet with reconstituted and fresh chopped mushrooms. Cook until wine has evaporated. Add tomatoes (or diluted half water–half paste) and cook for 30 minutes. Heat steaks quickly in sauce and serve on a heated platter.

Maiale Ubriaco

Drunkard's Pork — For 4

The verdant areas around Florence, Arezzo, and Siena are Chianti country. Hence the evolution of this recipe, using the ruby-hued wine. Santé — *both in the glass and on the plate!*

- 4 pork loin chops
- Bea's Garlic Salt (see page 31) to taste
- 2 tablespoons olive oil
- 1 clove garlic, crushed
- ¼ cup chopped parsley
- ⅛ teaspoon fennel seeds
- 1 cup Chianti wine

Rub pork chops with garlic salt. In a skillet with a cover, sear chops on both sides in hot oil. Sprinkle the crushed garlic, parsley, and fennel seeds over the chops; lower heat and fry slowly until meat is brown on both sides. Pour wine over the chops, and continue to cook slowly with cover on pan. Cook until wine has been completely absorbed. Serve at once on a heated platter.

Arista di Maiale della Nonna

Grandmother's Roast Pork — For 6

- 1 pork shoulder (4 to 5 pounds)
- 1 tablespoon chopped fresh rosemary
- 1 tablespoon chopped sage
- 2 cloves garlic, crushed
- 1 teaspoon salt
- 2 tablespoons olive oil
- 4 tablespoons butter, melted
- ½ teaspoon dried rosemary
- 1 teaspoon Bea's Garlic Salt (see page 31)
- Broth as needed

Skin and bone the fresh pork shoulder and open flat. Then mix first 4 seasonings and rub on meat, working into the crevices. Roll up meat and tie. Put meat in oiled roasting pan and cover it with a mixture of the oil and butter. Spread dried rosemary and garlic salt on top. Put in a 350°F. oven. Baste often while roasting and turn on all sides. Add broth if necessary for liquid. Roast 40 minutes to the pound or until meat thermometer registers 165°.

Pollo al Pian dei Guillari

Tuscan Fried Chicken For 4 to 6

Over twenty years ago, Santina, the custodian's wife of the Florentine villa where Beatrice and her family summered, made this chicken dish. It is a memory and a recipe to be treasured.

- 1 broiling chicken (2½ to 3 pounds)
- Bea's Garlic Salt as needed (see page 31)
- 2 extra-large eggs
- Juice of 1 large lemon
- Flour, for sprinkling
- Vegetable oil, for frying
- Olive oil, for frying
- Lemon wedges, for garnish

Wash and cut up chicken and dry. Cut thighs from legs at joint; cut breast into 4 pieces. In a deep bowl, mix garlic seasoning, eggs, and lemon juice. Roll chicken pieces in flour. Dip in egg mixture. Fry chicken in a mixture of vegetable and olive oil over moderate heat. After about 20 minutes, increase the flame so that the chicken becomes nicely browned. Serve garnished with lemon wedges.

Rognone Lazzaro

Veal Kidney, Lazzaro-Style For 4

If livers and kidneys have never been your thing, you may change your opinion after tasting this first "with your mind." The anchovy has a magical effect on the meat.

- 8 veal kidneys
- 2 tablespoons olive oil
- 1 clove garlic, crushed
- 1 anchovy, rinsed
- 4 tablespoons butter
- 2 tablespoons parsley
- 1 tablespoon lemon juice
- Salt and pepper to taste

With the point of a sharp knife, ease away the membrane and fat from the kidneys. Wash in salted water and rinse. Repeat. Separate the kidneys and slice thinly. Put into a hot skillet, shaking the pan over high heat so that the liquid is extracted from the kidneys. Drain. Put olive oil and crushed garlic in pan and heat. Add sliced kidneys and toss around quickly with pan over high heat. Do not leave over heat too long (this makes them tough). Mash anchovy with a fork, and add butter; stir together well. Remove from heat almost immediately. Add parsley and lemon juice, stir, and season. Pour into a serving dish.

Note: This became a favorite of the Lazzaro family after they had it for the first time in Piazza Santo Spirito in Florence.

Carciofi Fritti

Fried Artichoke Hearts For 4

Each region has its own way to prepare this favorite Italian vegetable. Tuscan food is known for its simplicity, and here is an easy yet delicious way to serve this all-season vegetable.

- 8 tiny tender artichokes
- Juice of 2 lemons
- Flour, for rolling
- 3 eggs, beaten
- Olive oil, for frying
- Salt (optional)
- Lemon wedges, for garnish

Remove hard outer leaves of the artichokes and trim remaining leaf tips. Slice in half lengthwise; remove the "choke" (the hairy or thorny center). Soak in water and lemon juice to cover for 1 or 2 hours. Cut each half into 4 parts. Dry and roll the pieces in flour. Dip in beaten eggs, and fry in olive oil until golden. Salt lightly if desired. Serve hot with lemon wedges.

Note: Canned artichokes may be substituted for the fresh. In that case, the trimming and soaking are not necessary, but they must be rinsed thoroughly.

Patate al Rosmarino

Roasted Potatoes with Rosemary For 4

Try this recipe and marvel at what a few sprigs of herbs can do!

- 8 good-quality large potatoes
- 2 tablespoons chopped fresh rosemary or 1 tablespoon dried and crumbled
- 2 to 3 tablespoons olive oil
- ½ teaspoon Bea's Garlic Salt (see page 31)

Peel and cut potatoes into 4 to 6 pieces, depending on size of potato. In a roasting pan crush the rosemary and olive oil together. Drop in potatoes, tossing them with your hands so that they are evenly coated with the oil. Bake in a 400°F. oven, moving them about often so that they brown evenly. When just about golden, add garlic salt and toss well. Serve with roasted meats, fish, poultry — or with almost everything!

Rapa Delcarte

Tender Turnips For 3 to 4

Turnips are an often misunderstood vegetable here in the United States, but in Italy they are eaten with relish. Here is a simple turnip recipe shared by Lena Delcarte, a friend from Franklin, Massachusetts. Her parents were from Monti in the province of Massa Carrara.

- 1 turnip, pared and sliced
- 1 medium onion, diced
- 2 tablespoons pork fat drippings
- 1 tablespoon flour (approximately)
- ¾ cup beef stock or bouillon
- ¼ teaspoon sage

Blanch the turnip slices (about 5 minutes) and drain. Sauté the diced onion in the pork fat drippings until transparent, stirring in the flour gradually to thicken. Cook 3 minutes. Add beef stock or bouillon and sage, and stir thoroughly. Lay in the turnips gently, cover, and cook until just tender (if there seems to be too much juice, cook uncovered until most of the juice has evaporated).

Zucchini in Casseruola

Zucchini Casserole

For 6 to 8

This is a wonderfully tasty, if rather rich, way to offer the zucchini so rampant in summer gardens — in Italy and here in America.

- 4 medium zucchini squash
- 1 tablespoon butter and oil combined
- 1½ cups *Besciamella* sauce (see page 133)
- 2 eggs, lightly beaten
- 2 tablespoons grated Parmesan cheese
- Salt and pepper to taste

Slice zucchini in ¼-inch rounds and fry in fat mixture until lightly browned; do not overcook. Mix cream sauce, eggs, cheese, salt, and pepper, and fold in zucchini.

Put the zucchini mixture in a well-buttered and floured 2-quart casserole dish, and place casserole in pan of water in a 375°F. oven. Bake for 40 minutes, remove from oven, and let stand for 5 minutes before serving.

Finocchio alla Santina

Tuscan Fennel (Anise)

For 4

Lesser known in this hemisphere than it deserves to be, the snowy fennel bulb, with its bright-green lacy foliage, is both delicious and versatile. Here is a cooked version of the vegetable revered by the Tuscans.

- 3 heads fennel
- ½ cup sweet butter
- ½ cup grated Parmesan cheese
- ¼ teaspoon salt
- ¼ teaspoon white pepper
- Dash each of nutmeg and paprika

Wash fennel heads and slice across in large rounds. Steam in a small amount of water; drain. Put in a serving bowl, and mix with the butter and half of the grated cheese. Season to taste with salt and white pepper, and mix well. Sprinkle with the remaining ¼ cup cheese and garnish with a shake each of nutmeg and paprika.

Note: Fennel, because of its strong licoricelike flavor, also takes well to a robust cheesy cream sauce or a simple tomato sauce. And, it is also refreshing when eaten raw.

Panzanella

Bread Salad

For 8

This is a country supper or lunch that travels handily to the fields, where the bright red tomatoes can be added still warm from the sun.

- 1 round loaf Italian bread
- 1 bowl iced water
- 6 teaspoons Balsamic vinegar
- Juice of ½ lemon
- ⅓ cup olive oil
- Bea's Garlic Salt to taste (see page 31)
- 4 celery stalks, cut in rounds
- 1 cucumber, sliced thin
- 4 scallions, with tops
- 6 to 8 leaves fresh basil
- 1 small fennel bulb, sliced
- 3 large ripe tomatoes

Slice the bread in thick slices, remove the crusts, and soak for a few minutes in the iced water. Break into bite-sized pieces and squeeze out the moisture in a clean kitchen towel. Refrigerate, still in the towel, until ready to pack or eat.

Make a dressing of the vinegar, lemon juice, olive oil and garlic salt; mix well. Put the remaining ingredients, except the tomatoes, in a salad bowl, interspersed with the cold, moist bread. Re-refrigerate or cover with plastic wrap if it's meant to "travel." Add the tomatoes, sliced or quartered, and the well-mixed dressing just before serving.

Biscotti di Noci Lazzaro

Nut Cakes

Makes 20

Although these biscuits are a specialty of Prato, they are eaten and enjoyed all over Italy. Their nutty crunch starts the day nicely with a cup of coffee, or enjoy them dipped in a sweet dessert wine.

- 3¾ cups all-purpose flour
- 1¼ cups sugar
- 1 teaspoon baking powder
- ¼ teaspoon cloves
- ¼ teaspoon cinnamon
- 3 large whole eggs plus 1 extra yolk, plus 1 extra white, beaten well
- 1 teaspoon grated orange or lemon rind
- 1 teaspoon almond extract
- ⅓ cup butter (very soft)
- 3 cups almonds and filberts, or more if desired

Sift flour into a mixing bowl with sugar, baking powder, cloves, and cinnamon. Beat 3 eggs and extra yolk with the citrus rind and almond extract. Add flour mixture to the eggs. Then add the softened butter and blend well. Put mixture on a floured board.

Preheat oven to 375°F. Blanch the nuts, remove skins, and chop nuts coarsely (they can be left whole if you desire). Add the nuts to the dough and knead in by hand. Spoon dough onto sheet pan about ¾-inch thick. Cut into strips 2 inches wide. Flatten out a bit with your fingers and brush with the beaten egg white. Place on a buttered sheet and bake for 30 minutes. Remove to a board and cut into pieces about ½-inch wide. Put cut side down on pan and bake for 3 minutes more to dry out cut sides.

Note: These biscuits keep indefinitely in a tightly closed jar or cookie tin.

Cenci di Connie

Connie's Fried Sweets

Makes 24

Beatrice's friend Connie makes this variation of the Tuscan classic, which translates into "rags" (because of their shape). The old country recipes use wine in the batter, but it toughens the pastry. This version melts in your mouth!

- 3 cups flour
- 3 tablespoons granulated sugar
- 1½ teaspoons baking powder
- 4 eggs
- Rind of 1 lemon, grated
- Oil, for frying
- Confectioners' sugar, for dusting

On a pastry board, sift flour, granulated sugar, and baking powder. Make a well in the center; into it break the eggs, along with the grated lemon rind. Begin to beat the eggs and gradually incorporate flour until all dry ingredients are mixed with the eggs. Knead for a few minutes until dough is smooth. Divide into 4 parts. Let dough rest for 15 minutes, covered. Roll out thin (one part at a time). Cut strips 1½ inches wide and 4 to 5 inches long. Knot each strip loosely (see sketch). Fry until very light in color. Before serving, sprinkle with confectioners' sugar.

Note: If you like, the strips may be rolled out by a pasta machine.

A short lengthwise slit is made in the dough strips for Cenci di Connie. *One end of the strip is then gently drawn through the slit to make a knot.*

Zucotto

Cream Pudding

For 8 to 10

This Florentine specialty has ingredients similar to the Gianduia *of Piedmont. However, this recipe is a good deal less complicated.*

Cake:

1 recipe Genoese Sponge Cake (see page 89)

Make cake and let cool. Then continue with recipe.

Filling:

- ¾ cup almonds
- ¾ cup hazelnuts
- ¾ cup liqueur of choice
- 4 cups heavy cream, plus extra for topping
- 1 cup confectioners' sugar
- 12 ounces semisweet chocolate bits
- 1 teaspoon vanilla
- Cocoa, for dusting

Blanch, skin, toast, and chop nuts. Line a 2- to 3-quart round glass bowl with plastic wrap, leaving extra at the top (see Note), and then with thin slices of sponge cake. Soak with liqueur. Whip 1½ cups cream with ½ cup confectioners' sugar. Add ½ cup chocolate bits and half of the nuts, and set aside. Melt the remaining 1½ cups chocolate bits and add ½ cup heavy cream. Add vanilla, mix well, and cool.

Pour the whipped cream–chocolate–nut blend into the lined bowl. Cover with another layer of sponge cake, soaking cake with the liqueur again. Whip the remaining 2 cups cream with the cool chocolate–cream–vanilla mixture; add the remaining ½ cup confectioners' sugar and the remaining ¾ cup chopped nuts. Spoon over soaked sponge cake. Cover with a last layer of sponge cake slices, soaking again with liqueur. Cover bowl with plastic wrap and put in freezer. When ready to serve, invert over a platter. Cover with sweetened whipped cream. Dust with cocoa, and decorate with additional chopped nuts.

Note: The plastic wrap will help lift pudding out of the mold when serving time comes.

EMILIA ROMAGNA
ADRIATIC SEA
Pesaro
Urbino
Ancona
Recanati
Camerino
Fermo
UMBRIA
ABRUZZI-MOLISE
E. Sears

The Marches

The Special Wines, Cheeses & Pasta of ***The Marches***

Wines of the Region

Dry reds: *Montepulciano Piceno, Rosso Piceno, Vallone*

Demi-sec red: *Rosso Montesanto*

Dry whites: *Orvieto, Verdicchio dei Castelli di Jesi, Verdicchio di Matelica*

Wines Available in the United States

Dry reds: *Rosso Piceno Superiore, Vallone*

Dry whites: *Faza Battaglia, Verdicchio dei Castelli di Jesi*

Cheeses of the Region

Bazzoto, Caciotta, Pecorino (mild or sharp and salty), *Raviggiolo, Ricotta, Slattato*

Pasta Specialty

Vincisgrassi — one of Italy's most famous dishes

Chi per man d'altri s'imbocca, tardi satolla.

He that depends on another man's table often dines late!

The name tantalizes — both fancy and logic want to play. Marshes . . . flat, swampy land? Let's look at a map. No, discard that explanation, for the region is either slashed by the green-hued Apennines or embraced by the sea. History books suggest that the topography of the region created natural military frontiers for the Papal and Frankish holdings. Thus, the derivation of the area's name: the points to which their ancient armies "marched"!

The rationale in support of the region's name is at least more satisfying than the controversy that has swirled around the name of the region's most famous dish, *Vincisgrassi.* Culinary eminences have sought etymological, historic, and anecdotal bases for their various theories, but to date there is still no answer to the centuries-old riddle. Those of us who have happily increased our waistlines with its delicious excesses might smugly say, "Who cares anyway? Something so sinfully delicious could bear a *number* and we would still pursue its caloric perfection!"

In fact, the Marches are a culinary puzzlement. Rustic food from the region's mountainous area is served with particular ingenuity and attention. Boundaries shared with five other regions (Emilia Romagna, Tuscany, Umbria, Latium, and Abruzzi) give a broad base to her cuisine, as is evidenced by the variety of recipes. A huge selection of pasta is to be had, much of it enriched with sauces of Emilian influence. Dropping to the seacoast, the inspiration for ingredients is not only national, but can be traced across the Adriatic and back in time to the small Renaissance courts whose home the Marches was for so long.

Outstanding among the many special Marchigiana dishes are *Brodetto,* a concentrated fish soup flavored with saffron and spices; *Olivette,* small, olive-shaped chunks of veal, stuffed and sauced; *Pan Pepato,* nougat of candied fruits and nuts; *Pasticciata,* a pizza-quiche cross; *Pizza Rustica,* a deep-dish pizza made with sausage and egg; *Porchetta,* a spit-roasted suckling pig, stuffed with peppers, garlic, and rosemary; *Tornedo alla Rossini,* filet mignon with ham, mushrooms, and lemon; *Datteri Marinati,* a local mussel in a spicy marinade; and the famous *Vincisgrassi.*

The Marchigiani are a cordial, friendly folk with artistry in their hands and hearts. There are more annual festivals to the arts held here than in any other region, save Rome. Urbino hosts the Renaissance Court Theatre; Pesaro has the International Festival of New Cinema and the Festival of Drama Groups; Fermo shows the Exhibitions of Reportages and Photographic Documentaries in August; Camerino the Ugo Betti International Theatre Awards (biennually); and Recanati is the September site of the Beniamino Gigli Opera Award.

For the traveler who is an *apassionato* of the performing arts, or who enjoys a more leisurely pace than that of the usual frantic guided tour, and most definitely for the epicure, the pleasures and rewards of the Marches are many . . . to see . . . to listen to . . . and to eat!

Pizza al Formaggio

Cheese Pizza — For 4

Not "pizza" as we think of it, but rather a particularly satisfying type of cheese bread. An ancient recipe from the city of Jesi, a Renaissance city whose fourteenth-century battlements must have inhaled the fragrance of many of these golden loaves.

Cheese Mix:

- ½ cup grated Parmesan cheese
- 4 ounces Swiss cheese, finely diced
- ½ cup grated pecorino cheese
- 4 ounces provolone cheese, finely diced
- 2 eggs
- 1 teaspoon salt
- 1 to 2 teaspoons olive oil

Mix the cheeses together and blend with the eggs, salt, and olive oil. Reserve.

Dough:

- 3¼ cups flour
- 1 teaspoon baking powder
- ½ teaspoon salt
- 1¼ cups warm water
- 2 packages dry yeast or 1 yeast cake
- 1 teaspoon sugar
- 2 tablespoons olive oil

To make the dough, in a large bowl, put 1 cup flour, baking powder, and sprinkle with the salt. Make a well in the center. Put in ½ cup of the warm water; add the yeast and sugar and let mixture foam. Then mix some of the flour back into the yeast, making a "pourable" batter as if for pancakes. Cover and let rise until spongy and bubbly. When ready, mix in the remaining 2¼ cups flour, the remaining ¾ cup warm water, and the olive oil. At the end add the reserved cheese mix and knead well to obtain a smooth dough that does not stick to the board.

Preheat the oven to "warm," 110°F. Put the dough into a large bowl or pan and coat with a little oil; cover with plastic wrap or aluminum foil. Put into the oven and turn off the heat. Let dough rise until doubled in bulk. Punch down dough and spread in an oiled 10-inch pizza pan. Let rise again for 40 minutes or more. Reheat oven temperature to 425°F. When ready, bake pizza in lower part of oven until golden (about 30 minutes). Serve warm.

Maccheroni Pesarese Imbuttiti

Filled Pasta, Pesaro-Style

For 4

The Southern Italians use the word "macaroni" in a generic way. Can you imagine anyone but a Lilliputian trying to fill the little cylinders we associate with the word?

Pasta:

- 18 large pasta shapes for filling (shells or tubes)
- 2 tablespoons olive oil

In salted water to which you've added the olive oil, boil pasta VERY *al dente*. Drain, and set aside to cool on a cloth-covered surface.

Filling:

- ½ medium onion, sliced thin
- ¼ cup butter, plus extra for sautéing and dotting
- 1 pound veal, chopped
- ½ pound chicken (skinned and boned)
- ½ cup broth of choice
- 2 chicken livers
- ½ pound boiled ham
- 1 cup cream
- 1 cup grated Gruyère cheese

Sauté the onion in ¼ cup butter until it becomes transparent. Add the chopped veal and chicken, and moisten with the broth. Cook until liquid is almost evaporated. In the food processor or meat grinder, chop poultry, chicken livers, and ham very fine. Moisten chopped meats with 2 to 3 tablespoons cream. Mix well and gently fill the pasta tubes. Butter a 9- by 13-inch Pyrex baking dish, spoon some sauce over bottom, and lay in the filled tubes. Spread with a sauce made of the remaining filling, thinned with the cream as needed. Sprinkle with the grated cheese, pour the remaining cream over the top, and dot with the remaining butter. Bake in a 400°F. oven until heated through, about 20 to 25 minutes (the edges should bubble and cheese will be browned).

Vincisgrassi

Regional "Lasagna"

For 8

A rich extravaganza of flavors. The Marches and Abruzzi both make this delicious dish. The two versions differ in that the Marchigian specialty is spelled with a "V" and is made exactly as this recipe is written. The Abruzzi version, spelled with a "P," departs in that it includes tiny meatballs tucked away between the pasta layers to surprise and delight you. Both presentations are delicious and quite clearly labors of love.

Pasta:

- 3 cups flour
- 1 cup semolina flour
- 8 tablespoons butter, softened
- ¼ cup dry Marsala wine
- 3 eggs

Make pasta according to instructions on page 38. Cut into strips the length of the pan (9 by 13 inches), and boil gently in salted water with 2 tablespoons oil for 2 minutes. Drain, and spread on a clean cloth to dry.

Sauce:

- 1/4 cup butter, plus 4 tablespoons for dotting and drizzling over top
- 1 onion, chopped
- 1 thick slice prosciutto, chopped
- 1 pound chicken giblets
- 1/4 cup dried mushrooms, soaked and chopped
- 4 tablespoons tomato paste
- 3/4 cup broth (chicken preferred)
- 1/4 teaspoon cinnamon
- 1/2 cup white wine
- Milk, as needed
- 1 pound chicken livers
- 1 recipe *Besciamella* (see page 133)
- 1 to 2 cups grated Parmesan cheese

In a skillet, melt the 1/4 cup butter. Add chopped onion and prosciutto, and sauté. Remove hard parts of giblets and chop in food processor or grinder, then put in skillet with mushrooms and sauté. Mix the tomato paste with the broth, and blend well into the other ingredients being sautéed. Add cinnamon and cook until ground chicken mixture is tender. Add wine and let it evaporate. Cook about 2 hours, adding milk often to prevent drying out. Sauté chicken livers for 3 to 4 minutes, dice, and set aside. Prepare 1 recipe (about 3 cups) *Besciamella* sauce, increasing nutmeg to 1/2 teaspoon. Reserve 1 1/2 cups.

Butter a lasagna pan (9 by 13 inches). Put down a thin layer of sauce, and layer in this order: pasta, cooked chicken sauce, thin layer of *Besciamella,* sprinkled diced chicken liver, grated cheese, and dots of butter. Continue layering in this fashion until all lasagna and chicken sauce are used. Cover with foil and refrigerate overnight.

Heat oven to 400°F. Spread the remaining *Besciamella* sauce over the top of the last lasagna layer (it may need to be thinned with a little milk). Bake for 10 minutes and lower the oven to 375°F. Bake 30 minutes longer or until the top is golden. Remove from oven and drizzle melted butter over the entire surface. Add more grated cheese and let set before serving. This dish should be eaten hot.

Naselli alla Marchigiana

Whiting Fish Porto Recanati

For 4

Porto Recanati is the beginning of the Macerata Riviera, and what could be more fitting than this delicate fish, fresh from the nets?

- 4 small whiting fish
- 2 onions, thinly sliced
- 1 clove garlic
- 1/3 cup olive oil
- 1 cup bread crumbs
- 1/3 cup butter
- 1 anchovy
- 2 tablespoons Balsamic vinegar
- Salt and pepper to taste

Clean, wash, and dry the fish. Then put on a plate and cover with sliced onions. Crush garlic into the olive oil and dribble the oil over the fish. Marinate 1 hour or more, turning fish often. Put fish on a grill and cook each side, moistening with the marinade. When almost cooked, sprinkle all sides of the fish with the bread crumbs, patting them onto the fish so that they will adhere. Baste with the olive oil marinade and continue to grill. In a small saucepan, put butter, anchovy, and vinegar. Mash the anchovy and sauté for about 5 minutes. Pour this sauce over fish, season to taste, and serve immediately.

Stufato Stile delle Marche

Meat Stew, Marches-Style

For 6

An area of many culinary influences, the Marches borrows seasoning techniques from each of its neighbors. This is an ancient recipe that lends itself well to pork, lamb, or veal.

- 2 sprigs rosemary
- 1 large clove garlic, crushed
- 1/3 cup olive oil
- 2 1/2 pounds meat of choice, cubed
- 1 cup dry white wine
- Bea's Garlic Salt to taste (see page 31)
- 1/8 teaspoon oregano (optional)
- 4 fresh tomatoes, peeled and chopped
- 2 tablespoons tomato purée

Chop rosemary with crushed garlic clove. Sauté in olive oil in a large skillet. Braise meat and fry until golden over moderate heat. Add wine and let it evaporate. Add garlic salt and oregano, if desired. Add the peeled, chopped tomatoes and tomato purée (you may wish to dilute the purée). Cook over low heat until meat is tender and sauce is concentrated. Adjust seasoning and serve.

Cavolfiore Fritto

Fried Cauliflower

For 4 to 6

Along with an abundance of wild vegetables, cream-colored cauliflower is a Marchigiana favorite.

- 1 cup flour
- 1 egg
- ½ cup white wine
- Salt and pepper to taste
- 1 cauliflower (about 2 pounds)
- Vegetable oil, for frying

In a bowl, put flour, egg, white wine, salt, and pepper. Mix and heat to obtain a thin paste; cover and leave for 1 hour. Wash the cauliflower and cut into florets. Boil cauliflower in small amount of water (it should be firm); drain and cool. In pan, heat ample oil. Dip florets in prepared batter, drop in hot oil, and fry until golden. Remove and drain on paper towels. Sprinkle with a little salt and serve immediately.

Frustingolo

Marchigiana Fruitcake

For 8 to 12

A Christmas holiday specialty of the Marches.

- 1 pound dry figs
- ½ cup white seedless raisins
- ⅓ cup chopped semisweet chocolate
- ½ cup almonds, blanched
- ¼ cup candied orange peel, chopped
- ½ cup walnut meats
- ½ cup sugar
- 1½ cups bread crumbs
- ½ cup olive oil
- Pinch of grated nutmeg
- ⅔ cup honey
- 1 tablespoon pine nuts

Soak figs overnight. Next day, in the same water bring the figs to a boil, lower heat, and simmer until soft; let cool in their juice. Plump raisins in hot water to cover.

Preheat the oven to 375°F. Drain figs, and put in a bowl. Add raisins, chocolate, almonds, orange peel, walnut meats, sugar, bread crumbs, olive oil, nutmeg, and honey. Mix well. Butter a 9- or 10-inch tube cake pan. Pour in fruit mix, and cover surface with pine nuts. Bake until firm, about 45 minutes. Test for doneness.

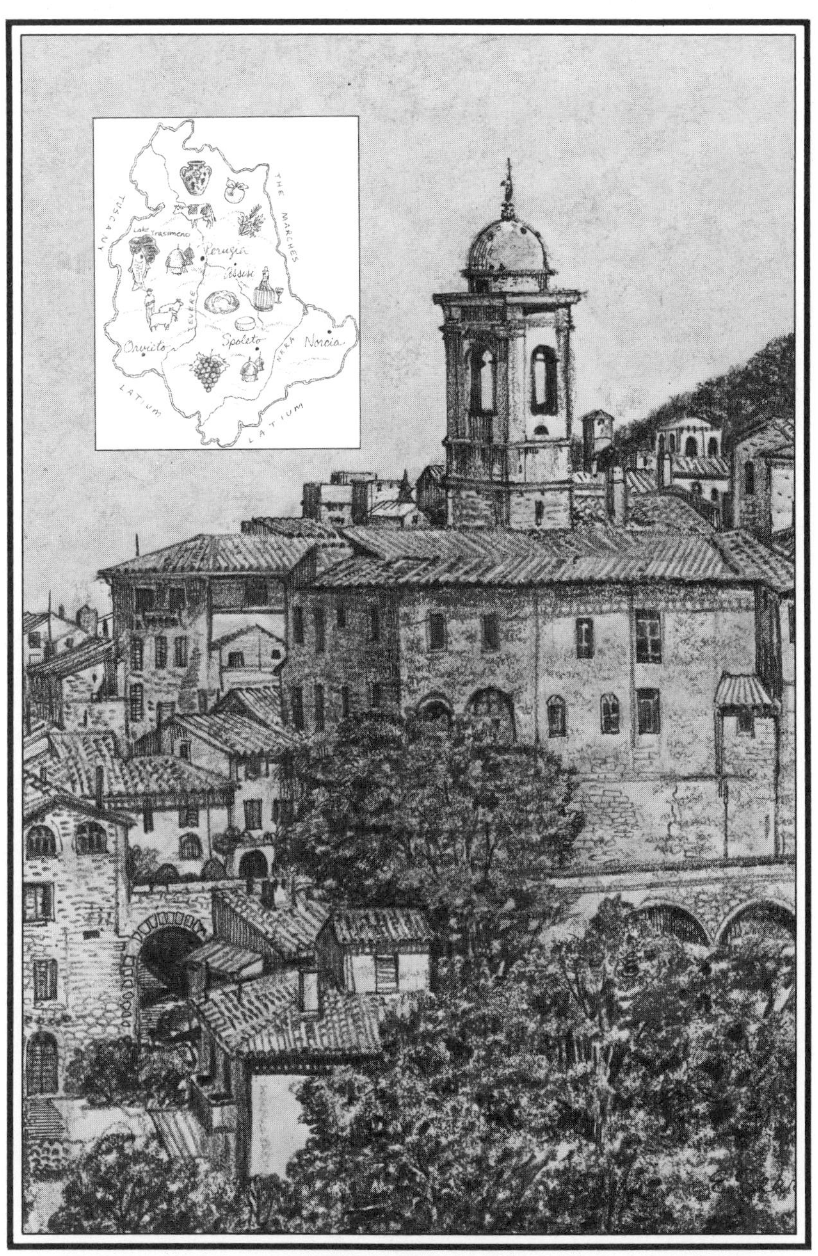

TUSCANY
THE MARCHES
Lake Trasimeno
Perugia
Assisi
TEVERE
Orvieto
Spoleto
NERA
Norcia
LATIUM
LATIUM

Umbria

The Special Wines, Cheeses & Foods of
Umbria

Wines of the Region

Dry reds: *Lungarotti, Rubesco Riserva*

Demi-sec reds: *Rubesco di Torgiano, Sacrantino*

Dry whites: *Orvieto, Torgiano*

Demi-sec white: *Greco di Todi*

Sweet white: *Orvieto*

Wines Available in the United States

Dry reds: *Lungarotti, Rubesco Riserva*

Sweet reds: *Lungarotti, Vin Santo*

Dry whites: *Lungarotti, Orvieto Classico Secco, Tenuta le Velette, Torre di Giano*

Demi-sec white: *Tenuta le Velette*

Sweet white: *Orvieto Classico Abbocato*

Cheeses of the Region

Cacciotte (a sheep's-milk cheese), *Caciofiore, Giuncata* (ricotta-like, salt-free), *Pecorino, Scamorza*

Other Specialties

Black truffles from Norcia, Amelian white figs, sausages, fennel

A chi piace el bere, parla sempre di vino.

He who is fond of drinking, talks always of wine.

Landlocked Umbria is the only region in Italy without an outlet to the sea; however, its hilly valleys are crisscrossed with tumbling rivers and mirrored in the clear expanses of Lake Piediluco and Lake Trasimeno. In Etruscan country the traveler has the feeling that things are much the same as in distant times.

A sharp bend in the road discloses one of Umbria's many walled cities. Gothic or Romanesque, each is girdled by olive trees planted in symmetrical rows. Nearby, fat sheep and pigs share grazing privileges, feeding on the acorns shed by the venerable oaks which shade the fields.

The open-range concept of livestock fattening (rather than forced feeding or penning) makes the pork from the area especially lean yet tender, and the same may be said for the succulent lamb. Wild herbs and the native olive oil are the constants in a cuisine which has remained relatively unchanged for centuries.

The most famous wine of the region comes from Orvieto, a tiny jewel of a medieval city that houses an Etruscan museum. During the annual wine festival, one may wander through the sandstone halls of the museum and imagine drinking from one of the graceful sepia and black-etched wine flasks. One instinctively stretches out a hand to the shining glass cases and longs to drink the fruit of the local vines in the old mode.

The Festival of Corpus Christi has been celebrated in Orvieto since 1264. All of Umbria pays special homage to the church holidays: the Festival of the Dove (also in Orvieto); the Festival of the Waters, held at the spectacular Marmore waterfalls; and the ancient Festival of Forgiveness. All of these occasions are marked with processions, special masses, and much good food. (*Porchetta,* a very special spit-roasted suckling pig, is only one of the traditional festival offerings.)

Not all of the special dishes of Umbria are holiday dishes. Among the other noted regional dishes are *Palombacci allo Spiedo,* roasted wood pigeons; *Agnello all'Arrabbiata,* spit-roasted lamb; *Salumi di Norcia,* a sweet sausage with pine nuts or raisins; *Pasta Aglio e Olio,* a pasta with garlic, olive oil, and ginger; and *Cardi alla Perugina,* breaded and fried cardoons, which are members of the thistle family.

Norcia is a kind of gastronomic cornucopia for the region. Freshwater fish, wood pigeons, and wild hare are spit-roasted, crispy, and flavored subtly by the smoke from a wood fire that uses wild herbs mixed with the kindling. A fundamental, rustic bread dough is common and is used for the local pizza, which is baked on special terracotta (*testi*) ovenware. The large number of sweets are almost all linked to specific *Giorni di Feste* (Feast Days).

Every block of the town has its own purveyor of pickled olives, spicy salamis, and baskets laden with herbs, dried mushrooms, and other fragrant, but not always identifiable (to us), merchandise. The shopkeeper will enter into good-natured haggling with you: hand-signaling and much smacking of lips will finally result in a laden basket and semaphoric instructions as to the best picnic spots. How often do we enjoy the same sort of intimate banter with our local greengrocer, baker, or butcher friends? Fortunately, Italy still retains that graciousness, that "people priority," most marked in the provinces and the smaller urban food shops.

Well, we're off to sample, no, *empty* our basket and raffia-wrapped Chianti di Orvieto. Isn't that the big tree by the brook where our friend from Norcia told us to eat? *Buon appetito!*

Minestra alla Perugina

Perugian Soup

For 4 to 6

2 carrots
1 celery stick
1 leek
1/3 cup olive oil
1 quart broth, or more as needed
1 pound ground beef, crumbled
1 hard-boiled egg
1 quart water
Grated Parmesan cheese

Slice vegetables and sauté in oil. In a separate large saucepan, heat the broth and add the crumbled hamburger. Pass the egg through a coarse sieve and add to the combined broth and vegetables. Add water and cook all together slowly until liquid has reduced by half; vegetables should be mushy. Serve very hot, sprinkled liberally with the Parmesan cheese.

Rotolo di Pasta Ripieno

Stuffed Pasta Rolls

For 6 to 8

This is a recipe culled and adapted from an ancient convent cookbook.

Pasta:

1 recipe Classic 3-Egg Pasta (see page 36)

Make pasta; set aside to relax dough while making the filling (below).

Filling:

1½ pounds spinach
½ pound pork breakfast sausage
1 package (3 ounces) cream cheese, softened
1 cup ricotta cheese
½ cup grated Parmesan cheese
3 eggs
½ teaspoon Bea's Garlic Salt (see page 31)
Dash of freshly grated nutmeg

Steam spinach; drain; squeeze dry and chop. Place in a large bowl. Peel skin off sausages, break up, and sauté over medium heat, pouring off the fat. Add meat to spinach, then add softened cream cheese, ricotta cheese, Parmesan, eggs, garlic salt, and nutmeg. Mix well and correct seasoning.

Divide pasta mass in half. Roll out each half on a floured board until it is 1/16-inch thick, turning it to maintain a rectangular form; trim if necessary. In turn, place each pasta rectangle on a cloth, spread each with half the filling, and roll it up jellyroll fashion. Wrap each pasta roll's cloth around it several times to secure it, and tie the ends with string. Fill a roasting pan with boiling water. Lay the rolls in the water and let them cook gently on top of the stove, rolling over several times, for 45 to 50 minutes. Remove from water and allow to cool. While they cool, prepare the sauce (below) and continue with the recipe.

Sauce:

- 1/2 cup butter
- 1 small onion
- 6 tablespoons tomato paste
- 3/4 cup water
- 1 bouillon cube
- 1/2 cup whipping cream
- Salt and pepper to taste

Sauté the first 3 ingredients together for several minutes until they are sauce consistency and the onion is beginning to turn transparent. Dilute with the water in which you have dissolved the bouillon cube, and continue to cook. When thickened, add the whipping cream. Taste to correct seasoning and discard the onion.

Assembly:

Grated Parmesan cheese as needed

Remove the filled pasta rolls from cloth and cut into 3/4-inch-thick slices. Place cut side down on a deep baking sheet. Pour sauce over slices, sprinkle with Parmesan cheese, and bake in a 400°F. oven for about 5 minutes. Then serve immediately.

Note: If you do not wish the dish as rich or as complicated, simply dribble melted butter over the filled pasta "wheels" and sprinkle with the cheese. Then bake as above.

Agnello Arrabbiata

Spicy Lamb

For 4

A savory recipe that dates from the Middle Ages.

- 3 lamb shoulders
- 2 cloves garlic, crushed
- 4 tablespoons olive oil
- Salt and pepper to taste
- 1 tablespoon chopped parsley
- 1 tablespoon capers, rinsed
- ¼ teaspoon oregano
- ¼ teaspoon mint leaves
- Salt and pepper to taste
- Pinch of cayenne pepper
- 8 Italian pickled olives
- 2 cups white wine
- Juice of 1 lemon

Cut lamb shoulders into bite-sized pieces. Mix garlic, olive oil, salt, and pepper in a large bowl. Marinate the lamb in the garlic marinade for at least 1 hour, turning it from time to time to be sure it is well covered. Put marinade into a large skillet over high heat and add parsley, capers, spices, and olives. Add the lamb. Cook briskly, moving the lamb to prevent scorching. When lamb is nicely browned, reduce the heat and add the white wine; cook, allowing the wine to evaporate. When meat is tender, remove to a heated serving platter. Add the lemon juice to the pan scrapings and pour over the lamb. Serve piping hot.

Scallopine Perugina

Veal, Perugian-Style For 4

Here the delicate flavor of the veal is enhanced by several "exotic" additions. Another recipe from the capital of Umbria.

8 veal scallops
2 tablespoons butter
2 tablespoons olive oil
2 ounces prosciutto, chopped
1 clove garlic, crushed
2 anchovies, rinsed
1 chicken liver, chopped
2 teaspoons capers, rinsed
½ teaspoon grated lemon peel
½ teaspoon sage
Salt and pepper to taste

Sauté veal in a mixture of the butter and oil, cooking for 8 minutes on one side, turning and cooking for 7 minutes on the second side. Remove veal to a warm platter. In same pan, put chopped prosciutto, garlic, anchovies, chicken liver, capers, lemon peel, and sage. Season with salt and pepper. Add more oil and butter if necessary, or if a richer sauce is desired. Stir until liver is cooked. Season the veal lightly and spoon sauce over top. Serve at once.

Filetti di Maiale con Capperi

Pork with Capers For 4

The addition of capers adds distinction — and surprise — to this easy-to-prepare pork dish.

¼ cup olive oil
8 pork scallops
¼ cup red wine
Juice of ½ lemon
Salt and pepper to taste
1 tablespoon capers, rinsed

Heat oil in a large skillet. Brown the pork scallops on both sides. Sprinkle with the red wine and lemon juice. Continue cooking over medium heat until meat is thoroughly cooked and tender. Season with salt and pepper and add the capers. Arrange meat on a warmed serving platter. Allow pan juices to reduce, pour over meat, and serve.

Peti di Pollo Trifolati Sontuoso

Sumptuous Chicken Breasts

For 4

A dish that most certainly must have come from the Renaissance courts. Not difficult to prepare, and memorable even without the truffle.

- Light oil, for frying
- 1 egg
- Salt to taste
- ½ cup flour
- 4 chicken breasts
- ⅓ cup butter
- 4 thin slices prosciutto
- ⅓ cup grated Parmesan cheese
- 8 slices truffle
- ¼ cup cognac
- ½ cup milk or light cream
- 2 cups cooked spinach or peas

Heat light frying oil in a large skillet. Beat egg in a deep plate, and add salt to taste. Flour the chicken breasts, dip in the egg, and flour again. Fry lightly in hot oil; do not allow to brown. Remove. Discard the oil and add the butter to the pan, allowing it to melt. Return the breasts to the pan, and cook slowly, over a very low flame, turning occasionally. Place a prosciutto slice on top of each breast, sprinkle liberally with Parmesan cheese, and top with truffle slices. Continue cooking very slowly for another 20 minutes. Pour the cognac over the tops of the breasts and allow it to evaporate. Then pour milk or light cream over the whole and stir with the pan juices. Remove the chicken to a heated platter over which you have spread a bed of spinach or peas. Cover to keep warm. Stir pan juices, allowing them to reduce if too thin. Correct seasoning, pour over the chicken, and serve at once.

Cardi al Forno

Baked Cardoons

For 4

As we have said before, cardoons are members of the thistle family, kissing cousins with the artichoke. However, in this case, it is the stem rather than the blossom which is eaten. A specialty of Perugia.

1 large cardoon
Juice of 1 lemon
1 teaspoon salt
1 cup flour
2 eggs
2 cups bread crumbs
Oil, for frying

Wash cardoon. Strip away the tough exterior with a potato peeler. Cut into 3-inch pieces and drop in water acidulated with lemon juice. Have a kettle of salted water boiling vigorously and drop in the cardoon pieces. Allow them to cook until just tender; drain and cool. Put flour in a dish while beating the eggs in another receptacle. Then dip the vegetable strips first in the flour, then in the egg, and then into the bread crumbs. Sauté in hot oil and drain on paper towels. Prepare the sauce (below) and continue with the recipe.

Sauce:

6 tablespoons butter
2 chicken livers
3 tablespoons olive oil
½ onion, chopped
½ pound ground beef
3 tomatoes, chopped
1 teaspoon Bea's Garlic Salt (see page 31)
Beef broth as needed
Salt and pepper as needed

In a skillet, melt the butter and sauté the chicken livers; set aside. In olive oil, sauté the onion until transparent. Add ground meat and cook until it begins to sizzle. Add chopped tomatoes and garlic salt, and simmer for 1 hour or more. If sauce becomes too thick or dry, thin with broth. Correct seasoning.

Chop sautéed chicken livers and add to the sauce along with the pan juices.

Assembly:

Butter, for dotting

Put a layer of cardoons in a small casserole, cover with a layer of sauce, and repeat until all cardoons and sauce are used up. The last layer should be meat sauce. Dot with butter and bake in a 400°F. oven for 20 to 25 minutes. Serve very hot.

Note: Grated Parmesan or mozzarella cheese may be added to layers or on top for variety. This recipe also works well with celery or fennel.

Torcolo Perugino

Umbrian Fruitcake

For 8 to 12

This is the classic sweet of Umbria.

- ½ cup seedless raisins
- ½ cup milk
- ¼ cup butter
- ½ cup sugar
- 3 eggs, separated
- 2½ cups flour
- ¼ cup citron, finely chopped
- ¼ cup candied orange peel, finely chopped
- 2 teaspoons anise seeds

Put raisins in hot water to plump. Heat milk and add butter. Beat together the sugar and 2 of the egg yolks. Beat the 3 egg whites until they form peaks, and fold into the beaten yolk mixture.

Preheat the oven to 350°F. On a pastry board, mound the flour. Make a well, pour in the egg mixture, and add in a little of the flour. Add the milk and butter, the drained raisins, chopped fruit, and anise seeds. Knead dough well, adding more flour if too moist or more milk if too dry: the dough should be quite soft. Butter a 10-inch tube pan, put in the dough, and brush the top with the remaining beaten egg yolk. Bake until straw or tester inserted into the cake comes out clean, about 40 minutes. Cool and remove from pan.

Pinoccate

Pine Nut Sweets

Makes 3 to 4 dozen

A specialty of Umbria, these pretty, sweet morsels are a Perugian Christmas treat.

- 3 tablespoons butter, melted
- 2 cups sugar
- ½ cup water
- 1½ cups candied peel (orange or lemon), chopped
- 1½ cups pine nuts

Prepare and have cookie sheets ready, lined with silicon baking paper or baking parchment. Brush paper surfaces lightly with melted butter.

Put sugar and water in saucepan. Place over low heat and cook to dissolve the sugar. Increase the heat, put a candy thermometer in the pan, and when thermometer registers 235°F. ("thread" stage), remove from heat. Beat vigorously until it begins to turn white. Add pine nuts and candied peel. *Work quickly.* If candy mass hardens, put over low heat with a little water to remelt. Continue to heat until thick but still soft. Put ¾-inch opening point on pastry-tube bag and fill with the nut mixture. Press out rosettes the size of quarters on the prepared paper. Let cool before serving.

UMBRIA
TUSCANY
LAKE BOLSENA
Viterbo
ABRUZZI E MOLISE
ROME
Frosinone
Latine
TYRRHENIAN SEA
CAMPANIA

Latium/Rome

The Special Wines, Cheeses & Sweets of
Latium/Rome

Wines of the Region

Demi-sec reds: *Cecubo, Merlot di Aprilia, Sangiovese di Aprilia, Velletri Rosso**

*There is no true "dry" red from this region.

Dessert red: *Moscato di Terracin*

Dry whites: *Cannellino di Frascati, Colli Albani, Est! Est! Est!, Falerno, Marino, Montecompatri, Zagarolo*

Demi-sec whites: *Cannellino di Frascati, Colli Lanuvini, Est! Est! Est!, Marino*

Dessert whites: *Cannellino di Frascati, Aleatico di Gradoli, Velletri (dolce)*

Wines Available in the United States

Demi-sec reds: *Boncampagni Ludovisi, Fiorano Rosso*

Dry whites: *Antinori, Est! Est! Est! di Montifiascone, Frascati Superiore, Gotto d'Oro*

Cheeses of the Region

Caciotta Romana, Fiore Molle, Mozzarella di Bufala, Pecorino Piccante, Provatura, Ricotta

Special Sweets

Crostate, Gelato, Maritozzi con la Panna, Pizza Dolce.

Il vino porta gioia la cuore e felicita' all' anima!

Wine brings joy to the heart and happiness to the soul!

Acknowledged as one of the great world cities, Rome and her seven hills are the fabled vault of a culinary wealth that is both ancient and constantly accruing.

Everywhere in Italy moderation at table is difficult, but in Rome it is practically impossible. Her epicurean pleasures are impossible to compute; but why try? Rome is an "open to the public" Fort Knox of food.

Just as New York would want to be considered the culinary showcase of the Northeast Coast; Chicago, the menu-maker for the Midwest; and Los Angeles would battle San Francisco for that title on the West Coast, so it is with Rome in Italy.

The early Romans believed, as do their modern descendants, that a laden table and overflowing wine carafes are marks of civilized and rational living. The laughter heard in the streets in front of every restaurant attests to the pleasure that is the privilege of dining well. Overindulgence is an omnipresent lure. While our American pioneer fathers practiced frugality, the Roman ancients blurred the lines between gastronomy and gluttony.

In Rome, all of the regional delights come together — from the humblest fare in a tiny *trattoria* in Trastevere to the elegant excesses of the Via Veneto's Hotel Excelsior.

By contrast, the tables of the rest of the region of Latium are plainly stocked with a limited but vigorous cookery that relies on lard, olive oil, and bacon, blended into what is known as *battuto.* The generous spirit of the *osterie* of Frosinone, Latina, Rieti, Viterbo, and the picturesque towns between, is a joy to experience — and all the more so as it is shared with the merry, rotund proprietors of these simple inns. Here, one has the opportunity to greet the *true* Italy: unpretentious, life-loving, and above all, *appassionati* of *food;* food that is fresh, plentiful, and cooked and consumed with enthusiastic appreciation. So we have Latium, the classic contrast of urban and rural, and hand in hand, the values innate in each lifestyle.

Any list of the culinary specialties of Latium and its great center city, Rome, only scratches the surface. The sampling given here merely indicates the rich variety: *Lumache,* snails in a ginger sauce; *Crostini alla Provatura,* a Roman version of our popular grilled cheese sandwich; *Spaghetti alla Carbonara,* an egg, bacon, and cheese-sauced pasta; *Abbacchio alla Romana,* a spicy roasted lamb; *Involtini,* meat rolls; *Trippa alla Romana,* Roman-style tripe; *Cipolline in Agro Dolce,* sweet and sour onions in tomato sauce; and *Suppli al Telefono,* rice cakes with a mozzarella center. Happily, recipes for a number of the fine Latium/Rome dishes follow.

Pizza Margherita

Roman-Style Pizza

For 4 to 6

This classic pizza is found in both the Campania and the areas around Rome. Whoever Margherita was, her ingredients never vary; if the succulent dish bears her name, this is the way it will be made.

- 1 recipe Basic Pizza Dough (see page 263)
- 4 or 5 large fresh tomatoes or 1 can (1 pound) plum tomatoes, crushed and drained
- Salt to taste
- ⅓ cup grated pecorino cheese
- 1 tablespoon chopped fresh basil
- 4 ounces mozzarella cheese, sliced
- Sprinklng of oregano
- ¼ cup olive oil

Roll dough into a round about 13 inches in diameter, and let it rest a few minutes. Then place it gently in a large pizza pan. With hands, spread dough out to the edges, making indentations around the outside edge with your thumbs and pressing the dough onto the edge of the pan. Purée tomatoes, and arrange over dough. Salt to taste. Spread with grated cheese and chopped basil. Spread a layer of the sliced mozzarella, sprinkle with oregano, and dribble olive oil over the entire surface. Heat oven to 475°F. Put pizza on the lowest rack. Bake until underside of pizza is golden (about 30 minutes).

Salsa Verde

Roman Green Sauce

Makes ½ cup

- 1 bunch Italian parsley
- 1 hard-boiled egg
- 2 anchovies
- 3 gherkin pickles (*cornichons*)
- 1 tablespoon capers, rinsed
- 2 tablespoons celery leaves
- 1 thick slice onion
- 1 teaspoon Bea's Garlic Salt (see page 31)
- ¼ cup olive oil

Place all ingredients except the olive oil in a food processor or blender and chop (do not purée). Add olive oil, stirring constantly until well blended. Serve with boiled meats or on salads.

Salsa Verde Cevolani

Green Sauce

Makes 2 to 3 cups

This sauce or dressing is delicious all by itself over a bed of lettuce. However, its more familiar use is as an accompaniment to Bollito Misto *(the Italian New England boiled dinner, recipe on page 60).*

- 2 bunches scallions
- 1 red pepper
- ½ cup chopped parsley
- 1 clove garlic, crushed
- 1 cup olive oil
- ½ teaspoon dry mustard
- 1 teaspoon capers, rinsed and chopped
- 2 hard-boiled eggs, finely chopped
- 3 anchovies, rinsed and mashed
- Salt and pepper to taste
- ⅓ cup vinegar

Finely chop the vegetables and parsley in a bowl. Add crushed garlic, olive oil, mustard, and chopped capers. Prepare the eggs and anchovies, add to vegetable mix, and season to taste. Add vinegar just before ready to use. Spoon into lettuce cups or over salad greens or vegetables.

Salsa Quattro Formaggi

Four-Cheese Sauce

For 4 to 6

Beatrice's comment on this Roman sauce is that it's "wonderful served on tagliatelle *or rice." Lotte's comment is that it's "wonderful on anything!"*

- ½ cup butter
- 1¼ cups heavy cream
- ⅔ cup diced Fontina cheese
- ⅔ cup diced Emmenthaler cheese
- ⅔ cup Parmesan cheese, grated
- ¼ cup diced provolone cheese

Place enough water in the bottom of a double boiler to heat the contents of the upper saucepan; pan should not sit "in" the water. Add butter and allow to melt. Add cream. When warm, add the cheeses, stirring constantly over a low flame. When all the cheese has melted, the sauce should be creamy. Keep warm in top of the double boiler until ready to serve.

Note: Swiss cheese is similar to Emmenthaler and may be used.

Spaghetti alla Carbonara

Spaghetti with Egg, Bacon and Cheese

For 4

Rome is generally credited with being the originator of this favorite. In truth, the woodsmen of the Apennines who made charcoal were the inspiration for this unusually filling pasta dish.

- ¼ pound unsmoked bacon, cut into small pieces
- 2 tablespoons olive oil
- 2 tablespoons butter
- 2 cloves garlic, crushed
- 3 eggs
- 3 tablespoons Parmesan cheese
- 3 tablespoons pecorino cheese
- Salt and pepper to taste
- 1 pound spaghetti, cooked *al dente*

Fry bacon pieces in a mixture of the oil and butter. Add garlic, and when it begins to color, remove and discard. Break eggs into bowl and beat well with both cheeses and pepper to taste. Put hot cooked spaghetti into the pan with the bacon and oil, and toss. Pour in egg mixture and continue mixing until eggs look like yellow cream. Season to taste, and transfer spaghetti onto a hot serving platter.

Fettuccine "Alfredo" Lazzaro

For 6

This is Beatrice's splendid rendition of the international favorite.

- ½ pound cream cheese
- 2 tablespoons milk
- 1 recipe *fettuccine* (use Classic 3-Egg Pasta recipe on page 36)
- 1¼ sticks (10 tablespoons) butter, softened
- 1 cup grated Parmesan cheese
- 1 cup heavy cream
- Salt and pepper to taste

Whip cream cheese with milk until very soft. Boil *fettuccine al dente* in salted water. Drain, and return pasta to kettle, keeping hot over a tiny flame. Add whipped cream cheese, butter, ½ cup grated Parmesan cheese, heavy cream, and salt and pepper. Keep tossing until pasta is totally covered and glistens with the sauce. Serve immediately, sprinkled with the remaining ½ cup Parmesan cheese.

Note: Use the bulk cream cheese purchased in delicatessens or cooperative food centers.

Suppli

Fried Rice Balls For 6 to 8

A Roman favorite, a variation of which is native to Sicily. The recipe given here is the Roman version. Adding ground meat, sausage, and peas to the center changes the name to the Sicilian arancine. *By either name, a treat!*

- ¾ cup raw rice to make about 2 cups cooked
- 4 eggs
- ⅔ cup grated cheese (half and half pecorino and Parmesan)
- 3 cups bread crumbs
- Salt and pepper to taste
- 6 to 8 small slices of mozzarella cheese
- 2 tablespoons water
- Blend of olive and vegetable oils, for frying

Cook rice. Then, while rice is still warm, break in 2 of the eggs. Add ⅓ cup of the grated cheese, and salt and pepper, if desired. Stir well to blend; refrigerate to cool. Put a ball of rice in your hand, top with a slice of mozzarella cheese, cover with more rice, and shape into a ball. Dip ball in a mixture of the remaining 2 eggs and water, and roll in a mix of the bread crumbs and ⅓ cup grated cheese. Fry in the blend of oils until brown. Serve at once, plain or with tomato sauce.

Abbacchio alla Romana

Baby Lamb, Roman-Style For 4 to 6

We've spoken about suckling lamb — this is the recipe that started it all. Ask your butcher for the youngest, tenderest member of his "flock."

- 3 tablespoons olive oil
- 2 tablespoons butter
- 2 cloves garlic
- 2 to 3 pounds young lamb, cut into bite-sized chunks
- 2 sprigs rosemary
- 2 anchovies
- 1 tablespoon white vinegar
- 1 tablespoon Bea's Garlic Salt (see page 31)
- White wine as needed

Melt olive oil and butter in a heavy skillet and sauté garlic until light golden in color. Remove garlic. Add the lamb and brown on all sides. Bruise rosemary leaves, rinse anchovies, and blend with vinegar and garlic salt. Add to the lamb, continuing to cook over a medium flame until vinegar evaporates and the meat is tender. If meat appears dry, moisten with white wine. Place meat on a heated serving platter, pour the sauce over it, and serve at once.

Note: Some of the ancient recipes add lamb kidneys to the dish. This works well if the lamb is a bit older; however the flavor may be too strong. Use your own judgment and your family's tastes to decide. The kidneys should be cleaned and cooked at the same time as the meat, and treated in the same manner.

Agnello Arrosto Lazzaro

Roast Lamb, Lazzaro-Style For 6

There is lamb, and there is lamb in Rome and its environs. This recipe can be found all over Italy, but it reaches a perfection of refinement in Rome itself. This is Beatrice's own recipe.

- 1 leg spring lamb
- 2 tablespoons rosemary
- 2 tablespoons parsley
- 1 teaspoon marjoram
- 1/8 teaspoon thyme
- 2 cloves garlic, crushed
- 1½ teaspoons salt
- ½ cup olive oil
- ½ cup butter, for dotting
- 1 teaspoon fresh ground pepper
- 6 potatoes, partially boiled
- 2 cups rosé wine

Clean leg of lamb and remove the cartilage from the ankle part of the leg. Place leg in a roasting pan.

In a food processor or using a mortar and pestle, grind the herbs, garlic, and salt together until they make a very fine paste. Poke some of this herb paste into small slits in the leg. Pour olive oil over the meat, and sprinkle with remaining herbs. Dot with butter and grind black pepper over the entire surface.

Preheat the oven to 475°F. Place lamb in oven and allow to sear for 15 minutes. Reduce heat to 325°F. Place the partially boiled potatoes around the roast. Continue cooking until a meat thermometer registers 155° to 160°F (the correct temperature for medium-rare lamb). Baste the roast frequently during the cooking process with the rosé wine, and turn the potatoes frequently so that they brown nicely.

Pollo alla Romana

Chicken, Roman-Style

For 4 to 6

The cross-pollination of recipes is nowhere more noticeable than in the country cuisine of Italy. This recipe is made in the identical way in the Marches with the exception of the use of tarragon as a flavoring.

- 1 chicken (about 3 pounds)
- ¼ cup olive oil
- ½ stick (4 tablespoons) butter, melted
- 1 teaspoon Bea's Garlic Salt (see page 31)
- 1 clove garlic, chopped
- ½ teaspoon chopped rosemary
- ¼ teaspoon dried tarragon
- ⅔ cup dry white wine
- ¼ cup tomato paste
- 1 cup chicken broth

Wash chicken, cut into serving pieces, and pat dry. Brush with mixture of olive oil, melted butter, and garlic salt. Put remainder of the oil-butter mix in a skillet and add the chicken. Cook over moderate heat, turning frequently, until browned on all sides. Add seasonings. Pour in the wine and allow it to evaporate over fairly high heat. Stir in tomato paste and add the broth; blend well, cover, and simmer for 30 to 40 minutes. Remove chicken to a heated serving platter. Let sauce thicken over a high flame, and pour over the chicken. This dish is usually served with a medley of fresh green peas and mushrooms.

Note: You may substitute a ½-pound can of tomatoes for the tomato paste; the flavor will be a little more delicate.

Spinaci alla Romana

Spinach, Roman-Style For 4

Propaganda to the contrary, Rome, not Florence, is really the seat of the true spinach lovers — and here is a green delight to impress the most elegant guest list.

- 3 tablespoons raisins
- 2½ pounds spinach
- ¼ cup butter
- 2 tablespoons olive oil
- 1 clove garlic
- 2 tablespoons pine nuts
- Salt to taste

Soak raisins in hot water to plump. Wash and steam spinach; when cooked, drain and cool; then squeeze dry. In a skillet, put butter, olive oil, and garlic. Fry garlic 2 minutes and remove. Add spinach, pine nuts, and raisins. Mix well; cook 5 to 10 minutes. Add salt to taste and serve immediately.

Carciofi alla Giudia

Artichokes, Judaic-Style For 6

One of the special Roman ways to serve these tender, green relatives of the thistle family — elegantly understated and wildly desirable for all that! The early Romans visited the Jewish ghettos to savor this delicacy.

- 12 tender small artichokes
- Juice of 1 lemon
- Salt and pepper to taste
- 1½ cups olive oil

Clean artichokes and remove tough outer leaves. Cut across tops about ¼ inch down; open, and with very sharp knife, cut around centers. Then scoop out thorny "chokes." Soak in water and lemon juice for 15 minutes. Hold artichokes upside down and press down hard to flatten and spread out leaves. Drain and dry. Sprinkle inside with salt and pepper. Place artichokes upside down in a skillet. Pour in the olive oil, and cook over low heat for 10 minutes, moving them around, turning them on their sides and finally, right side up, with the heat turned up a little, let them crisp. Cook another 10 minutes and serve.

Misticanza

Roman Mixed Salad

For 6

Waverly Root declares that this is the only salad native to Rome. Trying to trace the ancient roots of food customs is always fascinating, often frustrating, and seldom verifiable, so we graciously doff our hats to Mr. Root and give you this recipe, which we evolved from enjoying the dish with friends of ours from La Latina.

1 bunch roquette (ruca)
1 head of Romaine lettuce
3 large ripe tomatoes
2 medium fennel bulbs
12 small radishes
½ cup olive oil
2 to 3 tablespoons Balsamic vinegar
Salt and pepper to taste

Wash the roquette and lettuce thoroughly, reserving the outer leaves for other use. Crisp and dry in a cloth. Slice the tomatoes in quarters; squeeze slightly to remove excess moisture. Scrape the outside of the fennel bulbs with a potato peeler to remove the stringy portions and slice lengthwise into thin slivers. Make tiny radish roses.

Assemble by putting 2 lettuce leaves with several roquette leaves on the bottom of a chilled, flat salad plate. Place 2 tomato wedges on one side, stack a fair share of the fennel in a pretty, miniature haystack on the other side, and adorn each plate with radish roses. Prepare a dressing of the olive oil and vinegar, seasoned to taste, and pour over the salad just before serving. Top with a grating of freshly ground pepper.

Torta di Ricotta Lazzaro

Ricotta Pie — For 12

Imagine yourself picnicking in the Parco Borghese. The grass is cool and green, the pie is sweet, and your bottle of wine cool and relaxing.

Pasta:

1 recipe *Pasta Frolla* (see page 158)

Make pasta; set aside while you prepare filling.

Filling:

- 1½ pounds ricotta cheese
- ½ pound cream cheese
- ¼ cup dried sponge cake crumbs
- ¼ cup butter, softened
- Rind of 1 lemon, grated
- 1 cup confectioners' sugar
- 2 egg yolks, plus 1 whole egg
- ¼ cup brandy or rum
- ½ teaspoon vanilla

Beat together the ricotta cheese, cream cheese, cake crumbs, butter, lemon rind, and sugar until soft and well blended. Add 2 egg yolks, the whole egg, brandy, and vanilla. Beat to blend all the ingredients.

Assembly:

Roll out *Pasta Frolla* dough and fit into a 10-inch pie plate. Cut extra dough away from around the top edge of the plate. *Do not stretch dough when fitting into plate.* Pour in ricotta filling. Use extra dough to make strips for lattice top, then twist a long, slender strip and place it around top of plate to cover lattice ends.

Preheat the oven to 350°F. Bake pie for 30 minutes or more, or until crust is brown on bottom. If it seems to be taking too long, lower the rack and bake for a few minutes more.

Maritozzi alla Romana

Lenten Buns

Makes 12 buns

It is said that, in Rome, one's nose knows that it is Lent because of the communal odor of the baking maritozzi. *Read through the recipe, or better still, bake some* maritozzi, *and you will discover their kinship with our Easter Hot Cross Buns.*

- 3 cups flour
- 1 package (scant tablespoon) dry yeast
- ½ cup warm water
- 2 eggs
- ½ cup granulated sugar
- 1½ teaspoons salt
- 2 tablespoons olive oil
- ⅔ cup golden raisins, plumped
- ⅓ cup pine nuts
- 2 tablespoons chopped citron
- 2 tablespoons chopped candied orange peel
- 3 tablespoons butter, for pans
- ¾ cup confectioners' sugar
- 1 tablespoon boiling water
- ¼ teaspoon vanilla

In a bowl, sift the flour, and make a well. Put the yeast and warm water mix in the center, pulling in a little of the flour to make a semifirm batter. When it becomes bubbly, add eggs, granulated sugar, salt, and olive oil. Draw the remaining flour into the well, little by little, forming a dough with your hands. Turn the dough out onto a floured board. Knead until the dough is smooth and elastic. Place in a buttered bowl, turn once, and cover with plastic wrap.

Prewarm oven to 100°F. Turn the oven off and put dough inside to rise. Remove when doubled in bulk. Put dough on a breadboard, punch down, and make a hole in the center. Put in the raisins, pine nuts, chopped citron, and orange peel. Pull and knead to incorporate fruit and nuts into dough. When well mixed, break dough into 12 pieces, and shape each into a flat, oblong bun. Put buns on buttered sheet pans, leaving several inches between each bun. Let rise for 4 to 6 hours or until they are doubled in size. When ready, preheat the oven to 425°. Bake buns 15 to 20 minutes or until they are golden brown.

While buns are cooling, make a glaze of the confectioners' sugar, boiling water, and vanilla, and brush over the tops of the baked buns.

Pizza Dolce all'Antica

Dessert Pizza — For 8 to 10

Another ancient recipe, as the name implies. More a yeast cake than what we think of as a pizza. It makes a marvelous duo with a steaming cup of espresso *or* cappuccino. *Traditionally, in Rome, it is baked as a breakfast bread.*

- 1 pound Basic Pizza Dough (see page 263) or your own favorite bread dough
- 2/3 cup butter, softened
- 3/4 cup granulated sugar
- 1/2 teaspoon cinnamon
- 1/2 teaspoon salt
- 5 eggs, well beaten, plus 1 whole egg
- 1/4 cup minced citron
- 1/4 cup candied orange rind, chopped

Mix the butter into the dough. Add the sugar, cinnamon, and salt. Incorporate the 5 beaten eggs, citron, and chopped orange rind. Keep working the dough until it is smooth and light. Put ball of dough in buttered 10-inch spring-form pan. Press down with hands to even the surface and push out any trapped air. Cover with a towel and allow to rise overnight in a draft-free place. This bread requires a long rising period.

Preheat the oven to 375°F. Beat the single egg and brush it over the top of the dough. Bake 40 minutes. Serve plain, or with butter and jam.

Torta Gelata di Amaretto

Amaretto Ice Cream Pie

For 12

The Americanization of the Defazio family dates back to 1898 when Salvatore Defazio Sr. left Gaeta (Latium) at the age of 25. This recipe from a modern-day Defazio and the following are two New World adaptations of old Latium country dessert favorites.

24 chocolate sandwich cookies
1 quart vanilla ice cream
1 quart chocolate ice cream
4 ounces semisweet chocolate bits
2 cups whipping cream
3 tablespoons confectioners' sugar
½ cup amaretto
Chocolate shavings
Slivered almonds (optional)

Crush cookies in a blender or with a rolling pin. Press crumbs against bottom of a spring-form pan and ½ inch up the sides. *Do not mix with butter.* Bake 5 minutes in a 375°F. oven and let cool. Let vanilla ice cream stand at room temperature until partially soft and spread over chilled crust. Return to freezer. Place chocolate ice cream in a bowl to soften slightly. Melt chocolate bits in a double boiler and stir into chocolate ice cream until chips form in the ice cream. Pour mixture over vanilla ice cream. Whip cream sweetened with confectioners' sugar. Then add the amaretto; whip again until stiff, and spread over the pie. Decorate with chocolate shavings and slivered almonds if desired. Freeze, covered with foil. When ready to serve, cut with knife dipped in hot water.

Biscuit Tortoni di Cioccolata

Chocolate Biscuit Tortoni

Makes 12

The origins of this Italo-American favorite are clouded in mystery. Part of the confusion lies in that much of the world classifies it as a kind of ice cream, when in reality it is a frozen mousse. Whatever its ancestry, it is the perfect light ending for a hearty meal.

- 1½ cups chilled whipping cream
- ½ cup sugar
- 1 cup almond macaroon or vanilla wafer crumbs (24 cookies), reserving small portion for topping
- ½ cup toasted almonds, chopped
- ⅓ cup cocoa
- ¼ cup maraschino cherries, drained and chopped, plus 12 halves for garnish
- 1 to 2 tablespoons rum or dry sherry
- 1 teaspoon vanilla

Beat whipping cream and sugar in a chilled bowl with chilled beaters until stiff. Fold remaining ingredients into whipped cream. Divide, filling 2 small (2-inch) muffin tins or lined with the small paper cupcake wrappers. Sprinkle with reserved crumbs and decorate with a cherry half. Freeze until firm, at least 4 hours.

Granita di Caffè

Coffee Ice

For 8 to 10

- 2 cups ground Italian coffee
- 5 to 6 cups boiling water
- ½ cup sugar

Make drip *espresso* coffee, keeping water boiling, and pouring a little water at a time over the coffee grounds in filter paper. Add sugar to coffee, sweetening to taste. Freeze in same manner as for *Granita di Limone* (following).

Granita di Limone

Lemon Ice For 4 to 6

Here are two versions of an icy froth that deserves better than our usual title of "ice" or "sherbet." Try the golden version first, then treat your palate to the second, and then experiment with any favorite fresh fruit.

- 3 cups water
- ¾ cup sugar
- 1½ cups lemon juice
- Rind of 1 lemon, grated
- 1 egg white, beaten

Boil sugar and water, and add to combined lemon juice and grated rind. Add beaten egg white to the mixture. Put in a bowl and freeze. During freezing process, whip several times to mix surface ice with liquid underneath. This must be done 4 or 5 times to crystallize the entire amount of liquid and to make uniform, tiny ice shavings.

Abruzzi e Molise

The Special Wines, Cheeses & Sweets of
Abruzzi e Molise

Wines of the Region

Demi-sec red: *Cerasuolo d'Abruzzo* ("festive red for special occasions")

Demi-sec dark rosé: *Montepulcino d'Abruzzo*

Demi-sec whites: *Peligno, Trebbiano d'Abruzzo*

Wines Available in the United States

Dry reds: *Emidio Pepe, Dragani*

Demi-sec dark rosé: *Montepulcino d'Abruzzo*

Dry white: *Dragani*

Demi-sec white: *Trebbiano d'Abruzzo*

Dry sparkling rosé: *Cerasuolo d'Abruzzo, Dragani*

Cheeses of the Region

Butirri (with butter core), *Caciocavallo di Pescocostanzo, Fior di Latte Abruzzese, Pecorino, Ricotta, Scamorze di Rivisondoli*

Special Sweets

Cauciunitti (incorporating wine, olive oil, candied fruits, and nuts), *Confetti* (sugar-coated almonds of Sulmona used in the region for garlands, centerpieces, and as magical symbols), *Parozzo* (chocolate-glazed sweet from Pescara), *Taralli* (dried fruits iced with sugar), *Torrone* (chocolate-coated nougat made with nuts and dried figs), and *Zeppole* (cinnamon-flavored fritters for St. Joseph's Day).

Chi si contenta, gode.

He who is satisfied is happy.

"Austere," "imposing," and "harsh" are the adjectives one encounters in descriptions of the climate and economy of the Abruzzi e Molise area of central Italy. To a visitor, the reasons for such a dismal appraisal are not always apparent, or even important. What haunts the heart and the senses is the majesty of her Apennine goliaths, the rush of the rivers that interlace her plains and marshlands, and the sober integrity of villagers whose passage of time is marked by common observances of the changes of season — the national, family, and church holidays.

Traditionalists in every sense of the word, the Abruzzesi and Molise consider themselves "simple folk." Their colorful, hand-embroidered regional costumes are merrily worn for saints' days, harvest *feste,* and for the celebration of the happiest and most revered of ceremonies: the wedding. The world's notion of *the* Italian wedding certainly started here! Years dedicated to the fashioning of handmade lace-edged trousseau items are rewarded by marriage feasts and dancing to the music of the *ciarmelle* or *cornamuse* (bagpipes), and by days marked with happy reverence in the great books of the church, the hearts of the young, and the memories of the aged.

Food is important to all Italians, but the Abruzzesi punctuates each day with its preparation and appreciation. A strange metal and wood apparatus is to be found in every Abruzzi kitchen. It is called a *chitarra* (guitar), but it is not used for music-making. Rather, it is used for the splendid fashioning of the local specialty *Maccheroni alla Chitarra.* For this dish, a rectangle of pasta is laid over parallel steel wires and a rolling pin passed over the pasta, cutting it into slender strips. Topped with the local sauce and cheese, the dish is a filling and fragrant tribute to the food craft of these mountain folk.

Other specialty dishes of the Abruzzi e Molise region include *Brodetto,* a fish stew of vegetables, spices and vinegar; *Pincigrassi,* a pie of pasta, cheese, meatballs, and bechamella sauce; *Porchetta,* roast pig stuffed with rosemary, garlic, and pepper; *Salsicce di Fegato,* pig's liver sausage made with garlic and orange peel; and *Scapece,* fried fish pickled in saffron and vinegar (a favorite for over 200 years).

Seasonal food festivals honoring benevolent saints and the Great Purveyor of propitious crop conditions are many; among them, the Ortona Grape Festival, the strawberry festival of Capistrello, and the *Maielletta* and pork festivals at both Ripa Teatina and Campli.

Another exceptional rite of the region, although not food related, is the Procession of the Serpents. Held the first Thursday in May, it is said to be linked to the ancient cult of Dea Angizia. Here we encounter the bifocal attitudes and celebrations which predominate throughout the Mezzogiorno of Italy, the harmonious (or perhaps unconscious) coexistence of Christian and pagan beliefs.

Many might classify another culinary ritual of the region, the *panarda,* as a bacchanal. The *panarda* is a nonstop eating and drinking marathon and can be initiated by almost any valid reason for a party! The basic number of courses needed to qualify for this event is said to be thirty, but as many as twice that number have been recorded. It is boasted that the tower of cloth napkins used during a *panarda* would reach the top of the Basilica of San Bernardino in l'Aquila!

However, one of the loveliest culinary rituals — and a religious one — is the Abruzzi Christmas Eve dinner served before the holiday's midnight mass. You will find the menu and the recipes for this very special time grouped at the end of this section.

A traveler who goes to Italy only to "play" may not appreciate the Abruzzi e Molise, but if he or she goes to feast the eyes on grandiose scenery, nourish the soul, and happily fill the stomach, then this is a region to visit!

Zuppa di Sposalizio

Abruzzi Wedding Soup

For 8

Next to the bride, the Abruzzi wedding guests pay most attention to this traditional soup. But don't wait for a special occasion; make a pot right now, and it's even better on the second day.

Basic Chicken Broth:

- 1 roasting chicken (about 5 pounds)
- 2 cloves garlic
- 2 medium onions
- 2 whole carrots
- 2 celery stalks, with leaves

Clean and cover chicken with about 4 quarts water. Add garlic and vegetables and cook until skin retracts from the legs. Set aside to cool. Degrease broth as much as possible.

Mini-Meatballs:

- 2 slices bread
- ½ cup milk
- 1 pound ground beef
- ¼ pound ground pork
- 2 eggs
- 1 teaspoon Bea's Garlic Salt (see page 31)

In a bowl, wet the bread with the milk and squeeze dry. Add all other ingredients, working the mass with your fingers until well mixed. Form meatballs the size of marbles.

Assembly:

- Salt and pepper to taste
- 1 large head escarole
- 1 pound small pasta (optional)
- ⅓ cup grated pecorino cheese

Taste broth, and adjust seasoning. Remove chicken and skin; bone, and break meat into bite-sized pieces. Strain broth, discarding the vegetables. Wash the escarole well, towel it dry, and chop it into medium-sized pieces. Drop into broth and cook for several minutes; then add the meatballs. (A small pasta may be added at this time if desired — *semi di pepe,* egg bows, etc.) When all ingredients are cooked, add the chicken pieces and heat for several minutes, just until the meat is warmed. Serve in pretty soup bowls with grated cheese.

Zuppa di Lenticchie

Lentil Soup, Abruzzi-Style

For 4 to 6

A heavy hand with the pepper mill is an Abruzzi characteristic. This universal soup adds pasta to make it a "meal in a bowl."

- ½ pound dried lentils
- 2 onions
- 2 stalks celery
- 1 clove garlic
- 1 carrot
- 4 tablespoons olive oil
- 1 tablespoon butter
- Ham or pork bones
- 2½ quarts water
- 1 cup cooked small variety macaroni (about ½ cup raw)
- Generous grinding of black pepper

Soak lentils overnight in water to cover. In a food processor or blender, chop onions, celery, garlic, and carrot. In a large (5-quart) soup kettle, sauté chopped vegetables in a mixture of oil and butter. When almost dry, add lentils, bones, and water, and simmer until lentils are tender. Add cooked macaroni to the soup just long enough before serving to heat it through thoroughly. Then serve piping hot with a generous amount of freshly ground black pepper.

Vermicelli in Salsa Abruzzese

Fine Noodles, Abruzzi-Style

For 4

Meat is not an Abruzzi mainstay. Fresh vegetables, which grow in abundance, are used to flavor and color the excellent regional dishes. Here we have the brilliant yellow of squash flowers and saffron coloring a superb sauce.

- 1 medium onion
- ½ cup parsley
- 1 bunch squash flowers (about 1½ dozen)
- ¼ cup olive oil
- Pinch of saffron
- 1 cup hot broth, or more as needed
- Salt and pepper to taste
- 1 egg yolk, well beaten
- 3 tablespoons grated pecorino cheese, with extra for garnish
- 1 pound *vermicelli* pasta
- Freshly ground pepper to taste (optional)

Chop together the onion, parsley, and squash flowers. Put the olive oil in a skillet, and sauté the vegetables. Then steep the saffron in the hot broth; pour into the skillet and cook over medium heat, stirring frequently, for about 20 minutes. Strain through a food mill or purée in blender or food processor, adding more broth if the sauce is not liquid enough. Season to taste. Simmer for a few minutes, then add the well-beaten egg yolk and stir in the cheese.

Cook the *vermicelli* in boiling, salted water *al dente* and drain. Place in a deep serving bowl, pouring the golden sauce over the top. Add more grated cheese to garnish and freshly ground pepper if you like.

Maltagliate (Strenghozze)

Pasta with Lamb Sauce

For 4

Maltagliate *means "poorly cut" in classic Italian.* Strenghozze *is the same word in the dialect of the Mezzogiorno. The sauce is Beatrice's version of* Sugo d'Agnello Buon Gustaio di Chieti, *an Abruzzi staple lamb sauce.*

Pasta:

1 recipe Classic 2-Egg Pasta (see page 36)

Make pasta. Follow instructions for the preparation of the dough, but cut according to sketch.

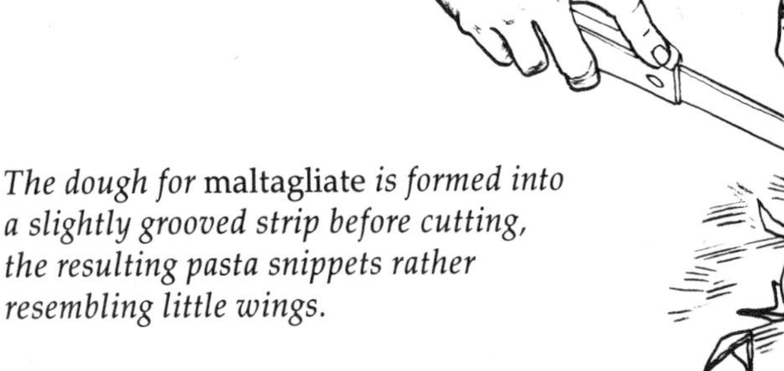

The dough for maltagliate *is formed into a slightly grooved strip before cutting, the resulting pasta snippets rather resembling little wings.*

Sauce:

- 1 medium onion
- 1 or 2 sprigs fresh rosemary
- 1 slice unsmoked bacon
- ¾ pound lamb shoulder
- Salt and pepper to taste
- 1 pound fresh tomatoes
- 1 can (1 pound) tomatoes
- ¾ cup white wine
- Water or broth as needed
- Grated cheese of choice

Chop together the onion, rosemary, and bacon. Sauté in saucepan until brown. Trim and flake (cut into small pieces) the lamb and brown in the bacon mixture. Season to taste. Peel, seed, and chop the fresh tomatoes and add them, along with the canned, to the tomato sauce. Add the wine and cook for 1½ hours over a very low flame; add water or broth if necessary during the cooking.

Cook the *maltagliate al dente*. Drain. Then spoon the sauce over the top, and serve with cheese of your preference.

Crespelli Ripiene d'Aquila

Crêpes, Aquila-Style — For 6

This crêpe dish is from the monument-studded city of Aquila. Although the hard-working folk of the Abruzzi also use pasta casalinga *(homemade), crêpes are often substituted and used in this part of Italy as a delicious base for the local cheeses and sauces. They are not always rolled into tubes but are sometimes layered flat into casseroles (as in* timballos*), featuring bits of meat, vegetables, and cheese mixed and melted together.*

Crêpe Batter:

- 2 cups flour
- 4 eggs
- ⅓ cup butter, melted
- 1¾ cups milk
- Salt to taste

Mix all ingredients and beat until smooth. Strain into a bowl, cover, and let stand for about 1 hour.

Filling:

- ¾ pound ground beef
- 1 medium onion, finely chopped
- 2 tablespoons oil
- 2 tablespoons butter
- 1 cup ricotta
- 1 small mozzarella, diced
- 1 tablespoon chopped parsley
- 2 tablespoons Parmesan cheese
- Broth as needed
- Salt and pepper to taste

Braise the beef and onion in the oil and butter. Add remaining ingredients and mix well. If filling mixture seems too dry, add broth until it is the right consistency. Season to taste.

Sauce:

Make a basic tomato sauce (Bea's on page 131 is a good one to use), using beef stock for the base.

Topping:

1 mozzarella cheese, shredded

1 cup grated pecorino cheese

Assembly:

To make crêpes, pour a little bit of the crêpe batter into a small buttered and heated iron skillet or crêpe pan. Roll pan to cover the bottom with a thin coating of batter. Cook over moderate heat until lightly browned (about 1 minute). Turn crêpe and cook quickly on the other side. Turn out onto a cloth or wooden surface. Continue in this manner (buttering pan after each crêpe) until batter is used up.

When crêpes, filling, and sauce are ready, spread each crêpe with a tablespoon of the filling, a bit of the tomato sauce, and shreds of mozzarella cheese. Roll up crêpe and place in a buttered baking dish. Repeat until all crêpes are filled and lined up in the casserole. Cover with the tomato sauce. Top with grated pecorino cheese and bake 20 to 30 minutes in a 350°F. oven.

Quaglie Stilo Abruzzi

Quail, Abruzzi-Style

For 4

Because these small game birds are meaty for their size, they are a great favorite with those lucky ones who bag enough to make a feast. A local risotto *with vegetable bits is traditionally served with them. The recipe may be followed for any game bird. Allow three quail per person.*

- 12 quail
- 1 cup olive oil
- 2 cloves garlic
- 6 sage leaves, bruised
- 12 thin slices fatback
- 2 cups white wine
- Salt and pepper to taste

Wash and dry the quail well, checking always for any hidden buckshot. Rub each bird with olive oil. In a hot (450°F.) oven, heat the remaining olive oil in a lasagna pan. Add the garlic cloves and sage, and push them around with a wooden spoon to flavor the oil. When the oil begins to smoke, put in 6 of the quail, turn them in the oil, then add the other 6, also coating them well with the oil. Sit quail on their "shoulders" with their feet in the air, and drape a piece of the fatback between the legs, forming a sort of fat "drip cloth" that will baste the birds. Cover the ends of the bones with aluminum foil so they don't char. Let them bake for 5 minutes at 450°, then lower the oven temperature to 350° and allow them to cook 10 minutes more. Remove the fatback before serving, and make a simple sauce using the pan drippings moistened with the wine. Salt and pepper the birds lightly and put on a platter. Then pour on the wine gravy and serve at once.

Trota ai Ferri

Charcoal-Broiled Trout For 1

The Abruzzi wives prepare the area's agile trout over their charcoal stoves. The men also sometimes spit-roast them at riverside, eating them unadorned but with good appetite nonetheless.

- 1 fresh trout
- 1 garlic clove, crushed
- 2 tablespoons fresh parsley
- Salt and pepper to taste
- 2 tablespoons olive oil
- 1 small orange, sliced

Wash and dry trout. Crush garlic and parsley together, and press onto outside of fish along with the salt and pepper. Grill over charcoal, turning once — 5 minutes on the first side and 4 on the other (the exact time is a variable, depending on the heat of your embers). Remove to a heated platter, dribble olive oil on top, and garnish with fresh orange slices.

Note: Fish gains flavor if allowed to sit for several minutes in a marinade of half white vermouth and half orange juice. This can also be used to baste during the cooking.

Cassata Abruzzese

Cassata, Abruzzi-Style For 10

Cassata *is perhaps the most famous of the Italian desserts, rivaling the spectacular presentation of our Baked Alaska. Although the best known is the one from Sicily (see recipe page 333), this version has two crunchy layers that make it particularly taste-appealing.*

Cake:

1 recipe Sponge Cake Genoese (see page 89)

In a 14- by 17-inch cookie tin (with a high lip), make the *Pasta Genoese.* Cut into 4 equal rectangles.

Cream Fillings:

¼ pound *torrone* (see Note)
¼ pound almond brittle
2 ounces semisweet baking chocolate
3 tablespoons cocoa
1 cup butter
6 eggs
1 cup confectioners' sugar

To make fillings, chop *torrone,* almond brittle, and chocolate separately. Put *torrone* and chocolate in one bowl, the almond brittle in another, and the cocoa in a third. Cream butter until light and creamy; add eggs, one at a time, alternating with small amounts of confectioners' sugar and beating well after each addition. Divide into 3 parts and add a third to each of the sweets-filled mixing bowls. Taste the cocoa-flavored "cream" and adjust for sweetness. Blend each mixture well but with a light hand. Remove 2 heaping tablespoons of each of the 3 mixes and blend together in a separate bowl.

Assembly:

Centerbe liqueur (see Note)
Slivered almonds, for garnish
Chocolate curls, for garnish

Place the first quarter (layer) of the cake on a serving plate. Drizzle liqueur lightly over the cake and spread with the cocoa cream. Add another cake layer, drizzle liqueur, and spread with almond brittle cream. Repeat with the third layer and chocolate-*torrone* cream. Top with the final layer of cake. Pour generous amount of liqueur over the top and ice with the triple-cream mixture. Decorate with slivered almonds and curls of chocolate, and refrigerate for several hours before serving.

Note: Centerbe is an Abruzzi liqueur, available in Italian specialty shops. If unavailable, rum or brandy may be substituted. *Torrone* is a kind of nougat, available in specialty shops that carry imported sweets.

An Abruzzi Christmas Eve Feast

Christmas Eve dinner throughout Italy is a time of special culinary observances, but nowhere is it more deliciously marked than in the Abruzzi. Boston broadcast-journalist Rosetta Romagnoli, a superb cook in her own right, shares her traditional family menu with us. The recipes, except for the *Cauciunitti*, serve 4. They can, of course, be increased for a larger gathering.

Insalata di Arancio
Pinzimonio (Finocchio)
Verza Vigilia di Natale
Capitone allo Spiedo
Cauciunitti

Insalata di Arancio

Orange Salad

4 navel oranges
½ head of white escarole
10 green olives
⅓ cup olive oil
Freshly grated black pepper

Peel and cut the oranges into bite-sized pieces. Wash and break the escarole leaves into a medium-sized salad bowl. Toss the oranges, olives, and olive oil with the escarole. Serve with grated black pepper.

Pinzimonio

Fennel Salad

Scrub several fennel (anise) bulbs thoroughly and remove the outer leaves. Slice the cores lengthwise and dip into olive oil seasoned with salt and pepper.

Note: This might be classified as an Italian "munchy."

Verza Vigilia di Natale

Christmas Cabbage

2 cloves garlic
½ cup olive oil
4 fillets anchovies, mashed
1 medium cabbage, cooked
Capers rinsed and drained (optional)

Grate garlic and steam until soft; drain. Fry the garlic in the olive oil until golden. Add the mashed anchovies and mix with the cooked cabbage. Top with rinsed and drained capers, if desired, and serve at once.

Note: Traditionally, the Italians abstain from eating meat on Christmas Eve.

Capitone allo Spiedo

Skewered Eel

1 cup olive oil
⅓ cup vinegar
1 clove garlic, minced
Salt and pepper to taste
An eel or eels, large enough to be cut into 16 two-inch pieces, skinned
12 bay leaves
Lemon wedges, for garnish
Black and green olives, for garnish

Blend the olive oil, vinegar, minced garlic clove, and salt and pepper to taste. Place 4 sections of eel on each skewer, separated by touching bay leaves to lend flavor during the cooking. Place in 375°F. oven and cook, turning frequently for about 25 minutes, or until eel is white and dry; baste with oil mixture while cooking. Serve at once, garnished with lemon wedges and black and green olives.

Cauciunitti

Abruzzi Christmas Pastries — Makes 20 to 24

In Beatrice's search through the tattered pages of her Old-Country cookbooks, she came across this rather inexact recipe for this traditional Abruzzi sweet. Close your eyes, think and feel *Italian; then relax and make a batch of* Cauciunitti *(or* Calgianetti *as they are variously called).*

- 1½ cups almonds, blanched and toasted
- 2 cups grape jelly
- ½ cup sugar, plus extra for sprinkling
- ¼ cup chopped citron
- ¼ teaspoon cloves
- Rind of 1 orange, grated
- A "little" semolina flour
- ¼ cup olive oil
- 1 cup dry white wine
- All-purpose flour (approximately 3 cups)
- Fat, for frying
- Cinnamon, for sprinkling

The day before: Chop the almonds. In a saucepan, put the jelly, sugar, citron, cloves, orange rind, and chopped almonds; cook until liquified, stirring to keep from burning. Add enough semolina flour to thicken slightly, and refrigerate for next-day use.

When ready, mix the oil and white wine, and add the all-purpose flour little by little, working with the hands, until you have a firm dough. Knead until smooth and elastic. Roll out dough (by hand or with your pasta machine on the medium setting). Cut pasta into 3- by 5-inch rectangles. Put filling in center of each, fold over, moisten edge, and seal well. Fry in deep fat (slowly — they should not be darkened by the frying process). Remove to paper towels to drain and sprinkle with cinnamon and additional sugar.

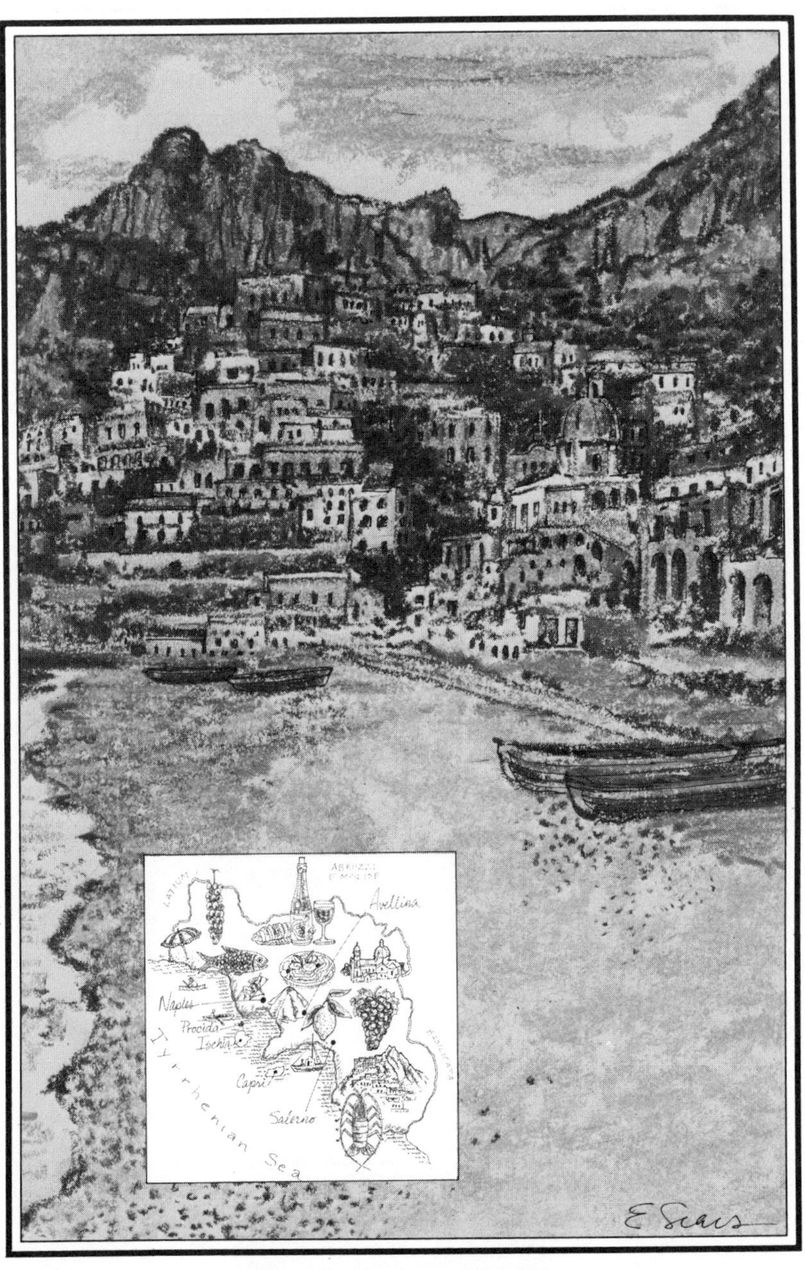
Avellina
Naples
Procida
Ischia
Capri
Salerno
Tyrrhenian Sea

Campania

The Special Wines & Cheeses of *Campania*

Wines of the Region

Dry reds: *Falerno, Gragnano, Ischia, Vesuvio*

Demi-sec: *Aglianico, Capri Rosso, Epomeo, Gragnano*

Dry whites: *Capri, Epomeo, Falerno* (wonderful!), *Forastera, Lacrima Christi*

Demi-sec whites: *Asprinio, Biancolella, Ischia, Ravello*

Dessert wine: *Sanginella*

Wines Available in the United States

Dry reds: *Taurasi Riserva, Mastroberardino*

Dry whites: *Fiano di Avellino, Greco di Tufo, Mastroberardino*

Dessert wines: *Amabile Mastroberardino, Lacrima Christi*

Cheeses of the Region

Butirri, Caciocavalli, Mozzarella (made from "bufalo" milk), *Pecorino, Provola, Provolone, Scamorze, Trecce*

Dove entra el bere, se n'esce il sapere.

When the wine is "in," the wit is out.

Travelers, writers, and hearty eaters have been extolling the virtues of the sun-drenched Campania shores for centuries. There, the semitropical climate stimulates nature to joyous excesses. The pastel-colored stucco walls of modest dwellings and enormous villas alike are ablaze with bougainvillea and oleander, and the streets fragrant with the odor of flowers and all that fine Neapolitan cooking!

Even the post-World War II determination to make Naples the center of noise, graffiti (seaports seem particularly fertile areas for spray-can political blather, and caricature), uncollected garbage, and other metropolitan detritus loses conviction in the face of so much natural beauty. Unpredictable Vesuvius hovers, sharing scenic honors with the special blue of the Mediterranean, and the islands of Capri, Ischia, and Procida, each with its special delights, lie a pleasant boat ride away.

Apart from the archeological treasures, so long ago buried but daily rediscovered, the volcano's primary legacy to the region is the rich, black lava soil. Everything grows here and several annual crops are harvested simultaneously. For example, supported between the symmetrical lines of olive trees are lathe-sustained beans, tomatoes, and other climbing plants. Grapevines coexist with slender poplars (high foliage allowing the sun to penetrate to the light-hungry vines). No inch of land, vertical or horizontal, is left barren. The valleys that drop away from the Amalfi cliffs provide marshy, optimum grazing conditions for the native *bufalo,* a white bovine indigenous to Campania and the "mother" of the popular mozzarella cheese — the prime, elastic ingredient of America's favorite ethnic food, the pizza!

Actually, the authorship of the pizza is fiercely contended in several regions of the "Boot," but on the western side of the Atlantic most of the Italian cuisine with which we are familiar has Neapolitan origins. Great pasta lovers, they share with the Sicilians the affectionate label of *mangiamaccheroni* (macaroni eaters).

Another strong culinary cord unites Campania to New England and all of the American coast cities — the daily catch from the Bay of Naples. It lends itself to the succulent triumphs of the kitchen arts also familiar to American coastal regions: the fish stews; *Fritto Misto del Golfo* (fish fry); and everyone's pasta "darling," *Spaghetti con le Vongole* (spaghetti with clam sauce). So here and "there," the sea's gifts are harvested and enjoyed, incorporated into a lifestyle where eating well is considered almost an art form.

Other noteworthy culinary treasures from the Campania region include *Bistecca alla Pizzaiola,* beef or veal cutlet sautéed with tomato sauce; *Fritto Misto,* fish fried with cheese, cauliflower, and potatoes; *Parmigiana di Melanzane,* baked eggplant; *Pepperoni Imbottiti,* stuffed peppers; *Sartù,* a rice casserole filled with cheese and meat bits; *Spaghetti al Pomodoro* (Campania is the home of *the* basil-flavored tomato sauce); *Calzoni alla Napolitana,* a delight-filled dough; and *Sfogliatelle,* flaky pastries filled with spiced ricotta and candied fruit.

Mozzarella in Carrozza

Grilled Mozzarella "Sandwich" For 4

The Italian name translates to "Cheese in a Carriage."

- 8 slices of bread, decrusted
- 1 large mozzarella cheese, sliced
- 1 tablespoon flour
- $1\frac{1}{2}$ tablespoons water
- Pinch of salt
- 2 eggs, well beaten
- Olive oil, for frying

Cover 4 slices of the crustless bread with equal shares of the sliced mozzarella. Then cover with the remaining 4 slices bread to make 4 "sandwiches." Make a thin batter of the flour, water, and salt. Brush the sandwich edges with batter and press the edges tightly together to seal. Dip the sandwiches in the beaten eggs. Let them rest for 10 minutes. Put olive oil in large skillet and fry the sandwiches until golden brown. Drain on paper towels and serve hot.

Note: A marvelous variation of this dish was served at La Gondola, a Mexico City Italian restaurant. A rinsed anchovy was placed between each pair of bread slices; the small, round slices of Italian bread were then lined up like a little train in a loaf pan, with a sauce of olive oil, chopped garlic, and shredded anchovy served on the side.

Pasta di Pane per la Pizzetta

Basic Pizza Dough

Makes three 12-inch pizzas, or two of the thicker Sicilian-type pizzas. This Basic Pizza Dough is a little lighter in texture than the Basic Yeast Dough following later in this segment.

- 4½ cups all-purpose flour
- 2 teaspoons sugar
- 1½ cups warm (110°F.) water
- 1 package (scant tablespoon) dry yeast
- 2 tablespoons olive oil, plus extra for oiling dough
- 1½ teaspoons salt

Put flour in a large bowl; make a well in the center; add sugar, water, and yeast; and incorporate a little flour at a time. Cover until it bubbles. Add olive oil and salt. Mix ingredients together until a rough mass is formed. Turn out onto a floured board and knead 5 to 6 minutes. Put a little oil in a bowl, add the dough, and turn once to oil on other side.

Warm oven to low (110°F.); then turn off. Cover dough bowl tightly and place in oven until tripled in bulk. Punch dough down, and divide into the number of pizzas desired. Knead the small ball of dough for a few minutes, adding flour if the dough seems too sticky. Rest dough. Flatten the dough with the heel of your hand into a circle about an inch thick (see Note). Then stretch out into the desired shape and size — ready for a filling of your choice.

Note: Experienced pizza-makers like Beatrice do wondrous things at this point with only their hands — stretching and tossing, a kind of "bread ballet." (I use a rolling pin: the results are satisfactory, if less creative. L.M.) Bea also sometimes adds 1 teaspoon baking powder to her pizza dough — for an even lighter texture.

Pizza Rustica

Country Pizza

For 6

More a two-crusted pie than the classic pizza to which we are accustomed, this specialty is appreciated over a wide area, with regional differences, of course. In the Marches, they add vegetables to the filling; in the Abruzzi, a Swiss-type cheese is included along with cinnamon and nutmeg. The one area of agreement is that the crusts are made not with a yeast dough, but rather with baking powder. In this recipe from Campania, a note is appended in the original old Italian that the mozzarella must be the real one, made from the milk of the bufalo.

Crust:

2¼ cups flour
⅔ teaspoon baking powder
1 stick (½ cup) butter
1 egg yolk
⅛ cup water

In a mixer, put flour, baking powder, and butter. When the mass has formed pea-sized balls, add yolk and liquid. Allow it to mix well. Remove the dough to a floured breadboard, and knead several minutes with the heel of the hand. Put in a plastic bag and let relax.

Filling:

3 Italian sausages
½ cup prosciutto
½ cup chopped pepperoni
½ cup chopped boiled ham
½ pound mozzarella cheese
1 tablespoon grated pecorino cheese
2 tablespoons grated Parmesan cheese
1 pound ricotta cheese
2 whole eggs
¼ teaspoon freshly ground black pepper
Salt to taste

Skin and break up sausages, then sauté, covered, over low heat. Remove cover and continue to cook to evaporate the liquid. Put into a large bowl. Add the chopped meats along with the cheeses and whole eggs. Mix all together well, add the freshly ground black pepper, and correct the seasoning with salt if desired.

Assembly:

- 2 tablespoons water, plus water to moisten dough
- 1 egg white

Preheat the oven to 400°F. Roll out ⅔ of dough to fill a 10-inch round baking tin, leaving an inch overhang. Pour in and spread the filling. Roll out the last third of the dough and place over the filling. Moisten the edge with water; fold up and over the dough overhang, pinching the two edges together between the fingers to seal. Then, with a sharp knife, make several slits in the top crust to allow the steam to escape.

Beat the egg white with a fork and add 2 tablespoons water; brush mix over the top of crust with a pastry brush. Put pizza in oven and bake for 15 minutes. Reduce heat to 325° and continue baking for 45 minutes. Five minutes before the end of the baking time, brush the top crust with the egg white mix again. Remove from oven and let cool for 5 to 10 minutes before serving.

Calzone Bella Napoli

Turnovers, Naples-Style

Makes: 2 large turnovers

- 1 recipe *Basic Yeast Dough* (see recipe on page 268)
- 1 pound ricotta cheese
- 1 egg
- ½ cup grated cheese (Parmesan and Romano, mixed)
- ½ pound mozzarella cheese, diced
- ¼ pound each prosciutto and salami
- Pinch of salt (optional)

Make dough recipe. Then in a large mixing bowl, put ricotta, egg, grated cheeses, chopped prosciutto and salami, and salt if desired. Blend together well. Stretch and roll out a large circle of dough about ⅛-inch thick. Put the filling on one half of the circle. Moisten the edges with water, fold over the other half of the dough, and press the edges firmly together to seal. Bake in a preheated 475°F. oven about 30 minutes.

Calzone Lazzaro

Stuffed Turnovers

Makes 2 large turnovers

Beatrice's version of everybody's favorite from Naples.

Dough:

1 recipe Basic Yeast Dough (see recipe on page 268).

Make dough; allow to relax while making the filling.

Filling:

1 pound ricotta cheese
2 eggs
¼ cup grated Parmesan cheese
¼ cup grated Romano cheese
¼ pound thinly sliced salami, chopped
4 slices of boiled ham, chopped
1 small mozzarella, sliced
¼ pound *capo colla*, sliced very thin (see Note)
Salt to taste

In a bowl, put ricotta and eggs and heat over pan of warm water. Add grated cheeses, chopped salami, chopped ham, mozzarella, and *capo colla*. Correct seasoning.

Assembly:

Preheat the oven to 450°F. Roll out about half the dough to make a 12-inch circle. Put half of prepared filling in center and spread it out over the dough. Moisten edges and fold half of dough over to form a half-moon shape. Pinch edges to seal securely. Bake for 30 minutes. Make a second round of dough, spread with remaining filling, and proceed in same manner as for first turnover.

Note: *Capo colla* is an Italian specialty dry cured luncheon meat. You may substitute prosciutto or more boiled ham.

Panzerotti Napolitana

Cheese Turnovers — For 8

The name of this Neapolitan favorite means "puffed bellies," and that is exactly what you may find yourself with after too many of these.

Dough:

- 3 cups all-purpose flour
- 1 teaspoon salt
- 4 tablespoons lard
- 1 egg, separated (reserve the white)
- 2 tablespoons water, or more as needed

Put flour and salt into a bowl, and cut in lard until dough balls are about the size of peas. Blend the egg yolk mixed with 2 tablespoons water into the dough. Add more water if necessary and knead until you have a pliable mass. Cover and allow dough to relax for 30 minutes.

Filling:

- ¾ pound ricotta cheese
- 1 cup grated Parmesan cheese
- 1 cup diced mozzarella cheese
- ½ cup grated provolone cheese
- 2 eggs
- ⅓ cup chopped parsley
- Salt and pepper
- Oil, for frying

Put ricotta in a bowl, and add Parmesan, mozzarella, provolone, eggs, parsley, and seasoning.

Make balls, each a little larger than a walnut, of the relaxed dough. On a floured board, roll out each one very thin, making 3-inch circles. Place a spoonful of filling on each. Moisten the edges with the reserved egg white. Fold in half to form half-moons. Heat a good amount of oil and fry the pastries a few at a time until golden. Drain on paper toweling.

These turnovers may be eaten plain, dipped in tomato sauce, or — omitting the parsley and pepper — they may be dipped in sugar and eaten as a dessert.

Pasta di Pane per Panzarotti, Calzoni e Pizza

Basic Yeast Dough   Makes three 12-inch pizzas, or 2 pizzas and 2 *calzoni*

3 to 4 cups all-purpose flour
1 package (scant tablespoon) dry yeast
1 cup warm water
2 teaspoons sugar
2 teaspoons salt
1 tablespoon olive oil

Put flour in a large bowl, make a "well" in the center. Put in yeast, water, and sugar. Let sponge foam. Add rest of the ingredients. Mix and knead. Then, in a greased bowl, let dough rise in a warm place, turning once, until doubled in bulk. Punch down and let rise again for 15 minutes. Roll out as desired.

Zuppa di Vongole

Sautéed Clams in Broth   For 4

The delicate pink and green liquid in which these clams float wafts a fragrance dear to the heart of the gentle folk from Campania.

4 pounds clams
1 cup water
½ cup olive oil
2 cloves garlic, crushed
¼ cup chopped parsley
2 tablespoons tomato paste
3 tiny hot red peppers
½ cup white wine
Salt and pepper to taste

Wash and rinse clams. Put in a pan, add 1 cup water, and place over heat, covered, until shells open. Shuck the clams, rinse them in the clam juice, and put them aside in a bowl. Strain the clam juice and reserve. In a saucepan, put olive oil and garlic. Sauté a few minutes. Add chopped parsley and tomato paste; again, sauté. Add the red peppers and heat for a few minutes in the sauce, then remove peppers and discard. Add the white wine and evaporate. Then, add the clams and the remaining clam juice. Cook for a few minutes; taste and add salt and pepper as wanted. Serve over toasted bread that has been rubbed with garlic.

Zuppa alla Santé di Signor Ciani

Signor Ciani's Health Soup For 8 to 10

Signor Ciani, "God rest his soul," lived a full and happy life. Much of its success may have been due to this soup, which he frequently made and shared with family and friends. The recipe can be traced back to his family in Campania.

Meatballs:

Prepare meatballs as for *Zuppa di Sposalizio* (see recipe on page 247). Shape the meat mass into tiny meatballs the size of marbles. Fry lightly in olive oil and put on paper toweling to degrease. When these are ready, continue with soup.

Soup:

- 2 carrots
- 1 bunch celery
- 2 onions
- 2 pounds spinach, chopped
- ¼ pound butter
- 2 quarts beef broth
- 1 quart water
- 1 pound tomatoes, fresh or canned
- 2 cups cooked rice (about ¾ cup raw)
- Grated cheese, for garnish
- Bea's Garlic Salt (see page 31) and pepper to taste

Chop vegetables coarsely and sauté in butter in a large soup kettle. Add the 3 quarts of liquid and the tomatoes. Cook until vegetables are tender (about 30 minutes). Place prepared meatballs in soup, and cook for another 15 minutes. Add rice and allow to heat for a minute or two. Adjust seasoning to taste. Serve hot with grated cheese on the side. *Salute!*

Salsa Marinara

Sailor's Sauce

For 6 to 8

This is a sauce that varies not only with region, but also with each cook within the region. The basic "constants" are as follows. However, a true marinara, *whatever its origin, always mixes oil and butter, never uses tomato paste, and never contains celery.*

- 4 tablespoons butter
- 4 tablespoons olive oil
- 1 clove garlic
- 1 medium onion, chopped
- 1 large can (2 pounds) tomatoes
- ¼ teaspoon oregano
- 2 basil leaves, crushed
- 1 tablespoon chopped parsley

Melt butter with olive oil and sauté the garlic and onion until golden. Remove the garlic clove. Add the tomatoes, and simmer with the herbs for 1 hour.

Variations:

Add 2 or 3 rinsed and crushed anchovies.

Add a pinch (or several, depending on your palate) of cayenne pepper.

Spaghetti alla Puttanesca

Spaghetti in Harlot's Sauce

For 4 to 6

Famous all over Italy, as much for its startling name as for its unique blend of flavors. The origin of the dish is obscure, but there's no reason why the diner can't fantasize: your version is as valid as anyone else's!

- ⅓ cup plus 1 tablespoon olive oil
- ¼ cup butter
- 2 cloves garlic, crushed
- 1½ pounds fresh tomatoes, chopped
- 1 tablespoon capers, rinsed
- ¾ cup pitted black olives
- ¼ teaspoon dried hot pepper, plus extra for garnish
- ½ teaspoon oregano
- ½ can anchovies
- 1 tablespoon chopped parsley
- Salt to taste

In saucepan, heat 1/3 cup olive oil and butter. Add crushed garlic, then add tomatoes, capers, olives, hot pepper, and oregano. Cook over high heat 20 to 25 minutes. Add anchovies and mash. Lower heat, and cook a few minutes more. Add parsley and season to taste. Cook spaghetti *al dente* in boiling, salted water with the remaining tablespoon olive oil; drain. Put spaghetti in a bowl. Mix with 2/3 of the sauce. Spoon remaining sauce over top. Serve hot, with extra hot pepper and grated cheese on the side.

Maccheroni in Bianco Marianna

Marianna's Macaroni

For 6

A sterling case for the versatility of pasta. This dish doesn't suffer at all from the absence of the ubiquitous tomato, and instead surprises us with the spring green of little peas and the tang of the mixed meats. Thank you, Marianna!

- 1½ pounds short macaroni, cooked *al dente*
- 4 ounces prosciutto
- 2 ounces Italian salami
- 4 ounces Fontina cheese
- 4 tablespoons flour
- 1 stick (8 tablespoons) butter
- 2 cups milk
- Salt and pepper to taste
- Pinch of nutmeg
- 1 cup heavy cream
- 1 cup grated Parmesan cheese
- 1 package (10 ounces) frozen peas or 2 cups fresh peas, cooked

Cook macaroni and drain. Cut prosciutto and salami in small, thin strips. Thinly slice Fontina cheese. Make a roux of flour and butter, adding milk gradually while whisking. Season with salt, pepper, and nutmeg. In the same pan in which macaroni was cooked, mix the pasta, heavy cream, and ½ cup of the Parmesan cheese. Add prosciutto and salami and mix well again. Add cooked peas. Spoon the mixture into a 2- to 2½-quart buttered casserole. Lay slices of the Fontina over the top. Then add the cream sauce and sprinkle with the remaining ½ cup Parmesan cheese. Put in 375°F. oven for 20 minutes or until top is golden.

Sartù

Rice Timbale

For 10 to 12

The *holiday dish of Campania, present at all grand occasions, and Italy's answer to the Spanish* Paella. *The amount of work involved in the preparation of this ancient dish serves the cook well, for it is truly a single-dish meal and can be made to feed a hungry horde. Reading through you will note that it is similar to* Vincisgrassi *in content, except that it uses rice instead of layered pasta.*

Sauce:

1 ounce dried Italian mushrooms
1 large onion
1 clove garlic, crushed
4 tablespoons olive oil
4 tablespoons butter
1 small carrot
1 stalk celery
1 slice unsmoked bacon
5 Italian sausages
1 cup tomato purée
1 cup broth
Bea's Garlic Salt (see page 31) to taste

Soak dried mushrooms in warm water until soft; drain, reserving liquid, and chop. Chop onion and garlic together. Put into a skillet with oil and butter. Finely chop the carrot and celery, and sauté with the bacon and sausages. Remove the sausages and set aside (they'll be used in the filling). Add chopped mushrooms and reserved liquid, and cook until liquid has evaporated. Add tomato purée, blend, and cook 10 minutes, then add 1 cup broth. Cook until oil surfaces and you have a good consistency. Discard the bacon, correct seasoning, and set aside.

Filling:

2 tablespoons butter
3 chicken livers
¼ teaspoon Bea's Garlic Salt (see page 31)
Cooked sausages (from the sauce recipe above), sliced
3 tablespoons white wine
1 box (10 ounces) frozen or 1½ cups fresh peas
½ cup broth

In a small saucepan, melt butter, add chicken livers and garlic salt, and cook 3 to 5 minutes. Then chop livers and replace in pan. Add sliced sausages. Add wine and let it evaporate. Put in peas and ½ cup broth. Cook only until peas are tender.

Cheese Mixture:

- 1 cup diced mozzarella cheese
- ½ cup diced prosciutto
- 1 cup grated Parmesan cheese

Blend all together well, and set aside.

Meatballs:

- ½ pound ground beef
- 2 eggs
- ½ teaspoon Bea's Garlic Salt (see page 31)
- ½ cup grated Parmesan cheese
- 1 tablespoon chopped parsley
- ¾ cup bread crumbs
- 2 tablespoons mixed olive oil and butter

Put the first 6 ingredients in a bowl and mix thoroughly by hand. Make little meatballs smaller than a walnut. Fry in oil and butter mixture, and set aside.

Rice:

- 2 tablespoons butter
- 2 cups raw rice
- ½ of the prepared sauce
- 4 cups broth, heated
- 2 eggs
- ⅓ cup grated Parmesan cheese
- Salt and pepper to taste

Put butter in a saucepan or deep skillet, add rice, and stir to coat well. Strain half of the prepared sauce into the rice, and cook to the point of absorption, stirring constantly. Add hot broth (broth should come to about 1 inch above the rice). Bring to a boil and cover. Lower the heat. When liquid is absorbed and rice is tender, beat the eggs and add along with the grated cheese. Correct seasoning if necessary.

Assembly:

Butter, for dotting
Grated Parmesan cheese, for topping
Bread crumbs (optional)

Now that you have every pot in the kitchen either dirty or in use, we are going to assemble this incredible casserole.

Butter well a large (3-quart or more) casserole. Pour in ⅔ of the rice. With a wooden spoon, spread the rice evenly over the bottom and up the sides, leaving a large hollow in the middle. On bottom of the "hollow," put some of the cheese mixture, some of the filling, and some of the meatballs. Spoon some sauce over all, then add some grated cheese. Repeat this layering, finishing with a layer of rice on top. Dot with butter and sprinkle with grated cheese, and add bread crumbs if you like.

Bake at 350°F. for 1 hour. The top should be golden and the kitchen should smell "heavenly"!

Calamaretti alla Napolitana

Squid, Naples-Style

For 6

Did you know that the principal difference between squid and octopus is in the number of tentacles? Octopi have eight while members of the squid family have ten! In Naples, this means two more of the chewy morsels to be consumed with gusto.

¼ cup olive oil
1 clove garlic, crushed
1 can (1 pound) plum tomatoes, crushed
½ cup sultana raisins
½ cup red wine
2 pounds small squid
½ cup pine nuts
½ cup black *Gaeta* olives, pitted
Salt and pepper to taste
1 tablespoon chopped parsley

In a skillet, put olive oil and crushed garlic. Sauté, but *do not let garlic brown.* Add crushed tomatoes immediately and cook for 30 minutes.

Soak raisins in warm red wine to plump. Clean squid as described on page 322. Add squid, pine nuts, pitted black olives, and plumped raisins to skillet. Cover pan, lower heat, and cook very slowly until squid are tender, about 30 minutes. If sauce should thicken too much, dilute with a little water. Cook a few minutes more. Adjust seasoning if needed, and put in serving dish. Sprinkle with chopped parsley and serve immediately.

Note: *Polpi alla Luciana* is another specialty of the region. It is made in the same fashion, omitting the pine nuts, olives, and raisins.

Tegamino di Pesce Zia Mary

Aunt Mary's Fish Casserole

For 4

A simple, hearty one-dish meal often made by Beatrice's Aunt Mary.

- 2 pounds cusk or haddock fillets
- Salt and pepper to taste
- 6 potatoes, quartered
- 1 can (1 pound) plum tomatoes, crushed
- 2 tablespoons chopped parsley, plus extra for topping
- 1 teaspoon oregano
- 1 clove garlic, crushed
- 1/3 cup olive oil
- Bea's Garlic Salt (see page 31)

Wash and dry fish fillets, salt and pepper them. Boil potatoes partially and drain.

Preheat the oven to 400°F. Place fish in an oiled 1½- to 2-quart casserole. Cover it with the crushed tomatoes, ring with the potatoes, and sprinkle with the parsley and oregano. Sauté garlic in olive oil and then pour over the casserole ingredients. Sprinkle with garlic salt, pepper, and additional parsley. Cook in preheated oven about 35 minutes or longer, depending on the tenderness of the fish used. Test with a fork, and when the fish flakes away, the dish is ready to serve.

Bracciole di Maiale Imbuttite

Stuffed Pork Rollups

For 6

The use of pine nuts, raisins, and capers reoccurs in the cuisine of Campania — here we find it accompanying pork.

8 slices pork loin, cut thick
½ cup raisins
¼ pound prosciutto
3 tablespoons capers
⅓ cup pine nuts
2 tablespoons bread crumbs
1 tablespoon butter, melted
2 tablespoons olive oil
2 ounces fresh salt pork, minced
½ cup tomato purée, thinned with 1 cup water
Salt and pepper to taste
Pinch of cayenne pepper

Ask your butcher to cut the pork loin slices a little thick. Then cut ("butterfly") the slices into 2 layers, leaving a hinge. (See sketch.) Flatten with a kitchen mallet to make a large, thin piece of meat. Soak raisins in water to plump. On a board, chop together prosciutto, capers, drained raisins, and pine nuts. Put mixture into a bowl and add the bread crumbs. Spread filling over each slice of pork and dribble butter over filling. Roll up meat and tie, or secure with a small skewer or toothpick.

The pork for these stuffed pork rolls is first "butterflied," then pounded, then filled and rolled. To "butterfly," the pork is sliced in two horizontally leaving a hinge at one end to make one large slice when folded open.

In a saucepan, put the olive oil and the minced salt pork. When salt pork begins to sizzle, add the pork rolls and fry. When nicely browned, add tomato purée thinned with water. Season with salt, black pepper, and cayenne. Cook over low heat for 1½ hours or until sauce is rather thick. Pour over pork rolls and serve.

Trippa Gusto di Raffaele

Tripe, Lazzaro-Style

For 6 to 8

No, you don't have *to eat tripe . . . but you may be missing the plate of your life!*

- 4 pounds tripe
- 2 bay leaves
- 1 tablespoon peppercorns
- ¼ cup butter
- ⅔ cup olive oil
- 1 onion, finely chopped
- 2 cloves garlic, crushed
- 4 tablespoons tomato paste
- ⅓ cup dry wine
- 2 pounds tomatoes, crushed
- 2 teaspoons chopped basil
- 2 tablespoons chopped parsley
- ¼ teaspoon oregano
- ⅛ teaspoon hot pepper
- ½ cup water, or as needed
- ½ cup grated pecorino cheese, plus extra for topping

Wash tripe, then boil with bay leaves and peppercorns until tender but firm. Put in colander to drain.

In a 5- to 6-quart pan, melt butter and add oil, chopped onion, and fresh garlic. Sauté until onion is soft. Add tomato paste. Sauté about 5 minutes; add wine and let it evaporate. Continue cooking, allowing the sauce to darken a bit. Add crushed tomatoes, and cook until oil surfaces and sauce is quite thick. Add basil, parsley, oregano, and hot pepper.

Cut tripe into thin strips 2 to 3 inches long. Add strips to sauce and cook until tripe is tender. (If sauce needs to be thinned out, add a little water.) When cooked, add the grated cheese. Serve hot with extra cheese and crusty bread.

Pepperoni Ripieni

Stuffed Peppers

For 4

The black volcanic earth of Campania produces unsurpassed vegetables. In this recipe, the glossy green of the region's giant peppers is joined by the cloud-hued cheese and the brilliant red tomatoes.

- 4 large green peppers
- 2 tablespoons plus ¼ cup olive oil
- 1 large onion, chopped
- 3 Italian sausages, skinned
- 2 cups bread crumbs of stale bread
- 2 tomatoes, crushed
- ⅓ cup grated pecorino cheese
- 1 tablespoon chopped parsley
- 1 teaspoon chopped basil
- 1 egg
- 1 clove garlic, crushed
- 10 stuffed green olives, cut up
- ¾ cup ricotta cheese
- Salt and pepper to taste

Prepare peppers. Remove top with stem, leaving a hole large enough for stuffing.

Put 2 tablespoons oil and onion in pan; sauté. Add skinned sausages and break up meat. When meat is cooked, add bread crumbs, crushed tomatoes, grated cheese, chopped parsley, chopped basil, egg, ¼ cup olive oil, crushed garlic, green olives, and ricotta. Correct seasoning. Mix by hand to blend well. Fill peppers. Stand up in a baking dish, fitting the peppers closely together. Bake at 375°F. for 1 hour, basting often with the juices formed. Serve hot.

Fritto di Fiori di Zucca

Fried Squash Flowers

For 4 to 6

As in Venice, the flower of the male squash is prized as a vegetable in Campania. In both regions, they are batter-wrapped, but in the Campania they are first stuffed. This is a specialty of Salerno.

Recipe is for approximately 1 pound of squash blossoms.

Batter:

- ¾ cup flour
- 1 egg yolk
- ⅓ cup water

Mix the 3 ingredients and beat well to remove all lumps. The batter should be thin, like heavy cream. Let rest 1 hour.

Stuffing and Frying:

- ½ cup bread crumbs
- 2 anchovies, mashed
- 1 tablespoon chopped parsley
- ⅔ cup grated mozzarella cheese
- ¼ cup grated Parmesan cheese
- ¼ cup olive oil, or more as needed
- Hot oil, for frying
- Salt, for sprinkling

Mix by hand the crumbs, anchovies, parsley, both cheeses, and olive oil. Add a little more oil if necessary to make stuffing hold together. Wash and dry squash flowers. Put a little stuffing in each flower and carefully close flower to hold stuffing. Dip each flower in prepared batter and fry in hot oil. Sprinkle lightly with salt and serve hot.

Struffoli alla Napolitana

Honey Cakes

Makes 1 ring or several dozen pastries

Merely a mouthful, but what a heavenly one! Made both in Campania and in Umbria (where they may also contain pine nuts).

Struffoli:

- 2 to 3 cups flour
- 4 eggs, plus 1 egg yolk
- Rind of ½ lemon, grated
- Rind of ½ orange, grated
- ¼ teaspoon salt
- ¼ cup butter, softened
- Oil, for frying

On a pastry board, sift flour and make a well; add whole eggs, yolk, lemon rind, orange rind, salt, and softened butter. Mix and knead thoroughly for a smooth dough. Cover and let dough relax for 1 hour. Break off small pieces of dough, larger than a filbert. Mold into a rough, round shape (do not overhandle dough) and drop into hot oil. Fry until golden; drain on paper towels.

The dough balls for Struffoli alla Napolitana *may be formed in any manner of ways — in a ring, in a single mound, or in individual shells.*

Sauce:

- 1 cup honey
- 3 tablespoons granulated sugar
- 2 tablespoons water
- ⅛ teaspoon ginger
- ½ cup candied orange peel, chopped
- ½ cup chopped citron
- ⅓ cup nonpareilles and/or pine nuts, for topping

In a 3-quart saucepan, bring honey, sugar, and water to boil. Then simmer until foam subsides and add ginger. Drop in the fried *struffoli* a few at a time, along with half of the chopped candied fruits. Mix, and spoon *struffoli* onto a buttered plate. Working with wet hands, form the pastries into a ring. Sprinkle with the remainder of the fruit, and the nonpareilles and/or pine nuts. (These may also be made individually.) The pastries will keep for a week if carefully wrapped in foil.

Zeppole

Fried Pastry Rings

Makes 24 rings

Crispy, crunchy little sweets, as irresistible for snacking as for enjoying with an after-dinner wine.

- ½ cup butter
- ¼ cup granulated sugar
- 1 cup water
- 2½ cups flour
- ¼ teaspoon salt
- 2 tablespoons brandy
- 4 eggs
- Oil, for frying
- ¾ cup confectioners' sugar
- ½ teaspoon cinnamon

In a saucepan, melt butter; add granulated sugar and water and bring to a boil. Add flour all at once and salt. With a wooden spoon, stir in brandy and mix so that pastry leaves side of pan and forms a ball. Put pastry in the bowl of an electric mixer. Then, beating at medium speed, add eggs one at a time, beating vigorously after each addition. Break off pieces of dough, roll into sticks ½-inch wide by 8 inches long. Form into "hoops," pressing the ends together to seal (using a #9 tube and pastry bag makes forming these "hoops" easier).

Have pan ready with hot oil and fry rings until golden. Remove to paper towels to drain. Sprinkle with confectioners' sugar mixed with cinnamon.

Pepatelli

Sweet and Spicy Biscuits

Makes 4 dozen biscuits

The classic, anise-flavored nut biscotti *are enjoyed all over Italy; this version from Campania reflects the temperament of the area — the name means "little peppery ones."*

- 5 cups flour
- 1½ cups sugar
- 2 tablespoons baking powder
- 4 eggs, plus 1 egg white for brushing top
- ¾ cup honey
- ½ cup chopped citron
- ½ cup butter, melted
- 1 teaspoon pepper
- ¼ cup candied lemon peel
- ¼ cup candied orange peel
- 1½ teaspoons cinnamon
- ½ teaspoon cloves
- ½ teaspoon baking soda
- 1 cup shelled filberts
- 1 cup shelled almonds
- 2 cups shelled walnuts

Preheat the oven to 350°F. In a large pan or bowl, put flour, sugar, baking powder, whole eggs, honey, citron, melted butter, and pepper. Chop lemon and orange peel together and add along with the cinnamon and cloves. Then dissolve baking soda in a little water and add. Mix all together, then add filberts, almonds, and walnuts. Blend well. (If too dry, add orange or some other fruit juice.)

Shape into bars 2 inches wide by the length of the cookie pan (this should make 5 or 6 bars). Bake for 30 minutes. Before removing from oven, brush egg white over surfaces. Put bars on a breadboard; cut into biscuits ¾-inch wide. Put biscuits flat on a cookie sheet and toast 4 or 5 minutes in oven. Remove and cool on board. Repeat until all biscuits are toasted. These keep well in a covered cookie tin.

ABRUZZI E MOLISE
CAMPANIA
ADRIATIC SEA
Foggia
Cerignola
Bari
Monopoli
Brindisi
BASILICATA
Taranto
Lecce
Santa Maria de Leuca

Apulia

The Special Wines & Cheeses of *Apulia*

Wines of the Region

Dry reds: *Castel del Monte, Primitivo di Gioia, Torre Quarto*

Demi-sec reds: *Aleatico di Puglia, Barletta*

Rosé: *Castel del Monte*

Sweet reds: *Mistella, Primitivo di Giola, Zagarese*

Dry whites: *Castel del Monte, Torre Giulia*

Sweet whites: *Malvasia Bianca, Moscato delle Murge, Moscato del Salento, Moscato di Trani*

Wines Available in the United States

Dry reds: *Salice Salentino, Torre Quarto, Primitivo di Manduria*

Cheeses of the Region

Burrate, Cacioricotta (for grating), *Manteche, Pecorino, Provole, Ricotelle, Ricotta Forte, Scamorze*

Buon vino fa buon sangue.

Good wine makes good blood.

Apulia is a mythic land, classically Mediterranean yet filled with historical and natural enigmas: Fantastic caves and grottoes, rivers which appear and disappear into swirling depths, and monolithic stone castles whose walls bear mute witness to the architectural feats of the twelfth through sixteenth centuries. There are ghosts here for those who believe, and strange, rushing winds to convince the doubting.

Today's Apulian landscape boasts vast panoramas of olive groves and vineyards. A fascinating local punctuation is supplied in Bari province by the *trulli*, the white-washed, beehive-shaped dwellings of ancient and undocumented origin. From a distance, a hillside of the stone "hives" reminds the traveler of clusters of wild mushrooms. The feel of Greece is pervasive here.

Contrasting with the "old ways" is the annual Bari Trade Fair, second in importance only to the yearly Milan Industrial Fair. The history of this September exhibition dates back to Levantine times and is parent to the axiom that the Barinese are born salespeople.

Fables and folk tales are the natural outgrowths of all ancient civilizations and Apulia has more than its share. The Italian counterpart of the "Lorelei" is said to wail from her rock off the shores of Vieste. Vesta, the story goes, was a local girl so beautiful that the jealous sirens of the sea kidnapped her and tied her to a boulder in a secret sea cavern. When sailors (including her husband) tried to rescue her, they were dispatched by a giant guardian octopus that hurled them against the Cagnano Varano, a huge outcropping of stone which still stands there as a wave-lashed sentry.

In Santa Maria de Leuca, a santuary to the Virgin, De Finibus Terrae, is the basis for another lovely belief: a visit to her shrine during one's lifetime insures a place in the Kingdom of Heaven. And so the legends go.

Eating, not "dining," is the rule here. Again, the rustic, country cooking arts are practiced in the home. Not for *le Puglie* the familiar comforts of the neighborhood *trattoria* so popular throughout the rest of Italy. Excellent pasta made of durum wheat (one of the three principal crops of the "heel" of the "Boot") is made in fantastic shapes, with even more fantastic names in the local dialects.

Vegetables are an integral part of the Apulian cuisine. Sweet peppers, picture-perfect tomatoes, miniature fennel, and bitter wild onions (*lampasciuni*), along with the local olive oil and "whispers" of garlic, form the backbone of the cookery.

Other special features of the Apulian menu include *Capocollo,* a strong smoked sausage; *Taranto* figs; *Popone di Brindisi,* a highly perfumed melon; *Capitone,* a spicy, roasted and pickled eel; *Zuppa di Pesce alla Gallipoli,* an especially spicy fish stew; and *Panzerotti,* pasta stuffed with anchovies, capers, and many other things. There is a version of *Panzerotti* in the recipes that follow, along with a sampling of other Apulian gustatory treats.

With the longest coastline (440 miles) in the country, fish and shellfish are natural mainstays of the cookery. Mussel farming is an important industry, Taranto oysters are a national prize, and fish stews vie for, and rival, all honors for similar entries from the North.

Sheep graze the rocky hillsides and feast on the natural wild herbs which flavor both their meat and that of the black pigs indigenous to the same slopes. Open spit and clay casserole cooking reach perfection here.

No food profile of little-visited Apulia would be complete without a mention of its bread. Among the best in Italy, it is made from something pridefully called "traveling yeast." The rising agent of the large, round loaves is never bought — a small piece of "starter dough" is *borrowed* from a neighbor and passed on from house to house, mother to daughter. The original leaven is said to be hundreds (some believe, thousands) of years old. A baker's dream, a joy to eat, and impossible to duplicate, it's just another of the mysteries of Apulia.

Orecchiette con Braciolette

For 6

Translating foreign food terms into English is often great fun. This recipe translates literally to "Little Ears." It is actually a special feast particularly enjoyed in Apulia.

Pasta:

1 recipe Semolina Pasta for 6 (see page 36)

Make pasta. When dough is ready for "forming," make "ropes" 1 inch in diameter. Then cut crosswise slices ¼-inch thick. Lay the resulting circles on a floured cloth. Press center of each with the broad blade of a knife, leaving an impression like an *ear* (see sketch). Let "ears" dry until ready to cook; set aside and continue with recipe.

Beef Rolls:

- 6 thin slices beef, cut about 5 inches by 5 inches
- Bea's Garlic Salt (see page 31) and pepper to taste
- 6 slices prosciutto or other cold cut, such as mortadella
- 6 slices pecorino cheese
- 2 tablespoons chopped parsley
- ¼ cup olive oil
- 1 onion, chopped
- ½ cup wine (red and white mixed)
- Several spoonfuls pan drippings
- 1 can (28 ounces) tomatoes, peeled
- Blend of grated cheeses, for topping

Pound beef slices with a kitchen mallet until very thin. On each meat rectangle rub a little garlic salt and pepper. Lay on a strip of prosciutto and a slice of cheese. Sprinkle with chopped parsley and roll up the rectangle. Tuck in sides and continue to roll. Tie with a heavy thread. In a Dutch oven or similar pot, put the olive oil and brown the beef rolls on all sides. Add the onion and continue to cook until the meat has browned properly and the onions are golden. Moisten the rolls with the wine and let it evaporate. Add strained meat drippings (from a previous roast).

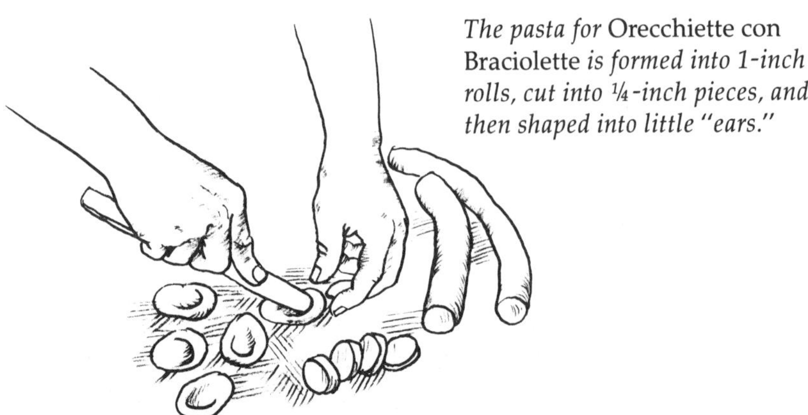

The pasta for Orecchiette con Braciolette *is formed into 1-inch rolls, cut into ¼-inch pieces, and then shaped into little "ears."*

Strain the tomatoes and add to pot, cooking slowly until the gravy has naturally thickened.

Boil the set-aside pasta *al dente* in salted water and drain. Remove the string from the meat, moisten the pasta with the sauce from the meat pan, sprinkle with cheese, and serve at once with the meat.

Cavatieddi con la Ruga

Pasta with Roquette For 6

This Apulian specialty requires a special "hand" for forming the pasta. (I learned by practicing with clay under Bea's watchful eyes.)

Pasta:

1 recipe Semolina Pasta (see page 36)

Follow instructions for making pasta in recipe for *Pasta Fatta in Casa* (see page 38). When ready, roll out the dough in a rope the thickness of your middle finger. Cut into 1-inch pieces. Shape the *cavatieddi* by taking each piece, pressing middle and index fingers down on the ends and pulling them toward you. This will curl up the pieces. Keep the rest of the dough covered while working. Dry the shapes on a floured cloth for 45 minutes. Cook *al dente* in salted water.

Assembly:

- 1 pound roquette greens
- Bea's Garlic Salt to taste (see page 31)
- 1 cup tomato sauce (your choice or see Sauces in index)
- ½ cup grated pecorino cheese

Cook roquette in garlic-salted water; drain well. Cook the pasta and drain. Put pasta and roquette in bowl. Mix with the tomato sauce of your choice and serve immediately covered with pecorino cheese.

Note: Roquette greens can be bought in season at most supermarkets. A good substitute would be Swiss chard.

Panzerotti

Little Stuffed Bellies — For 6

Panza *means "belly" in most Latin tongues (remember Sancho Panza, Don Quixote's sidekick?); thus the English name for this dish. These succulent little turnovers are made in the same way as the* Panzerotti Napolitana *are made in Naples. The only difference is in the filling.*

Dough:

Proceed as in the recipe for *Panzerotti Napolitana* (see page 267) using the filling below.

Filling:

- 2 cups ricotta
- 2 eggs
- 3 or 4 anchovies
- Salt and pepper to taste
- Olive oil, for frying

Mix filling ingredients together well. Make small, thin circles of the prepared dough about 5 inches in diameter. On half of the circle put a spoonful of filling. Moisten edges and fold dough over filling. Seal well all around. Fry in hot olive oil. Serve hot.

Spaghetti ai Frutti di Mare

Spaghetti with Sea Bounty For 6

An Apulian fisherman's reward when the catch is good! Preparing the mussels and clams for this dish takes time but the result is worth it!

2 pounds mussels
2 pounds clams
½ pound medium shrimp
2 cloves garlic, crushed
½ cup olive oil
1 pound ripe fresh tomatoes
1 pound cusk, haddock, or other similar fish
⅓ cup chopped parsley
1½ pounds spaghetti
⅓ stick (about 3 tablespoons) butter

Put scrubbed mussels and clams in a quart of water in a broad pan with a cover. Heat just until the shells open, discarding any which will not open (the mussels will open first). Detach the opened mussels and clams from their shells, rinsing off any sand in the cooking broth. Strain the broth through a clean cloth and reserve. Steam shrimp (covered in 1 cup water) 3 or 4 minutes to cook; remove shells and devein. Set aside.

In a saucepan, sauté the garlic in the olive oil. Seed and crush the tomatoes. Add tomatoes and strained shellfish broth to skillet. Cook until thickened. Add the fish, mussels, clams, and parsley, and simmer until fish is cooked. Then, at the last, add the shrimp just to heat through.

Boil pasta *al dente*, drain, and put into a large, deep bowl. Toss with butter. Spoon sauce over pasta and serve.

Note: There are two schools of seafood pasta eaters: those who like grated cheese and those who consider it a sin against the guardians of culinary purity. If you like cheese on your ocean-flavored pasta, by all means use it.

Calamare in Umido

Squid Stew

For 6

Don't care to try a squiggly squid? This venerable recipe from Foggia may change your mind.

- 1 small squid (2½ to 3 pounds)
- 2 pounds fresh or canned tomatoes
- 2 cloves garlic, chopped
- 3 tablespoons chopped onion
- ½ cup olive oil
- Bea's Garlic Salt (see page 31)
- ⅓ cup chopped parsley

Clean squid and cut into bite-sized pieces. If using fresh tomatoes, peel, seed, squeeze out excess juice, and chop (if using canned tomatoes, drain). In a broad saucepan, sauté the garlic and onion in 2 or 3 tablespoons of the olive oil. Cook until white pieces of the garlic surface. Add tomatoes and garlic salt to taste. Cook until thick. In a skillet, put the remaining oil and cook the squid, turning constantly until liquid evaporates. Put squid and pan juices into the tomato sauce and cook over low flame for about 10 minutes. Just before serving, sprinkle with chopped parsley. Can be eaten alone or served over pasta.

Agnello Agro Dolce di Bari

Sweet and Sour Lamb, Bari-Style For 6

The Apulian cook has an imaginative way with seasoning. She will tie a bouquet of unrelated herbs together, toss it into the cooking vessel, and create culinary magic. This recipe, working with the basically strong flavor of the sheep from the Murge Highlands, is a specialty of the city of Bari.

- 2 tablespoons olive oil
- 2 tablespoons butter
- 1 sweet onion, chopped
- 2 to 3 pounds lamb, cut into 1-inch chunks
- 3 tablespoons tomato purée, diluted in 1/3 cup water
- 1/3 cup vinegar
- 2 tablespoons sugar
- 1/2 teaspoon Bea's Garlic Salt (see page 31)
- 3 chopped basil leaves
- Sprig each rosemary and mint, crushed together

In a 2- to 2½-quart casserole, heat olive oil and butter. Add chopped onion. Add lamb and fry with the onion. When lamb is well browned, add the diluted tomato purée. Cover casserole and cook slowly. When almost cooked, add vinegar, sugar, garlic salt, chopped basil, and crushed mint and rosemary leaves. Cook to allow herbs to release their flavors but don't overcook; serve hot.

Tortiera di Patate e Funghi

Potato Mushroom Casserole For 6

Because so much of the cooking of Apulia is highly spiced, this filling, subtly flavored casserole often appears on the local tables.

- 1 ounce dried Italian mushrooms
- 2 pounds potatoes, washed and peeled
- 2 pounds fresh mushrooms
- Bea's Garlic Salt to taste (see page 31)
- 3 slices day-old bread, crumbled
- 1 tablespoon chopped parsley
- 1/2 cup olive oil
- 1/2 cup grated pecorino cheese

Soak dried mushrooms; when soft, chop. Cut potato slices ½-inch thick. Clean fresh mushrooms and slice. In a well-buttered 2-quart casserole, put half of the sliced potatoes, sprinkle with a little garlic salt, and cover with a layer of sliced fresh mushrooms. Make a mixture of bread crumbs, chopped parsley, garlic salt, ¼ cup olive oil, and chopped dried mushrooms. Sprinkle half of the mixture over the fresh mushrooms. Repeat layering of potatoes and mushrooms. Top with remaining bread crumb mixture. Pour remaining ¼ cup oil over the entire top. Top with grated cheese and bake at 375°F. for 1 hour.

Melanzane al Forno

Baked Eggplant Brindisi

For 4

Next to the red of the tomato, the regal purple of the eggplant is the most familiar hue of Italian kitchens.

- 4 small eggplants
- 5 slices day-old bread
- ⅔ cup grated pecorino cheese
- 1 cup pitted black olives
- 3 teaspoons capers
- ¼ cup plus 2 tablespoons olive oil
- 2 tablespoons chopped parsley
- Bea's Garlic Salt to taste (see page 31)
- Pepper to taste
- Dry bread crumbs, for topping

Cut eggplants in half and scoop out pulp, reserving the shells. Put pulp in bowl and chop. Tear stale bread into pieces and make crumbs. Mix bread crumbs, grated cheese, black olives and 2 teaspoons capers. Add chopped eggplant pulp and mix well. In a skillet, put ¼ cup olive oil and sauté the mixture. Remove from heat, and add remaining teaspoon of capers, chopped parsley, and 2 remaining tablespoons olive oil. Blend well. Season to taste.

Heat kettle of salted water to boiling point, add eggplant shells, and cook for 5 minutes. Drain well and put on oiled baking sheet. Fill eggplant shells with stuffing. Sprinkle dry bread crumbs over surface and bake at 400°F. for 20 to 25 minutes. Excellent hot or cold.

Diti di Apostoli

Dessert Biscuits

Makes 20 biscuits

As we call certain familiar cookies "ladyfingers," these digit-shaped sweets are lovingly called "Apostles' Fingers."

- ¾ pound fresh ricotta cheese
- ⅓ cup granulated sugar
- ¼ cup cocoa
- ¼ cup maraschino or other *white* sweet liqueur
- 4 egg whites
- 1 teaspoon olive oil
- 2 teaspoons butter
- 1 cup confectioners' sugar

In a mixing bowl, put ricotta, granulated sugar, cocoa, and liqueur. Blend well with wire whisk. Beat egg whites, not stiff, but foamy and syrupy.

Heat a 6- or 8-inch skillet; add oil and butter. Drop a spoonful of the egg white into skillet, and move pan around so egg white will spread out thinly. Continue to cook these "baby crêpes" until all of the beaten egg white is used. When done, remove from pan.

In center of each "crêpe," put a heaping tablespoon of ricotta mixture. Spread it out a little, fold one edge of pastry over filling, and press to close. Fold other edge back over center to meet the folded edge, and press lightly to hold (see sketch). Sprinkle with confectioners' sugar. Serve with wine or a light dessert. Keep in refrigerator in a tin or a covered bowl.

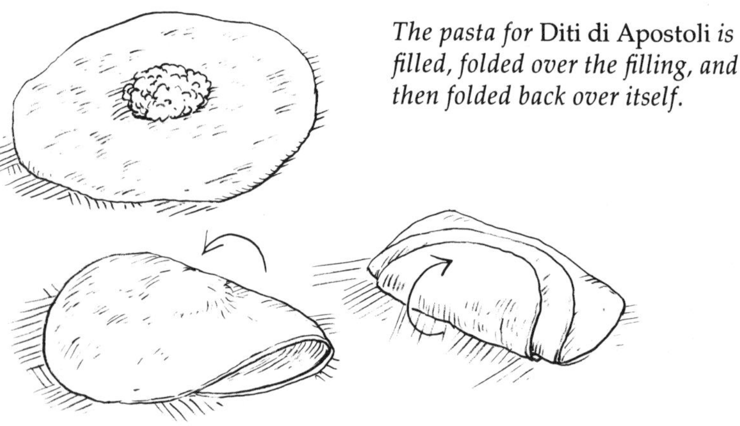

The pasta for Diti di Apostoli *is filled, folded over the filling, and then folded back over itself.*

Calabria/Basilicata

The Special Wines & Cheeses of *Calabria/Basilicata*

Wines of Calabria

Dry red: *Savuto*

Demi-sec reds: *Ciro di Calabria, Lacrima*

Sweet whites: *Balbino d'Altromontone, Greco di Gerace, Moscato di Cosenza*

Wines of Basilicata

Demi-sec red: *Aglianico del Vulture*

Sweet sparkling whites: *Malvasia del Vulture, Moscato del Vulture*

Wines Available in the United States

Dry red: *Aglianico del Vulture*

Cheeses of the Region

Butirrini, Caciocavalli, Mantechine, Mozzarella, Pecorini, Provolini, Ricotta (dolce e salate), Scamorze

Confartarse congli agliett.

Console yourself with garlic.

As children we were taught to visualize the geographic outlines of Italy as a boot. The toe of that boot is Calabria, and its instep, Basilicata. To continue the imagery, the toes of footwear normally take the brunt of wear and time, and so it is with these two Southern regions. Mother Nature has battered their terrain with earthquakes, parched their crops and people with drought, ravaged their fields with overtilling (necessary because so little of the land is arable), and has, in general, made life bleak and onerous.

This explains why so many of the Italian immigrants to the United States came from these regions of Italy. The *vivere con gusto* so inherent in the Latin peoples was stifled. Flight was the only answer — flight to a new land, to new fields, and to a new and better life.

What are the memories of yesterday and the realities of today? Between the mountains and the silvery Tyrrhenian and golden Ionian shores, little has changed. Farmers, at constant odds with the elements, tend their vegetables, wheat fields, and olive groves. Grapevines grow among Greek and Roman ruins. Wild licorice shrubs are rampant. Game is prized for the table, and in some of the thickly wooded areas, wolves are both the hunters and the hunted.

Most primarily agricultural societies fill the time between harvest and planting with creative pursuits. So, too, do the inhabitants of Calabria and Basilicata. Handmade crafts abound, among them woodcarving. Oxen yokes, wool spindles, and trousseau chests are intricately carved and hand-painted. Wild animal motifs are frequently central in the artisanry of Basilicata. Wrought iron, copper, stone, and rush are all native materials which often become objects of whimsy and beauty in the skillful hands of the Lucanians (Lucania is the older name for Basilicata).

Calabria, which shares with Basilicata the reputation for being the least prosperous and most afflicted region, stands alone when it comes to local customs and superstitions. In Palmi, the Museo Etnografia e Folklore Calabrese documents these religio-pagan beliefs — some awesome, some charming, but all fascinating and original. For example, one way to keep the "Evil Eye" from entering a house is to spread newspapers in front of the doors and windows. The "Eye" is purportedly illiterate but apparently able to count. While it peruses the pages looking for numbers among the letters, one presumes (and hopes) that it will become bored and go on to the next house! The practice of black and white magic is not uncommon, and *stregas* (witches) are part of the folklore.

The cooking of the dual region is spicy. Affection for hot peppers and the influence of the Near East is reflected in many dishes. Ginger is a frequently found spice, and the odd tang of the *megalollo* (a lemony-orange hybrid) can be traced in many of the vegetable and wine-based sauces. The fillip of crushed mint leaves is another Oriental influence. In all of the South of Italy the eggplant is King, Queen, and the whole royal family, and because of the broad ingenuity in its use, deservedly so.

Melanzane al Funghetto is only one of the area's eggplant delights. And eggplant is not the only area delight: others include *Pasta Sciutta,* pasta with a tomato and ginger sauce; *Lasagne Imbottite,* a timbale of pasta and meatballs; *Manate,* long strands of pasta to fill a dish; *Mostaccioli,* a hard sweet biscuit; and *Turridu,* a small iced pastry.

Magic, melancholy, and *melanzane* — the ruling triumverate of Calabria/Basilicata.

Pizza con la Ricotta

Calabrian Pizza

For 6 to 8

This is really a "Pizza Pie" with thin pizza crusts — delicious, but not at all calorie-caring!

- 1 recipe Basic Pizza Dough (see page 263)
- 1 pound fresh ricotta cheese
- 1/4 pound prosciutto, diced
- 2 hard-boiled eggs, diced
- 1/3 cup chopped parsley
- 1/2 cup grated pecorino cheese
- Salt and pepper to taste
- Olive oil, for brushing

Make Basic Pizza Dough recipe. Divide dough into 2 parts, one part slightly larger than the other. Oil a large pizza pan and roll out the large dough ball to fit the pan.

When ready, spread ricotta over the dough. Sprinkle prosciutto, diced eggs, chopped parsley, and grated pecorino cheese over the ricotta. Season with salt and pepper.

Roll out second circle of dough to exactly the size of the pan. Moisten the edges of the bottom dough round and lay the top dough round over the filling, sealing the edges together well with the fingers. Prick top with a fork. Brush olive oil over the entire surface. Bake in a preheated 425°F. oven until top is golden, about 45 minutes. This pizza version may be eaten either hot or cold.

Note: If you prefer, substitute sausage for the prosciutto.

Maccheroni di Fuoco

Fiery Macaroni — For 4

The adjective in this recipe's title has nothing to do with flavor, but rather with the brilliant red of this savory sauce from Basilicata.

- 1 cup olive oil
- 4 cloves garlic, crushed
- 6 sweet red peppers
- Salt to taste
- 1 pound large shaped pasta (macaroni, *tortiglioni*, *penne*, etc.) cooked *al dente*
- Blend of grated cheeses, for topping

In ½ cup of the olive oil, fry 3 garlic cloves for a few minutes. Add the red peppers, and sauté for several minutes (watch them closely, as they have a tendency to burn quickly). Remove from oil and purée peppers and garlic in a food processor or blender. Pour the remaining ½ cup olive oil into the original pan and add the remaining clove of garlic. Add the red pepper purée, stirring briskly so that the color does not darken. Adjust seasoning. Remove the garlic clove and pour over the cooked pasta. Serve with grated cheese on the side.

Schiaffettoni

Filled Pasta Tubes For 4

Deft hands are needed to duplicate this Calabrian specialty. The trick is to pinch one end of the pasta tubes closed with your thumb and forefinger while filling them from the top, and then easing your handiwork gently into your prettiest red, white, and green casserole dish — the colors in honor of Italy's own colors.

- 1 package *cannelloni*
- 4 Italian sausages, peeled
- 5 slices salami
- ½ pound hamburger meat
- 2 hard-boiled eggs
- ¼ cup olive oil
- 1 teaspoon Bea's Garlic Salt (see page 31)
- Pepper to taste
- Broth or bouillon as needed
- 1½ cups prepared tomato sauce (see Note)
- ⅔ cup grated pecorino cheese

Cook the *cannelloni al dente* in salted water, drain, and lay on cloth to dry. Chop the peeled sausages with the salami, ground meat, and hard-boiled eggs. In a skillet, put the olive oil and sauté the meat mixture seasoned with garlic salt and pepper until the meat juices have evaporated. Add broth as necessary to keep meat mixture moist, stirring frequently, and allow to cook about 20 minutes. Drain away any excess juice before filling the *cannelloni* tubes. Arrange a layer of the filled pasta carefully in the bottom of a well-buttered 9- by 9-inch baking dish.

Mix the tomato sauce with any remaining meat, and allow to simmer for about 5 minutes. Spoon some of this sauce over the first layer of pasta, sprinkle with grated cheese, and repeat with additional layers of pasta, sauce, and cheese until the dish is full. Bake in a 375°F. oven for 10 to 15 minutes or until heated through.

Note: Use the *Salsa di Raffaele* on page 316, your own favorite, or choose from the many tomato sauces in the Index.

Vermicelli alla Carrettiera

Wagoner's Pasta

For 4

Sometimes known as Vermicelli alla Trainiera, *this dish is made in both Calabria and Basilicata in a spicier version than that which originates in areas around Rome.*

- 2 slices stale bread, decrusted
- ½ cup olive oil
- 2 cloves garlic, crushed
- ¼ cup chopped parsley
- 1 onion, chopped
- Salt and pepper to taste
- Pinch of oregano
- 1 pound *vermicelli* noodles

In a food processor or blender, make fine crumbs of the decrusted stale bread. Then, in 2 tablespoons of the olive oil, sauté the crumbs until crispy. Put remaining olive oil in a separate roomy pan, add crushed garlic, parsley, and onion, and sauté until onion is transparent. Season with salt, pepper, and a generous pinch of oregano.

Boil *vermicelli* in salted water *al dente*. Drain, put pasta in pan with sauce, and toss well. Sprinkle with the crispy crumbs *instead* of grated cheese. (This pasta may, however, be served with additional grated cheese if desired.)

Spaghetti di Maratea

Spaghetti with Raw Tomato Sauce

For 4

It is this Basilicatian recipe for which Beatrice most often uses her Salsa di Pomodoro Crudo. *You can do the same.*

Make *Salsa di Pomodoro Crudo* following Bea's recipe on page 82.

Boil 1 pound spaghetti in salted water, drain, and put into a deep serving bowl. Toss with 2 tablespoons of olive oil. Pour the sauce over the pasta and mix. Set the bowl in a pan of very hot water and cover. Allow to "steep" for 10 minutes. Add grated cheese if desired.

Spaghetti e Carciofi

Artichoke Spaghetti

For 4

This recipe is taken from an old Calabrian cookbook. It does not work well with the large artichokes most common in American markets. Substitute the frozen or canned product.

- 8 small artichokes
- Juice of 1 lemon
- 3 tablespoons olive oil
- 2 ounces unsmoked bacon
- 1 clove garlic, crushed
- 1 pound spaghetti or rigatoni
- ⅓ cup grated pecorino cheese
- ⅓ cup chopped parsley

Cut artichokes into halves and remove chokes; cover with lemon juice and set aside. Heat large pot of water for boiling pasta. In a large saucepan, put the olive oil, the unsmoked bacon, and the crushed garlic. When the garlic begins to brown slightly, place the drained artichokes in the pan and sauté together for about 5 minutes, adding a little water if necessary.

Boil pasta in salted, boiling water until *al dente;* drain. Toss into artichoke "sauce," and mix well. Add grated cheese and parsley and serve at once.

Pasta al Sugo d'Arrosto

Pasta au Jus

Makes about 1 cup

A tip from Beatrice, with roots in Calabria: If you are planning a roast meat or fowl entrée, try serving *al dente* linguini which you've sauced this way. Remove the excess fat from the roasting pan and stir in ¾ cup light cream. Cook until slightly thickened, pour over the pasta, and top with a generous grating of Parmesan cheese. The yield will vary with the amount of pan juice but should lightly sauce approximately 1 pound of pasta, serving 6.

Spaghetti con Tonno e Funghi Secchi

Tuna and Mushroom Pasta For 6

The wonderful dried, wild mushrooms from Calabria and Basilicata give this Lenten pasta its special flavor.

- ½ cup olive oil
- 2 cloves garlic
- ¼ cup dried Italian mushrooms
- 2 pounds tomatoes, peeled, seeded, and chopped
- 1 can (10 ounces) tuna (in oil), drained and broken into chunks
- Pepper and salt to taste
- 1½ pounds spaghetti
- Chopped parsley, for garnish

Put oil in a saucepan and heat the garlic cloves; do not allow them to brown. Soak mushrooms in tepid water until soft; chop coarsely and drain. Add to oil and garlic. Add tomatoes. Cover the pan and let contents simmer for about 45 minutes. If the mixture seems too dry, add a bit of water from time to time. When mixture has reached a sauce consistency, add the tuna and cook for a few minutes longer. Taste and season.

Boil spaghetti *al dente* in salted water; drain, put in bowl, and spoon sauce over pasta. Grind fresh pepper over top and garnish with chopped parsley.

Strangolapreti Fritti

Crispy Fried Pastries Makes 24

A sweet version of gnocchi, *the name for which translates to "The Priest Strangler," reoccurs in several parts of Italy (Abruzzi and Campania, for example). The name always refers to a fritterlike dish. These "fritters" are sometimes filled with meat or vegetables, but in Southern Italy, they are usually sweet.*

- 3 cups all-purpose flour, sifted
- 3 eggs
- Rind of 1 lemon, grated
- Pinch of salt
- Olive and vegetable oil, mixed
- Confectioners' sugar, for sprinkling

Put sifted flour on a pastry board, making a well in the center. Add the eggs, lemon rind, and salt. Incorporate the ingredients, pulling flour in from the outside of the well, and beating together with the eggs to make a firm dough. Knead energetically for a few minutes. Let dough rest, covered, for 10 minutes. Put about an inch of blended olive and vegetable oil in a 2-quart saucepan; heat oils to 365°F. (test with a thermometer if you have one). Make "ropes" of the dough the thickness of a little finger, cutting the ropes into pieces 1 inch long. With your finger, press down in the center of each piece, and then roll it over a cheese grater lightly to pattern it (see sketch for making *Gnocchi Zanleoni* on page 100).

Drop a few of the pastries into the hot oil and fry until golden. Remove and drain on paper towels. Continue until all pastries are fried. Sprinkle with confectioners' sugar and serve with a dessert wine.

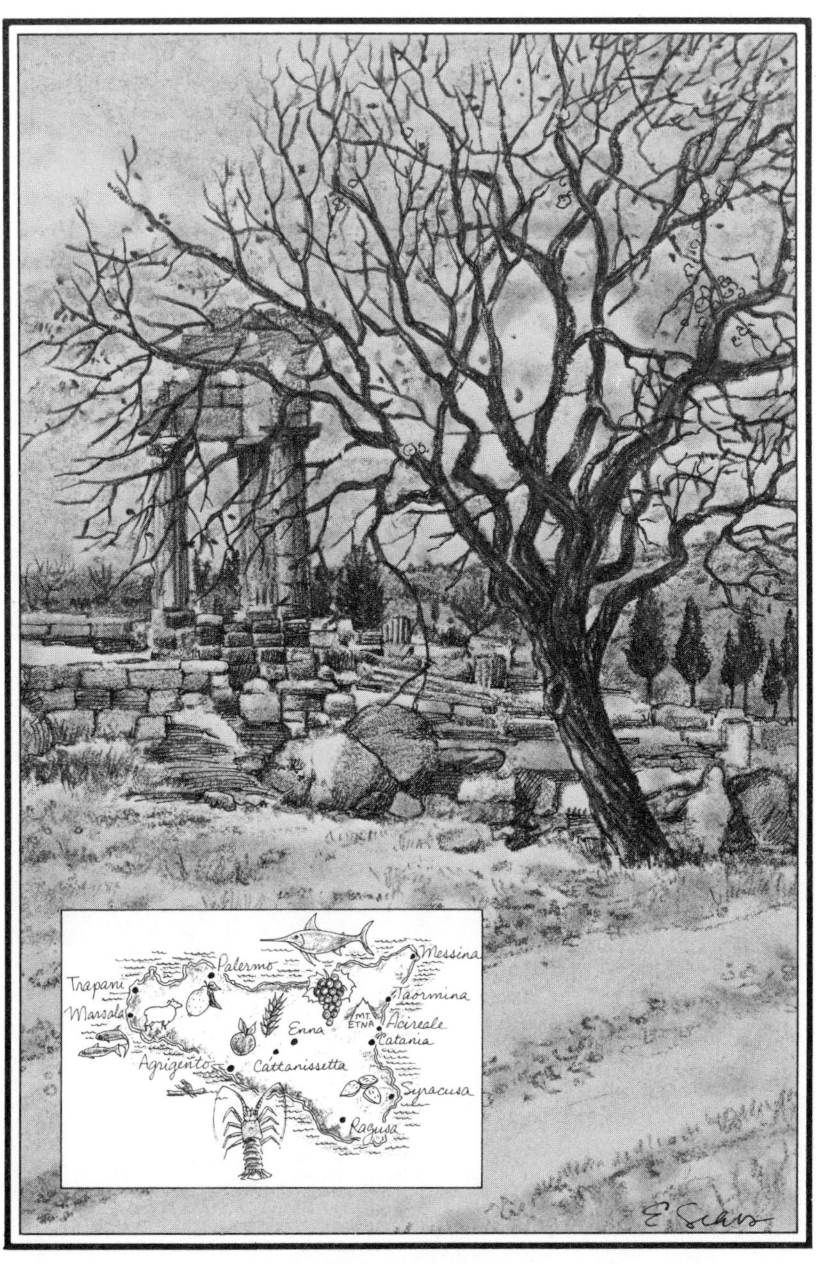
Palermo
Messina
Trapani
Marsala
Taormina
MT. ETNA
Acireale
Enna
Catania
Agrigento
Cattanissetta
Syracusa
Ragusa
E. Schas

Sicily

The Special Wines & Cheeses of *Sicily*

Wines of the Region

Dry reds: *Ambrato di Comiso, Cerasuolo di Vittoria, Eloro, Etna Rosso*

Demi-sec reds: *Corvo di Salaparuta, Corvo Rosso di Casteldaccia*

Dry whites: *Albanello di Siracusa, Corvo Bianco di Casteldaccia, Corvo di Salaparuta, Eloro, Etna Bianco, Mamertino, Moscato di Pantelleria* (Italy's famous muscatel), *Zucco* (a "tonic")

Sweet whites: *Albanello di Siracusa, Malvasia di Lipari, Mamertino, Moscato dello Zucco, Moscato di Noto, Moscato di Pantelleria, Moscato di Siracusa, Zucco*

Marsala: Deserving of separate mention, Sicily's Marsala has been produced for over two centuries. It is a fortified wine and is offered in both sweet and dry varieties.

Wines Available in the United States

Dry reds: *Casa Vinicola Duca di Salaparuto, Corvo Rosso*

Dry whites: *Casa Vinicola Duca di Salaparuta, Columba Platino, Corvo Bianco*

Sweet wines: *Ala (cherry-flavored), Casa Vinicola Duca di Salaparuta, Marsala, Pellegrino*

Dry sparkling: *Casa Vinicola Duca di Salaparuta, Corvo Blanc de Blancs*

Cheeses of the Region

Caciocavalli, Pecorini, Provole, Ricotte

To scorzo le cipolle, e a te ti bruciano gli occhi!

I peel the onions, and *you* complain *your* eyes are burning!

Exotic and passionately devout Sicily, the largest and most scenic of the Mediterranean islands, merits volumes all to herself. Her cultural tapestry is so colorful and intricate of design that it would take several lifetimes to separate effectively the threads that have shaped her customs and cuisine. Greek, Roman, Byzantine, Norman, and Saracen have all contributed to the richness and verve of Sicilian cookery.

Sicily, situated three miles from the Italian mainland (just off the toe), is pasta country. Wheat, which once filled the granaries of the Romans, has been the base crop of the agricultural economy of the area for over two thousand years. Next in importance are blood oranges, lemons, tangerines, and a variety of citrus hybrids, which flourish and perfume the semi-arid landscape, their dark green foliage lending visual counterpoint to the silvery groves of olive trees, splendid in their silent symmetry.

For a region beleaguered by the caprice of Mt. Etna, sirocco winds, and rainfall too scant to be measured, the yield wrested from the land is a tribute to the agricultural artistry, industry, and tenacity of the Sicilian *paesani*. Each winding into another valley surprises with a different view of growing things — a rustic cornucopia of subtropical produce.

For centuries, the Islanders have been followers of the sea. Great sailors and fishermen, their families learned and practiced the patience and resignation required of loved ones left ashore — a common bond with their New England seafaring-family counterparts. As New England's Salem and Gloucester "widows' walks" were used for silent prayer and vigil, so too were the rocks and cliffs around the harbors of Messina, Taormina, Acireale, and myriad small ports and inlets that circle Sicily.

The tuna haul from the waters surrounding Sicily is the basis of a prospering canning industry and also the inspiration for a unique annual festival called the *Mattanza del Tonno* or *Tonnara* (held off the island of Favignana). The ritual starts with the laying of a complex system of nets (according to tides, water temperature, and the judgment of the "chief" of the *mattanza*). Huge schools of tuna are entrapped and the ensuing thrashing struggle against death attracts the fishing community and curious tourists alike.

The specialty dishes of the Sicilian region incorporate all these elements, and others as well. Some of the best known are *Arancine,* rice balls with meat, cheese, and egg centers; *Maccheroni con le Sarde,* pasta with a sauce of pine nuts, fennel, olive oil, spices, and fresh sardines; *Anelletti di Calamari Gratinati,* rings of squid baked with spices and bread crumbs; *Frutti della Martorana,* a special sweet; *Mostardas,* gelatins of wine must, quince, and prickly pears; *Cannateddi con le Uova,* an Easter bread baked around a hard-boiled egg; and *Gelati, Spongate, Cassata,* and *Gelu,* all ice creams. A number of the Sicilian specialty dishes appear in the pages following, including *Caponata,* the spicy eggplant appetizer; *Farsu Magru,* a beef or veal roll stuffed with spices and eggs; and *Cannoli,* the delicious filled and fried sweet pasta treat.

Sicily is also the land of crafts, and the celebration and reverence of folk customs. Logically, therefore, it is the site for the annual International Folklore Festival. Fireworks light the skies, regional delicacies are sold and savored, and the world-famous hand-decorated donkey carts add a "clip-clop" timpany to the scene.

Is this really the twentieth century, or has an impish time machine had its way with us? No matter, let's throw away the operating manual and the ignition key, find a *cannoli* vendor, a shady spot, and enjoy!!

Caponata Siciliana

Sicilian Vegetable Relish

For 6 to 8

This dish is almost as famous as the capricious Etna itself. Omnipresent on all Sicilian tables, it is rich in number of ingredients, complex in flavor, and — above all — offers a delicious contrast to everything. It is served both as an appetizer and as a relish with meat.

- 1 medium eggplant
- 5 onions
- ½ cup olive oil
- 1 pound tomatoes, peeled, seeded, and sliced
- 2 tablespoons capers in brine, rinsed
- 3 center stalks celery, sliced
- 1 cup each pitted black and green olives
- ⅓ cup vinegar
- 1 tablespoon sugar
- Salt as needed

Slice eggplant and put in colander, sprinkling salt on each layer. Let sit for 2 hours, allowing the dark bitter moisture to drain out. Slice onions and fry them in ¼ cup of the olive oil. When onions are golden, add the tomatoes. Then, add the rinsed capers, sliced celery, and pitted olives, and continue to cook. When tomatoes are cooked, remove pan from heat. Dry eggplant slices; fry in remaining ¼ cup olive oil and add to tomato mixture. Mix vinegar and sugar and pour over the mixture. Toss together well and season as needed. Put pan on heat, and cook slowly until the vinegar evaporates. Remove from heat. Serve hot or cold.

Note: This relish can be placed in sterilized jars, refrigerated, and kept for weeks. It can also be frozen, although the texture changes slightly.

Impanata Siracusana

Sausage and Broccoli Pie

Makes 2 pies

Archimedes, one of Syracuse's favorite sons, might well return in spirit for a taste of this local favorite. This recipe is one of Mamma Francesca Lazzaro's. These pies make a delicious appetizer or a light one-dish meal.

Dough:

1 recipe Sourdough Bread (see page 312)

Following recipe, make dough and divide into 2 parts; divide each section again with one larger portion for the base, reserving a smaller portion for the top. Then let dough relax for a few minutes.

Filling:

- 1/3 cup olive oil
- 6 large onions, sliced
- 10 Italian sausages
- 1 large bunch broccoli, broken into pieces and cooked

Preheat oven to 400°F. In the olive oil, sauté onions and sausages. When cooked, slice sausages. Add cooked broccoli, and sauté all together for 5 to 10 minutes. Oil bottom of two 8- or 9-inch pie plates.

Assembly:

- 1/2 cup grated Parmesan and pecorino cheeses combined
- Olive oil, for brushing

Roll out relaxed dough, stretching with rolling pin until you have 4 circles, two about 2 inches smaller in diameter than the other two. Fit larger pieces of dough into pie plates. Spoon filling mixture evenly into each pie plate. Sprinkle with grated cheeses. Spoon pan juice over each and cover the filling with smaller stretched circle. Bring bottom dough over the top piece, pinching between the fingers to seal (see sketch). Make a steam escape hole in the center of each pie.

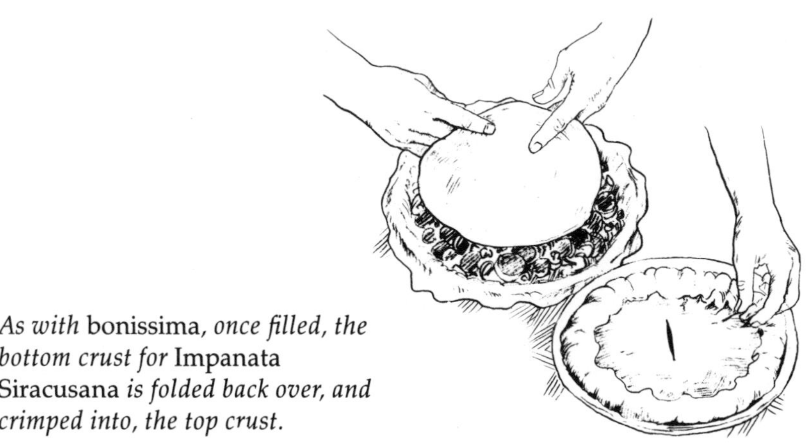

As with bonissima, *once filled, the bottom crust for* Impanata Siracusana *is folded back over, and crimped into, the top crust.*

Brush tops with olive oil, and bake on rack below center of oven until nicely browned top and bottom. When done, immediately remove pies from pie plates by sliding out of the plates onto a cooling rack — if left in pans, the bottoms become soggy.

Insalata di Calamari Lazzaro

Marinated Squid

For 4 to 6

Called scabeccio *in Liguria and* scapace *in Campania, this method of "pickling" is also used in Spain, where the dish is called* escabèche.

- 3 pounds squid
- ½ cup white wine
- 3 tablespoons vinegar
- 2 bay leaves
- 1 whole garlic clove, plus 1 clove, crushed
- 1 green pepper, thinly sliced
- 1 red pepper, thinly sliced
- 1 red onion, thinly sliced
- ¼ cup chopped parsley
- ¼ teaspoon oregano
- 1 teaspoon celery seed
- Olive oil to cover
- Juice of ½ lemon
- Bea's Garlic Salt to taste (see page 31)
- 18 or so each green and black olives, sliced

Clean squid, cut sac into rings and the tentacles in fourths. In a skillet, put the wine, vinegar, 1 bay leaf, whole garlic, and the prepared squid, and cook 10 minutes; then drain. Wilt the sliced peppers and onion in boiling water and drain. Put squid into a bowl with the vegetables. Add the remaining bay leaf, chopped parsley, oregano, crushed garlic, celery seed, olive oil, lemon juice, garlic salt, and sliced olives. Marinate all day or overnight, turning squid frequently. Serve as an appetizer or as a delightful light summer main dish.

Note: For more detailed instructions on preparing squid, see illustration on page 322.

Sicilian Bread

Sourdough Bread

Makes 1 large loaf or equivalent

No meal in sunny Sicily is served without the fresh bread baked daily in every household.

Sourdough Starter:

- 1 yeast cake (see Note)
- ¾ cup warm water (90° to 110°F.)
- 1¾ cups bread flour

Dissolve yeast in warm water. Put flour in a bowl, make a well in the center, add dissolved yeast, and stir. When thick, put mixture into a large jar, cover with a plastic bag, and let stand overnight at a warm room temperature. A strong sour odor indicates it is ready. This is your "starter dough."

Sourdough:

- 6 cups flour
- 1 tablespoon salt
- 2 cups warm water (90° to 110°F.)
- 1 yeast cake (see Note)
- 2 teaspoons sugar
- Sourdough "starter" (from above)
- 1 tablespoon cornmeal
- 1 egg white, mixed with 2 tablespoons water, and beaten
- 2 tablespoons sesame seeds

Put 2 cups flour and salt in an electric mixer bowl with a dough hook; make a well; add water, yeast cake, and sugar. Mix on low speed. Add sourdough starter and beat on high speed 2 or 3 minutes more. Add remaining 4 cups flour by hand. Turn out onto a breadboard and knead 15 to 20 minutes until very smooth and elastic, beating several times with rolling pin to remove air. Let rise; cover and let relax 15 to 20 minutes. Remove from mixing bowl; divide dough as desired — make a round shape and cut across on top; or make ropes, and coil one end toward center, then coil the opposite end, forming a letter "S."

Put loaf, or loaves, on a baking sheet covered with cornmeal. Brush loaves with egg white and water mixture. Sprinkle with sesame seeds. Let rise 50 to 60 minutes. Preheat oven to 375°F. and bake on lowest rack 45 to 50 minutes with a pan of hot water in oven to provide steam. This gives the bread its nice firm crust.

Note: To substitute dry yeast, use 2 packets (scant tablespoon) for each cake.

Zuppa di Pesce

Fish Chowder Testaverde — For 10

This Sicilian fish chowder comes to us from Salvatore Testaverde of Gloucester, Massachusetts — a man with a love of freedom of expression (which most definitely includes cooking) and a vast, first-hand experience with the sea.

4 pounds haddock fillets
1 onion, coarsely chopped
1 clove garlic
2 tablespoons olive oil
4 cups water
1 stalk celery, minced
½ tomato, mashed
3 potatoes, peeled and diced
1 can evaporated milk
Salt and pepper to taste

Cut the fish fillets into 1-inch chunks. In a large, deep skillet, sauté the onion and garlic clove in the olive oil. Add ½ cup of the water, the celery, and the mashed tomato; simmer for a few minutes. Add the remaining 3½ cups water and the potatoes, and continue to cook over low heat. When the vegetables are almost cooked through, add the fish chunks and cook on the same low flame until the fish is snowy white (do not overcook, as fish will fall apart). Add evaporated milk, salt, and pepper, and bring just to the boiling point; *do not allow to boil*. Serve at once.

Zuppa di Funghi

Agrigento Mushroom Soup

For 4

In the legendary "Valley of the Temples" in Agrigento, wild mushrooms grow underneath the flowering almond trees. This regional soup reminds one of the classic French onion soup in that its concentrated flavor results from the excellence of its raw materials, and not only from the artistry of the chef.

- 1 onion, chopped
- 4 tablespoons olive oil
- ½ stick (4 tablespoons) butter
- 1 clove garlic
- ½ ounce dried Italian mushrooms
- 1 pound fresh mushrooms, sliced
- 1 quart beef bouillon
- 2 eggs
- Bea's Garlic Salt (see page 31)
- ¼ cup chopped parsley
- ¼ cup combined grated pecorino and Parmesan cheeses

Sauté onion in olive oil and butter. Add garlic, and fry all together. When golden, remove garlic clove and discard. Soak dried mushrooms in warm water to cover until soft; chop. Drain, reserving liquid. Add sliced fresh mushrooms and soaked dried mushrooms to sautéed onions and fry together. Add beef bouillon and the reserved mushroom water. Cook 20 minutes.

Just before serving, beat 2 eggs in a bowl. Add garlic salt, parsley, and grated cheeses. Mix well and add to broth, stirring quickly. Serve immediately with butter-fried toast squares and more blended cheeses on the side.

Pasta 'Ncaciata

Sunday Special Casserole

For 6

This specialty of Messina is really a one-dish meal.

- 4 small eggplants, thinly sliced
- Salt and pepper as needed
- ¾ cup olive oil
- 2 pounds tomatoes
- 1 clove garlic, chopped
- 6 basil leaves, chopped
- ½ pound ground veal, chopped
- 1 cup shelled peas
- 3 chicken livers, chopped
- 1 (½-pound) mozzarella cheese
- 3 slices Italian salami
- 1½ pounds macaroni
- 2 hard-boiled eggs, sliced
- Grated pecorino cheese, for topping

Sprinkle eggplant slices with salt and layer in a colander for 1 hour or so to allow bitter moisture to drain out. Dry on paper towels and then fry in ½ cup olive oil. Drain again on more toweling. Then line a large baking pan with the eggplant, covering the sides as well as the bottom. Crush tomatoes.

In a large frying pan, sauté the garlic in the remaining ¼ cup olive oil. Add 3 basil leaves, tomatoes, chopped veal, and peas. Season with salt and pepper, cover, and cook over moderate heat for 30 to 40 minutes. Add chopped chicken livers and sauté until done, about 5 to 10 minutes. While the veal mixture is cooking, cut the mozzarella and the salami into strips, and boil and drain the macaroni. Put the macaroni, mozzarella, and salami together into a bowl and toss with the remaining 3 leaves basil, the sliced boiled eggs, and any small pieces of eggplant that may not have been used to line the casserole.

Pour the meat sauce over the pasta, mix gently, then pour mixture into the casserole. Sprinkle with pecorino cheese, and bake 20 to 25 minutes in a 375°F. oven. Remove, and let sit at room temperature for 10 minutes. Place a serving platter over the molded casserole and invert, then serve at once.

Salsa di Raffaele Lazzaro

Ralph's Sauce

Makes 2 cups

This is a classic tomato sauce for pasta and a variety of other dishes. It is also a great favorite of Beatrice's grandson, Raffaelino. Butter is used instead of the oil in many regions.

- ⅓ cup olive oil
- 1 medium onion, chopped
- 2 cloves garlic
- 2 tablespoons tomato paste
- 1 can (28 ounces) plum tomatoes, peeled
- 1 bunch parsley
- 1 bunch fresh basil
- Bea's Garlic Salt (see page 31)

Put olive oil into a large saucepan. Fry the onion, and when golden, crush the garlic into the pan. *Do not brown garlic.* Add tomato paste and sauté a few minutes. Add plum tomatoes and continue to simmer until oil surfaces. Chop parsley and basil together and add to the tomato sauce. Season as needed with the garlic salt.

Note: This sauce freezes well.

Pasta Palermitana

Thin Noodles, Palermo-Style

For 4

Yellow, green, and red sauce, punctuated with the black Sicilian olives—what a wonderful thing to do to pasta!

- 2 yellow sweet peppers
- 1 pound ripe tomatoes
- 12 black Sicilian olives
- 4 tablespoons olive oil
- 2 cloves garlic
- 2 anchovies
- 1 eggplant, peeled and diced
- 4 fresh basil leaves
- 1 teaspoon capers, rinsed
- Salt and pepper to taste
- 1 pound *vermicelli* or other pasta
- Grated pecorino cheese, for sprinkling

Roast peppers, peel off skins, and cut into thin strips. Peel, cut, and squeeze out seeds of tomatoes; pit the olives. Heat olive oil in a skillet and brown the garlic cloves; discard cloves when browned. Add anchovies, diced eggplant, and tomatoes. Sauté; add olives, basil, capers, and pepper strips. Mix and cook slowly, partially covered, and season to taste.

Boil *vermicelli al dente* in salted water. Drain, put into a bowl, and spoon sauce over pasta. Sprinkle the grated cheese over the top, toss, and serve at once.

Pasta Melanzani e Ricotta Salata

Eggplant and Ricotta Pasta

For 4

What a fresh idea for the eggplant lover! And Southern Italy certainly has eggplant — and that special light that enriches its purple velvet skin. Try this multicolored pasta dish — it's as tasty as it is pretty.

- 3 medium eggplants
- Salt and pepper as needed
- 1¼ pounds tomatoes
- ⅓ cup plus 2 tablespoons olive oil
- 2 cloves garlic, crushed
- 2 anchovies, rinsed
- ¼ cup chopped basil
- 1 pound spaghetti
- ⅔ cup grated hard ricotta cheese

Cut eggplant into ¼-inch slices. Salt, and lay in a colander for 1 hour or so to drain away bitter moisture. Peel tomatoes, squeeze out liquid and seeds, and chop the pulp. In a skillet, place ⅓ cup olive oil and the mashed garlic. As the garlic begins to color, add the tomatoes, anchovies, and basil, and season with the salt and pepper. Cook for 20 to 25 minutes. Dry eggplant and fry in the remaining 2 tablespoons olive oil. Remove and sprinkle with salt and pepper.

Boil pasta *al dente* in salted water. Drain and pour into bowl. Spoon on the tomato sauce and stir. Add fried eggplant and the grated ricotta cheese. Mix well and serve.

Note: If you prefer, the tomatoes needn't be peeled.

Cannelloni alla Siciliana

Sicilian Stuffed Pasta

For 4

The glory of the Sicilian table.

Beef Ragù:

- 2 pounds lean beef
- Flour, for dredging meat
- 6 tablespoons butter, plus extra for browning beef
- 1 slice unsmoked bacon (fatback)
- ½ onion, chopped
- 1 clove garlic, crushed
- 1 bay leaf
- 1 cup red wine
- 2 whole cloves
- Pinch of nutmeg
- Bea's Garlic Salt to taste (see page 31)
- Broth as needed

Flour beef, and brown in butter; set aside. In a heavy skillet or Dutch oven, heat 6 tablespoons butter, unsmoked bacon, chopped onion, and crushed garlic. When mixture begins to sizzle, add browned beef, bay leaf, red wine, cloves, pinch of nutmeg, and garlic salt to taste. Cover meat and cook over a low flame until tender (about 4 to 5 hours). Turn meat occasionally and add broth, if necessary, to ensure ample sauce. Remove meat from pan and grind with its juices, reserving sauce in pan.

Pasta:

- 1 recipe Semolina Pasta (see page 36)

Make pasta and roll out thin. Cut into 3- by 4-inch rectangles. Boil in salted water for 2 minutes. Spread out on a clean cloth.

Assembly:

- ¾ cup grated caciocavallo cheese
- 2 eggs

On each rectangle of pasta, spread ground meat, sprinkle with grated cheese, and roll up loosely.

Place pasta rolls side by side in a well-buttered 1½- or 2-quart baking dish. Cover with layer of meat sauce and sprinkle with grated cheese. Repeat the process with succeeding layer(s) of *cannelloni*, sauce, and cheese. Place pan in a 350°F. oven for 20 minutes. Remove and set aside.

In a separate bowl, beat 2 eggs well; pour over the *cannelloni* and put back in oven. Bake until eggs are set, and serve at once.

Spaghettini con Vongole in Bianco

Spaghetti with Clam Sauce — For 6

This is the recipe we all know for white *clam sauce, but nowhere does it taste quite as good as when made from the delicate clams from the waters around the Sicilian islands off Trapani.*

- ½ cup olive oil
- 2 cloves garlic, crushed
- 1 pint clams, chopped, with juice
- ⅓ cup chopped parsley
- Pinch hot pepper (optional)
- Salt to taste
- 4 tablespoons butter
- Freshly ground black pepper
- 1½ pounds thin spaghetti
- Grated cheese (optional)

In a saucepan, put olive oil and garlic. Heat, and when small pieces of cooked garlic surface, add the chopped clams, parsley, hot pepper, clam juice, and salt. Allow mixture to come to a boil. Remove from heat; add butter and freshly ground pepper.

Cook pasta *al dente* in salted water; drain but leave a few spoonfuls of water. Pour pasta into a bowl. Add clam sauce, and mix; it should be a little juicy. Serve hot, with cheese if desired.

Risotto alla Siciliana

Sicilian Rice

For 6 to 8

One of the most savory of all Italian rice dishes, perhaps because of the presence of the region's famed pecorino cheese.

1 package (10 ounces) frozen artichokes
Juice of 1 lemon
2 cloves garlic
2 small onions
¼ cup olive oil
¼ cup butter
3 anchovies
2 cups raw rice
4 cups boiling water, more or less
½ cup grated pecorino cheese

Cut artichokes into halves and remove chokes (the thorny centers); slice very thin and soak in lemon juice and enough cold water to cover.

In a large saucepan with a cover, sauté the garlic and onions in the oil and butter until lightly golden. Add the anchovies, mashing them with a fork, and then add the drained artichoke slices. Cover and cook for 15 minutes or more. Add rice and ½ cup of the boiling water; stir constantly, adding more water as needed until rice is cooked. When ready, stir in grated cheese and serve at once.

Crispeddi di Pachino

Crispy Fritters of Pachino

For 6

Ralph Lazzaro's mother, Mamma Francesca, made these typical fritters either with clams or anchovies.

3 cups flour
1 package (scant tablespoon) dry yeast
1 cup warm water
1½ cups freshly minced clams
⅓ cup chopped parsley
1 teaspoon Bea's Garlic Salt (see page 31)
Blend of olive and vegetable oils, for frying
Cayenne pepper, for sprinkling

Put ½ cup flour into a bowl, make a well in the center, add the yeast, and stir in ½ cup of the warm water. Mix well, cover, and let rise for 1 hour in a warm, draft-free place. Add remaining 2½ cups flour and ½ cup water. Mix in clams, parsley, and garlic salt to make a soft dough; mix well. Then let rise again. When light and spongy, drop by spoonfuls into hot fat. Fry until golden and crispy, and sprinkle with a speck of cayenne pepper.

Note: If preparing the recipe with anchovies in oil, use 1 (2-ounce) can. Chop fine, and add when you would the clams.

Polipo Siciliano

Octopus, Ralph Lazzaro-Style

For 4

This tender delicacy serves four, except when it is served to Professor Ralph — then it is a loving dish for one!

- 1 octopus
- ¼ cup butter
- ¼ cup olive oil
- 3 cloves garlic

Clean octopus, removing sac, eyes, and the thin reddish skin. Have ready a kettle of boiling water. Dip octopus in the boiling water 3 times, counting to 5 with each dipping. Then drop octopus into boiling water and boil 20 minutes. Put a clean dish towel over pan, put a cover over the towel (see Note), and boil 20 minutes more. Remove octopus to a dish and cut into pieces.

Mix the olive oil and garlic to make a garlic sauce. Serve in small bowls for dipping the octopus pieces.

Note: This is the best way of cooking to produce a very tender octopus. Beatrice and octopi-loving friends have been unable to scientifically document *why* the "cloth over the pot" method works such tenderizing wonders, but it does. It is not necessary to beat or pound the mollusk to make it tender.

Calamaretti Fritti di Marta

Marta's Fried Squid

For 8

Marta, Beatrice and Ralph's daughter, has grown up with the extraordinary culinary advantage of "on site" exposure to the treasures of the Lazzaro kitchen. As a creative personality herself, she is a fine cook in her own right. In this recipe, she adapts from the Sicilian cuisine.

- 1 squid (about 3 pounds)
- 1 cup flour
- 1½ cups fine cornmeal flour
- ¾ cup milk
- ¾ cup evaporated milk
- 3 eggs
- Blend of olive and vegetable oils, for frying
- Lemon wedges, for garnish

Holding the squid by the sac with one hand, pull off the tentacles with a firm but gentle motion. Wash well under running water to be sure that all sand and sac ink are rinsed away. Cut the tentacles above the eyes and throw away everything below (see sketch). Peel away as much of the pinkish outside membrane of the tentacles as

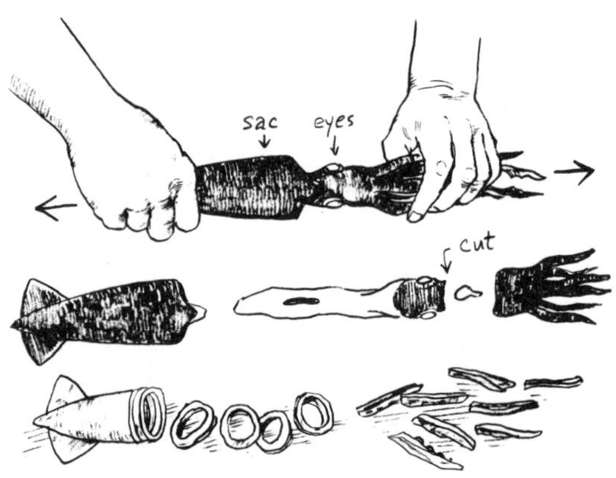

To prepare squid for use, first clean. Then, holding sac in one hand and tentacles in the other, gently pull the sac innards out away from the sac. When free, cut through above the eyes, reserving the tentacles and discarding the innards. Remove bone from sac, clean thoroughly, remove skin, and cut into rings. Then, under running water, clean and partially skin tentacles before using.

you are able. Cut each tentacle into 4 or 5 pieces. Remove the spine or cartilage from the sac and rinse again well. Then peel off the pink outer skin of the sac and rinse again. Cut the sac into ¼-inch rings. Then drain all of the squid pieces on a clean cloth.

Mix the flours together well and toss the pieces of squid a few at a time in the mix. Then shake off the excess flour. Beat the milks and eggs together and dip each squid piece into the milk-egg mix, then back into the flour. Again, shake off the excess. Drop into hot oil and fry a few at a time, draining on a paper towel, until they are all fried to a golden brown. Serve with lemon wedges.

A Conza per l'Aoste

Lobster Stuffing

This recipe — another from Salvatore Testaverde — should be enough to stuff a dozen 1- to 1½-pound lobsters.

- 12 lobsters (1 to 1½ pounds each)
- 1 sweet pepper
- 2 medium white onions
- 3 stalks celery
- 10 small green olives, pitted
- 1 pound seasoned bread crumbs (without oregano)
- 2 cloves garlic
- Salt and pepper to taste
- 1 small apple, peeled
- 2 small fresh tomatoes
- 1 can mushroom pieces
- 2 sprigs Italian parsley
- 3 tablespoons Italian grated cheese
- Olive oil as needed

With a large chef's knife, remove the head, sac, and feelers from each live lobster. Turn lobsters on their backs and slice each down the middle of each underside; split in two lengthwise, leaving a back "hinge." (Be careful not to cut all the way through.) Then remove the intestinal tract, setting aside the tomalley (green liver) if possible.

Put the remaining ingredients in a bowl, and mix together well, moistening with the olive oil as needed to "bind." Add any tomalley to the stuffing — it is a delicacy and gives great flavor.

Use stuffing to fill each lobster's body cavity. Place lobsters in a baking dish or dishes, heads to tails, adding 1 inch of water to dish. Cover with aluminum foil and seal tightly shut. Bake at 375°F. for about 1 hour or until lobster shell is completely *red.* (Test after 40 minutes; reseal if not done yet, adding a little water.) Serve at once.

Farsu Magru

Sicilian Stuffed Meat Roll

For 6

This is the Sicilian version of the Emilian specialty, Rotulato di Manzo. *The filling ingredients are similar, but are handled quite differently.*

Meat:

- 1 or 2 large slices bottom round (about 2 pounds), cut 1 inch thick and butterflied

Pound the butterflied meat thin and into a rectangle. (If you don't have a butcher "butterfly" the beef, follow the instructions for "butterflying" pork on page 276.)

Filling:

- 4 whole eggs, plus 2 yolks
- 3 Italian sausages
- ½ pound ground beef
- 3 slices bread
- ½ cup milk, for moistening bread
- ¼ cup grated pecorino cheese
- ¼ cup chopped parsley
- ¼ cup olive oil
- 1 clove garlic, crushed (optional)
- Bea's Garlic Salt to taste (see page 31)
- Salt and pepper to taste
- ¼ pound salami
- ¼ pound mortadella
- ¼ pound soft cheese, sliced
- 1 onion, chopped
- ½ cup red wine
- 1 can (6 ounces) tomato paste

Hard-boil 2 of the eggs; set aside. Skin and break up sausage. Then put sausages into a bowl with the ground beef; add bread moistened with milk, 2 raw eggs and 2 yolks, pecorino cheese, parsley, and 2 tablespoons of the olive oil. If you wish, add crushed garlic. Season to taste and mix well. Cut the salami and the mortadella into strips and add to mix.

Lay the butterflied beef rectangle flat and spread it with the sausage mixture. Add the sliced cheese, distributing evenly. Slice hard-boiled eggs thin and layer them over the cheese. Roll up meat and tie it well. Put remaining olive oil and chopped onion in a roasting pan. Brown the meat roll in the oil-onion mix, turning it until it is seared on all sides. Add red wine and tomato paste and bake in a 350°F. oven for about 2 hours. Turn frequently and baste with the pan juices. Meat is cooked when inserted fork is easily removed. Serve meat roll sliced, accompanied by pasta flavored with the pan juices.

Scallopine di Maiale alla Marsala

Marsala Pork

For 4

Approaching Ragusa from the Syracuse Road, one scans the deep ravines for grazing animals. Goats and sheep may be seen in small flocks, but the area is best known for its fine pork — pork that is the source for Sicily's spicy sausages.

- 2 tablespoons olive oil
- 4 tablespoons butter
- 1 clove garlic
- 8 slices pork (approximately 2 inches by 4 inches)
- Salt and pepper to taste
- ½ cup dry Marsala wine
- 1½ teaspoons flour
- Small red chili peppers, for garnish (optional)

Put oil and 2 tablespoons butter in a skillet. Add and fry garlic, and remove when golden. Fry the slices of pork and season with salt and pepper. Remove meat to a dish and keep warm. Pour into the pan the dry Marsala and the remaining 2 tablespoons butter mixed with the flour. Cook a few minutes to thicken sauce. Correct the seasoning, and pour over the cooked meat. Serve immediately with chili peppers on side if desired.

Pollo al Limone

Lemon Chicken Lazzaro — For 4 to 6

Here we have the subtle Bolognese hand in the Sicilian kitchen. This specialty of Beatrice's has a large fan club.

1 chicken (2½ to 3 pounds)
1 stick (8 tablespoons) butter
2 tablespoons olive oil
½ teaspoon Bea's Garlic Salt (see page 31)
2 teaspoons marjoram
1 teaspoon fresh sage
Juice of 2 lemons
1 cup water (approximately)
1 tablespoon cornstarch
Lemon wedges, for garnish

Cut chicken into serving pieces. Melt butter, add oil and pour in just enough of the butter-oil mixture to cover the bottom of a shallow 9- by 13-inch baking pan. Rub chicken with garlic salt, marjoram, and sage. Put in baking pan and spoon the remaining oil-butter mixture and lemon juice over top.

Bake at 350°F., basting frequently and adding water as needed to prevent juices from drying. Turn once or twice during cooking process so that the chicken pieces brown evenly. When tender, remove to a serving plate. Put cornstarch in pan and mix with juices, add about ½ cup water and whisk. Cook until thickened. When ready, strain sauce over chicken pieces; garnish with lemon wedges and serve immediately.

Carote Marsala

Carrots with Marsala — For 4

The slender carrots of Southern Italy are an orangy hue not to be equaled anywhere else in the world — perhaps it's the special Sicilian sun!

1½ pounds young carrots
Salt as needed
4 tablespoons butter
4 tablespoons olive oil
2 tablespoons sugar
⅓ cup dry Marsala wine

Scrape carrots and cut into thin strips 3 to 4 inches long. Blanch in salted water until barely cooked. Drain well and cool. In a warm skillet, melt butter and oil, then add carrots and sauté, stirring continuously. Sprinkle with sugar and continue to cook until carrots are glazed. Sprinkle the dry Marsala over the carrots and let it evaporate. Serve with roast or chicken.

Broccoli Stufati

Spicy Stewed Broccoli

For 8

A thoroughly Sicilian treatment for a favorite green vegetable, which in this Southern landscape has florets tinged with blue.

- 2 pounds broccoli
- ½ cup olive oil
- 1 onion, sliced
- ½ cup sliced pitted black olives
- 5 anchovies, rinsed and chopped
- 2 ounces caciocavallo cheese, thinly sliced
- Salt as needed
- ⅔ cup red wine

Clean, wash, and divide broccoli into florets. On bottom of a 2-quart casserole, put 1 tablespoon of olive oil, some sliced onion, and several sliced black olives. Dribble over this a little more oil, and cover with some of the anchovies and the thinly sliced cheese. Cover cheese with a layer of broccoli, dribble oil over it, and sprinkle with a bit of salt. Repeat the layering, with the last layer just broccoli and cheese. Pour wine over the contents and add the remaining oil. Cover and cook casserole over very slow heat for about 1½ hours. When cooked, the liquid should have evaporated.

Cannoli

Ricotta-Stuffed Pastry Tubes

Makes 10 to 16

Whether the origins of these cannoli *can be traced to history, religion, or simply pure delighted gastronomy, the dedicated sweet glutton could not find a better way to go than sated by the crunchy richness of these specialties of the Sicilian kitchen. The ricotta filling may contain sweetened cocoa, chopped citron, and/or pistachio or pine nuts. The "package" is what is important; the filling changes according to whim, imagination, and private hankerings!*

Pastry:

- 1½ cups all-purpose flour
- ½ teaspoon baking powder
- 1 teaspoon cocoa
- 4 teaspoons granulated sugar
- 3 tablespoons butter, softened
- ½ to ¾ cup white wine (preferably Marsala)

Sift dry ingredients into a bowl, add butter, and work it into the flour. Gradually add wine to make a firm, but not hard, dough. Knead dough until smooth and elastic. Then let dough relax in a plastic bag for 1 hour. Meanwhile, make filling.

Filling:

- ½ pound cream cheese
- 1 cup confectioners' sugar
- 1½ pounds ricotta cheese
- 2 teaspoons vanilla

Beat cream cheese with sugar. Add ricotta; then vanilla. Beat until smooth and refrigerate until needed to fill pastry tubes.

Assembly:

- 1 egg white
- Vegetable oil, for oiling and frying tubes
- Confectioners' sugar, for dusting

When pastry and filling are ready, beat egg white with a little water and set aside.

Then roll out half of the dough into a very thin, flat sheet. Cut into circles with a 4-inch round cutter. Oil outsides of metal cannoli tubes. Wrap pastry loosely around each tube, moisten end with egg white, and press against other end to seal.

Fill skillet halfway with vegetable frying oil. Fry 2 or 3 tubes at a time until golden. Slide fried pastry off tubes, and drain on paper towels. Repeat with other half of dough as needed.

Fill tubes with ricotta mixture. (A large pliable plastic pastry bag fitted with a large tube is good to use for filling pastries.) Do not fill too many at a time; the pastry softens and does not stay crisp. Dust with confectioners' sugar and serve.

Note: The pastry bag and tube may be put into a plastic bag and refrigerated so that the filling is always ready to fill *cannoli.* In that way you can fill as many at a time as you need. The optimum is a flaky, between crunchy and crumbly, pastry tube, with a super-rich, very cold filling.

Pastaciotti Celi

Sicilian Pastries — Makes 24 or more

Mary Celi is a melodious-voiced lady from Boston's North Shore. This recipe of hers for the traditional Sicilian delight is similar to the Ravioli Dolce *of Emilia Romagna, although the Emilian version is deep-fried and this one baked. For the filling, use the* Savor di Frutta *on page 152.*

Dough:

- 5 cups flour
- 7/8 cup granulated sugar
- 1 cup confectioners' sugar
- 1/2 teaspoon salt
- 1 cup vegetable shortening
- 1 cup margarine
- 2 eggs, plus 4 yolks

Sift flour, sugars and salt into a large bowl. With a food processor or by hand, chop in shortening and margarine and "work" until dough is broken up into the size of little peas. Lightly beat eggs and yolks together, and add to dry mixture. Mix well until a ball is formed.

Press down with the heel of the hand. Put dough into a bowl to relax, and refrigerate.

Filling:

1 recipe *Savor di Frutta* filling (see page 152)

Make filling; set aside.

Assembly:

Confectioners' sugar, for dusting

When ready, on floured board, roll out piece of dough as for cookies (about ¼-inch thick). Cut into circles with a 3-inch cookie cutter and put a mound of fruit filling in the center of each. Moisten edges of dough, and cover with another circle of dough, pressing the edges together to seal. Repeat procedure until all dough is used.

Heat oven to 375°F. Place pastries on a cookie sheet and bake until lightly golden. When cool, sprinkle with confectioners' sugar.

Pignolata

Pine Nut Puffs

For 8 to 12

Messina has a mammoth sweet tooth, as does most of Sicily, and pine nuts are used in a variety of ways to satisfy this yearning. In this recipe the fried dough is used to imitate the nuts.

- 3 to 4 cups cake flour
- 7 whole eggs, plus 5 eggs, separated
- 3 tablespoons butter, softened
- ¼ cup *grappa* or brandy
- Oil, for frying
- 2 cups sugar
- Rind of 1 lemon, grated

Sift the flour into a mound on a pastry board; make a well and put in it the whole eggs and the 5 extra yolks. Add soft butter. Mix all together well, adding the *grappa* a little at a time, then knead until smooth. Work the dough into rolls about the thickness of a finger, and cut into 1-inch-long pieces. Then fry in hot oil until golden; remove and drain on paper towels.

In a skillet, caramelize 1½ cups sugar. Gather all fried pieces into a bowl, and pour the caramelized sugar over them. Shape into a mound. (See sketch.) Beat the 5 egg whites in an electric mixer. Cook remaining ½ cup sugar with water until it spins a thread (at 238°F.). Pour sugar syrup onto the egg whites gradually while still beating. Add lemon rind. Put spoonfuls of meringue all over the *pignolata* mound, and serve with a good white dessert wine.

Note: If you prefer, this dessert may be divided into individual portions before serving, but it makes quite a splash left in its single tower. The spun sugar will allow it to be pulled apart quite easily at the table.

The dough for pignolata *is worked into finger-sized rolls about 1 inch long. These are then fried, drained, covered with caramelized sugar, and shaped into a single mound or into individual shells.*

Sfincioni Dolci di Riso

Rice Biscuits

For 6

A Sicilian "fast food" that is usually thought of as a snack, a kind of small sandwich. This version is more closely related to the omnipresent biscotti, *differing in that it is fried instead of baked. These biscuits are eaten with relish at the end of a meal with a glass of cool dessert wine.*

- 2 cups rice
- 2 cups of milk, or more as needed
- Rind ½ orange, grated
- ¼ teaspoon cinnamon
- 1¼ cups granulated sugar
- ¾ cup all-purpose flour
- 1 package (1 tablespoon) dry yeast
- Vegetable oil, for frying

Boil rice in salted water until half cooked; drain. Return rice to pan, add 1 cup milk, let it come to a boil, lower heat, and cook until milk is absorbed. If rice is not quite soft enough, add a little more milk. Remove from heat and let cool. When cold, add orange rind, cinnamon, ½ cup of the sugar, flour, and yeast. Mix well and let rise for an hour or two.

Shape rice mixture into ovals or rounds and have a pan ready with very hot frying oil about 1 inch deep. Fry cakes, 2 or 3 at a time, until golden. Drain well on absorbent paper and roll in remaining sugar.

Note: Eliminating the orange rind, cinnamon, and sugar, the same recipe may be used to make a fried rice cake that can be served with melted cheese, sandwich meats, or as a *vol-au-vent.*

Cassata Gelata Lazzaro

Ice Cream Cake

For 10 to 12

Here is the cassata *we all know and love, again with Beatrice's special touch.*

- 1 pint pistachio ice cream
- 1 pint coffee ice cream
- 2 pints heavy cream
- ½ cup confectioners' sugar, plus 2 tablespoons for whipped cream
- ½ teaspoon almond extract
- ¼ cup crushed macaroons
- ½ cup toasted almonds, chopped
- 4 each red and green maraschino cherries, chopped

Put a round 2-quart bowl in the freezer to chill. Remove and spread pistachio ice cream around sides and bottom of bowl about 1 inch thick. Cover bowl with waxed paper and return to freezer. When firm, spread the coffee ice cream in the same fashion, keeping a well in the center. Return to freezer. Whip 1 pint of heavy cream. Add ½ cup sugar, almond extract, crushed macaroons, chopped almonds, and the chopped maraschino cherries. Mix well and fill the hollow. Cover with plastic wrap and chill overnight.

Beat the remaining pint of heavy cream with the remaining 2 tablespoons of sugar until quite stiff. Put into a pastry tube and refrigerate until ready to serve. Unmold the *cassata* on a serving plate. Decorate with the whipped cream, piping it prettily out of the pastry tube. If you like, you may top with more cherries or almonds, but Bea prefers the purist's approach — just that wonderful mound of deliciousness waiting to be enjoyed!

"The Grape King"

A Chat with Ferdinand Martignetti

"Of course, we have time; . . . friendliness, along with service, was one of the basic ingredients in my father's inventory when he started the business on Prince Street in the early twenties."

After several "strike outs" with another large purveyor of food and liquor in the Boston area, the warmth and candor of Ferdinand Martignetti and his son Carmine were a refreshing and welcome change. Telling them about this book, I explained that we wanted to include local vineyard names for each Italian region, especially for those readers having the good fortune to travel extensively in Italy. And, beyond that, that we wanted our readers to know which wines are exported from Italy and available here, for enjoyment with each regional delicacy. Once this information was in hand, we wanted to know even more.

"Ferdinand, please tell us about the beginnings of the business and your family."

"Well, my father was a *big* man. He weighed over 250, and although he measured five feet ten, there wasn't an ounce of 'flab' on him; he was solid muscle. We youngsters — five in all — always thought he was the handsomest man in the world . . . and so did my mother!"

Carmine-Antonio Martignetti, Ferdinand told us, was born in 1897 in Monte Falcone, Province of Avellino in Campania. (Avellino translates into the "land of the chestnut trees," and indeed the countryside is studded with their sculptural silhouettes and enriched with their fruits.) He married Carolina Martignetti (no relation), and together they immigrated to Boston. "My mother was busy having and rearing us," Ferdinand recalled, "but they both dreamed about and saved for the store they were determined to start."

"My father's first job was working with a Mr. Rubin in the clothing industry. He learned his English with a Yiddish accent, and never lost it . . . . Talk about 'melting pots,' the North End of those days was a microcosm of everyone — and full of opportunity for anyone willing to work hard! For my parents, and all of us kids, the store was *everything*! I can remember as a really *little* kid sitting on the floor of the store and stacking cans. . . . We were always a very competitive but close family, each trying to outdo the other. . . . I suppose we thought it was a kind of game. . . . It sure didn't hurt us!"

"All Italian families made their own wine in those days, and my father was always interested in grapes. In season, the freight cars used to come in from California to the Charlestown freight yards loaded with 2,500 cases per car. They called my Dad the 'Grape King.' Talking about his size and strength, it probably had to do with tossing around those wooden cartons . . . but he was a fiery one anyway. In fact, one of my family's favorite stories has to do with the Yard. My father and his employees used to finish the grape-selling days with a lot of cash stashed in their pockets. One night, one of the 'crew' was jumped by a thief and yelled for help. Father climbed to the top of the nearest freight car, ran along the tops of several cars, and finally downed the thief, coming out of nowhere like Superman. . . . He got the money back, and of course, the story spread and his reputation grew. . . . Nobody 'messed' with Poppa; he took care of what was his!"

After Prohibition the most natural thing in the world for the Martignettis was to apply for a liquor sales license and really get into the business of wine. And by this time, the Prince Street store had moved to Salem Street, where it is today, catering to the third generation of customers.

Speaking of the store, Ferdinand summed it up beautifully, "We have an open door policy. . . . Know why? When the store first started, my Dad used to take the door off its hinges and leave the entrance wide open, no matter how cold it was. He insisted 'the people gotta get in!' "

And the people are still "getting in" and enjoying that special Martignetti Old World atmosphere and the feeling of *neighborhood*.

Index

D

E

F

G

I

J

L

M

Q

R

S

T

U

V

W

Z